Grounds of Engagement

THE NEW BLACK STUDIES SERIES

Edited by Darlene Clark Hine and Dwight A. McBride

A list of books in the series appears at the end of this book.

Grounds of Engagement

Apartheid-Era African American
and South African Writing

STÉPHANE ROBOLIN

UNIVERSITY OF ILLINOIS PRESS
Urbana, Chicago, and Springfield

First Illinois paperback, 2019
© 2015 by Stéphane Robolin
1 2 3 4 5 C P 5 4 3 2 1
∞ This book is printed on acid-free paper.

The Library of Congress cataloged the cloth edition as follows:
Robolin, Stéphane Pierre Raymond, 1975– author.
Grounds of engagement: apartheid-era African American and
South African writing / Stéphane Robolin.
pages cm. — (New Black studies series)
ISBN 978-0-252-03947-8 (cloth : alk. paper)
ISBN 978-0-252-09758-4 (e-book)
1. South African literature—Black authors—History and
criticism. 2. South African literature (English)—Black authors—
History and criticism. 3. American literature—African American
authors—History and criticism.
I. Title. II. Series: New Black studies.
PR9358.2.B57R63   2015
820.9'896068—dc23   2015010759

Paperback ISBN 978-0-252-08482-9

For
Sis Bongi
&
Evie

Contents

Acknowledgments

This book is about the literary relationships between black South Africans and African Americans that developed across the period of South African apartheid. It focuses on active engagements through the circulation of literature, through personal interactions, and through exchanged ways of seeing the world. It asks us to reconsider relation not as an inevitable condition but as something actively sought and produced. Sometimes, that relation is achieved with generative yet too frequently unacknowledged outcomes. It seems appropriate, then, that I begin this study by acknowledging the transactions and engagements that led to the production of this book.

I have accrued some of the most delightful debts over many years. John Beasley set me on this course long ago by inviting me to answer his challenging questions and, more, by inspiring me to pose my own; his friendship remains essential. Gaurav Desai, Supriya Nair, and Felipe Smith are my Teachers with a capital "T"—exemplary intellectuals and pedagogues; I regard them with more gratitude than they will fully know. Wahneema Lubiano, Ian Baucom, Grant Farred, Barbara Herrnstein Smith, and Maurice Wallace brilliantly guided me through an earlier phase of this project; their critical engagement and encouragement were simply indispensable. This book bears their continuing impress on my thinking; I hope they will each find their fingerprints on what follows. From the beginning, Wahneema has offered her radiant intelligence and keen mentorship, which inspire and sustain me still. Karla Holloway made a place for me and has unsparingly shared with me her wisdom and faith ever since.

Jill Petty, Jené Schoenfeld, Suzanne Schneider, and Doug Taylor made graduate school not just bearable but outrageously fun and rewarding; Jacques Khalip, Mendi and Keith Obadike, Rebecca Wanzo, Jaqueline Looney, and Becky Thompson helped extend those rewards. At Wake Forest University, Mary DeShazer, Dean Franco, Jonathan Marks, Jessica Richard, and Lisa Sternlieb dialogued with me about my project in generative, doubly thoughtful ways as it was taking shape. I thank friends and former colleagues from my time at Williams College, as well: Devyn Benson, María Elena Cepeda, Kenda Mutongi, Wendy Raymond, Neil Roberts, Mérida Rúa, and Leslie Wingard. Erica Edwards forever remains my ideal co-teacher and neighbor. Vince Schleitwiler and Ji-Young Um have offered illuminating conversations across seminar and dinner tables. James Manigault-Bryant and Rhon Manigualt-Bryant have been perceptive, ever-engaging interlocutors. I have learned in different ways from Dorothy Wang and Joyce Foster, along with Maggie Bishop, the meaning of big-hearted comrades-in-arms.

I have benefited greatly from ongoing engagements with colleagues and students in and beyond my department at Rutgers: Ousseina Alidou, Luc Barton, Melissa Bobe, Margarita Castromán, Cheryl Clarke, Ann Coiro, Barbara Cooper, Brittney Cooper, Harriet Davidson, Phedra Deonarine, Richard Dienst, Mark DiGiacomo, Gabrielle Everett, Regina Hamilton, Doug Jones, Ann Jurecic, Ryan Kernan, Renée Larrier, Rick Lee, Alamin Mazrui, Miranda McLeod, Meredith McGill, Richard Miller, Taylor Moore, Megan Paustian, Melanye Price, Barry Qualls, Jonah Siegel, Sushil Sivaram, Shatema Threadcraft, Alexa Valenzuela, Rebecca Walkowitz, Carolyn Williams, and others named later who read my manuscript. I remain indescribably grateful for the support, intelligence, and kindness that Abena Busia, Michelle Stephens, and especially Cheryl Wall have each so freely offered.

Farther afield, I thank a variety of people for their thought-provoking engagements over the years: Rita Barnard, Kerry Bystrom, Margo Natalie Crawford, Brent Hayes Edwards, J. Martin Favor, Simon Gikandi, Avery Gordon, Michael Hanchard, Peter Hudson, Tsitsi Jaji, Candice Jenkins, Meta DuEwa Jones, Minkah Makalani, Rosalind Morris, Aldon Nielsen, Rob Nixon, Ifeoma Nwankwo, Taiwo Adetunji Osinubi, Sonali Perera, Maboula Soumahoro, Greg Tate, Courtney Thorsson, Andrew van der Vlies, Deborah Vargas, Jennifer Wenzel, and Edlie Wong. Emails, meals, and even transatlantic conversations with Yvette Christiansë, who has taken generosity to new heights, have crucially sustained me along the way. In Botswana, Tom Holzinger's graciousness and the late Howard Head's insight made research a pleasure. In South Africa and beyond, scholars and writers have shared time and crucial expertise with true magnanimity. Thanks to Minesh Dass, Ingrid de Kok, Dorothy Driver, Isabel Hofmeyr, Sopelekae Maithufi, Dilip Menon, Bhekizizwe Peterson, Ashlee Neser, Meg Samuelson, Véronique Tadjo, and Shaun Viljoen. During a brief visit at Wits University, Michael Titlestad greeted me with consummate collegiality. Mongane Wally Serote very kindly granted me an interview. Keorapetse Kgositsile agreed to an interview years ago, and it has developed into a conversation that warmly continues.

Bongi Dhlomo-Mautloa is among the wittiest, shrewdest, and most generous people I know. She and the Fam took me in with open arms and have not let go. I partially dedicate this book to her, for it would have been unimaginable without her: a discussion about her 1999 exhibition *FLASHES* set this study in motion, and she's been a source of guidance ever since. Siyabonga, Sis Bongi, ngemihlaba/namazwe amangalisayo owakhayo nangokugqugquzela iThemba.

Insightful colleagues, former students, and friends gave precious time and energy to comment on my manuscript at different moments. Erica Edwards, Al Howard, Olabode Ibironke, Nicholas Gaskill, Andrew Goldstone, Colin Jager, Annette Joseph-Gabriel, Mukti Lakhi Mangharam, Carter Mathes, Sarah Novacich, Edward Ramsamy, Margaret Ronda, Claire Schwartz, Felipe Smith, Michelle Stephens, Doug Taylor, Cheryl Wall, Dorothy Wang, Anisha Warner, and two anonymous readers all offered vital feedback. Erica, Carter, and Doug have seen this project through from its inception to completion with sage advice; this project aside, I thank each of them for years of deep insight and friendship.

This project grew under the auspices of several seminars, each composed of remarkable constellations of people and ideas: "Race, Justice, and the Politics of Memory," organized by Srinvas Aravamudin and Charlie Piot in the John Hope Franklin Humanities Institute at Duke University; "Interrogating the African Diaspora," a Mellon-funded summer seminar organized by Jean Muteba Rahier, Felipe Smith, and Percy Hintzen; "Narratives of Power," organized by Deborah Gray White and Donna Murch via the Rutgers Center for Historical Analysis; and "Race, Space, and Place in the Americas," organized by Mia Bay and Ann Fabian at Rutgers's Center for Race and Ethnicity. I remain grateful to the conveners and participants in each. I gained much from sharing an early portion of this book as a talk at Wits University, jointly sponsored by the English Department and WISER.

This work would not have been possible without the libraries and archives—true treasures—and the experts who have shared their essential knowledge and skills with consummate professionalism. That includes the librarians at Yale University's Beinecke Library; the late Taronda Spencer at the Spelman College

Archives; Kathleen Shoemaker and staff at Emory University's Manuscripts, Archives, and Rare Books Library; the incomparable Gasenone Kediseng and Scobie Lekhutile at the Khama III Memorial Museum; and Ann Torlesse and the staff at the National English Literary Museum. I am enormously appreciative of staff at the University of Illinois Press, including Larin McLaughlin, who took on this project with enthusiasm, and most especially Dawn Durante, who saw this book through with extraordinary support and dedication. Thanks also to Darlene Clark Hine and Dwight McBride for their inclusion of this book in the New Black Studies series.

Kim Kupferman, Brian Moore, and Becca Olson—patient friends—have been sources of laughter and replenishment. I thank Leatha Shockley and Foster Shockley, whose bottomless encouragement, along with that of Teresa Shockley and Thomas Hotes, has meant so much. Alicia, Olivia, Hudson, Harper, and Henslee have made an uncle's heart burst with joy. My sister, Melody Rice, and brother, Sébastien Robolin, cheered me on when it mattered most. My father, Claude Robolin, taught me to aim high; he and Angelika Brennecke-Robolin shared a confidence in my abilities that has pushed me along. My grandmother, Yvette Menetrier-Stoffel, my aunt, Sylvette Menetrier, and—above all—my mother, Aline Robolin, have accompanied me on this journey with sustenance, love, and powerful inspiration. My mother is my first and best teacher.

My partner, Evie Shockley, has been my truest colleague, most engaged interlocutor, and best friend. In addition to reading innumerable drafts with her discerning pair of eyes, she has shown me the astonishing beauty of language, intellectual challenge, tenderness, and brilliance. I dedicate this book to her also. For the years of love, joy, and unshakable support well beyond the writing of this book, I offer my most profound gratitude.

. . .

Chapters 1 and 5 incorporate edited portions of the following original publications: "Remapping South African and African American Cultural Imaginaries" in *Global Circuits of Blackness: Race, Citizenship, and Modern Subjectivities*, edited by Jean Muteba Rahier, Percy Hintzen, and Felipe Smith (University of Illinois Press, 2010), and "Black Transnationalism: 20th-Century South African and African American Literatures" in *Literature Compass* (9.1). I gratefully acknowledge the following authors, estates, and institutions: excerpts from "Johannesburg Boy" by Gwendolyn Brooks, copyright © 1987, reprinted by consent of Brooks Permissions; excerpt from "living as a lesbian underground: a futuristic fantasy" in *Living as a Lesbian* by Cheryl Clarke, copyright © 2014, used by permission of the author and Sinister Wisdom/A Midsummer Night's Press;

excerpts from "Constructive Engagement," "The Garden," "Obsolete Geography," and unpublished letters by Michelle Cliff, copyright © 2014, used by permission of the author; excerpts from unpublished letters by Bessie Head, copyright © 1977, The Estate of Bessie Head, reproduced with permission of Johnson & Alcock Ltd.; "Question and Answer" from *The Collected Poems of Langston Hughes* by Langston Hughes, edited by Arnold Rampersad with David Roessel, Associate Editor, copyright © 1994 by the Estate of Langston Hughes, used by permission of Alfred A. Knopf, an imprint of the Knopf Doubleday Publishing Group, a division of Random House LLC (All rights reserved. Any third party use of this material, outside of this publication, is prohibited. Interested parties must apply directly to Random House LLC for permission) and also reprinted by permission of Harold Ober Associates, Inc.; excerpts from "When Brown is Black," "Brother Malcolm's Echo," and "Point of Departure: Fire Dance Fire Song" by Keorapetse Kgositsile, copyright © 1971, used by permission of the author and Doubleday, an imprint of the Knopf Doubleday Publishing Group, a division of Random House LLC, all rights reserved; excerpts from Harvard class notes by Jim Kornish, used by permission of the author; hand-drawn map and excerpts from Harvard course material and 1966 Columbia University paper by Richard Rive, used by permission of the Estate of Richard Rive and David Philip Publishers; image of *From South Africa to South Carolina* album cover and excerpts from "Johannesburg," "Let Me See Your I.D.," and introduction to "Johannesburg" by Gil Scott-Heron, used by permission of the Estate of Gil Scott-Heron; letter facsimile and excerpts from unpublished letters by Alice Walker, reprinted by permission of The Joy Harris Literary Agency, Inc.; excerpt from "South African Communion" and email by Afaa Michael Weaver, copyright © 2000, used by permission of the author and Sarabande Books; excerpts from "I Choose Exile" manuscript by Richard Wright reprinted by permission of John Hawkins & Associates, Inc., and the Estate of Richard Wright.

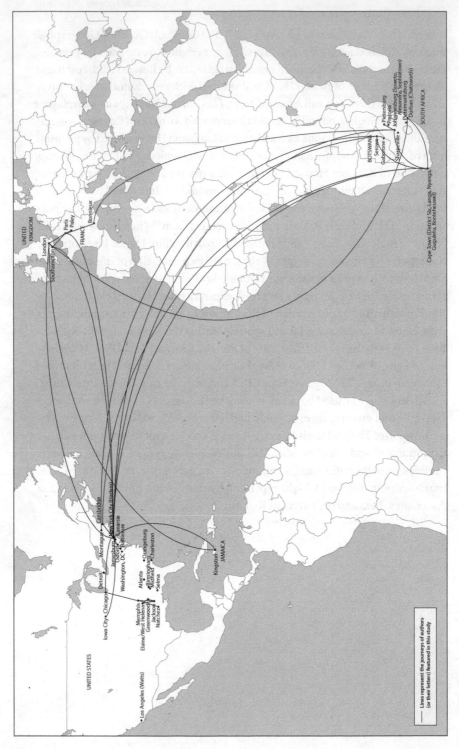

Figure 1. Map of places featured in *Grounds of Engagement*.

Lines represent the journeys of authors (or their letters) featured in this study

UNITED KINGDOM

London
Southampton
Paris
Paley
FRANCE
Bordeaux

UNITED STATES

Iowa City
Detroit
Chicago
Cambridge
Montague
New York City (Harlem)
Coney Island
Canarsie
Baltimore
Washington, DC
Atlanta
Orangeburg
Richfield
Charleston
Birmingham
Selma
Memphis
Elaine/West Helena
Greenwood
Jackson
Natchez
Los Angeles (Watts)

JAMAICA
Kingston

BOTSWANA
Serowe
Gaborone

SOUTH AFRICA
Pietersburg
Pretoria
Johannesburg (Soweto, Alexandria, Sophiatown)
Pietermaritzburg
Durban (Chatsworth)
Sharpeville
Cape Town (District Six, Langa, Nyanga, Guguletu, Bonteheuwel)

CHAPTER 1

Introduction

Imagining a Transnational Ground

In 1953, Langston Hughes was at work collecting African stories, poems, plays, and essays for what would become his 1960 anthology, *An African Treasury*. Inspired by rising U.S. interest in African affairs, Hughes corresponded with a variety of promising young writers from across the African continent to solicit work that could fit within the pages of his new project. Having served as a judge for a literary contest in the famed South African *Drum* magazine, he was positioned to seek an array of South African writers, including Bloke Modisane, Peter Abrahams, Peter Clarke, Phyllis Ntantla, and Todd Matshikiza—all of whom appeared in the anthology alongside other authors. Hughes's correspondence with the writers focused on formal publishing matters but, to varying degrees, also involved amicable discussions about the political and literary developments of their day. Some of the exchanges flourished into long-term literary friendships, and all of them attest to the centrality of Hughes as an ardent, if humble, engineer of transnational black literary circulation. Perhaps more importantly, this correspondence underscores how significant cross-cultural connections have been for black writers' personal and professional development the world over.[1]

Among Hughes's South African contacts was Richard Rive, a young aspiring coloured-classified writer living in Cape Town.[2] Rive eventually traveled to New York City to earn his master's degree at Columbia University's Teachers

College in 1966 and, while there, relied on Hughes, who lived nearby in Harlem, for insights and books. For twelve years prior to Rive's initial trip, their letters crisscrossed the Atlantic as the writers laid out their respective interests, views, and literary preoccupations. Early in their exchange, Hughes and Rive compared and contrasted the racial politics of their countries. In a July 1954 letter to Hughes, for example, the young Rive poignantly described the lay of the land for his American would-be mentor by referencing various parts of Cape Town. But his geographically dense report did more than introduce Hughes to an unfamiliar area; it also crucially underscored the escalating segregation under the apartheid mandates of the Nationalist Party–led government that had assumed power six years earlier. Racial segregation had long held sway across South Africa, but here, Rive charted its very evident markers writ across his landscape under the new dispensation. Rive lamented how the astounding beauty of the Western Cape was "desecrated with signs reading 'Blankes alleen' or 'Whites only.'"[3] Despite the city's proud liberal tradition that (as of Rive's writing) still permitted the limited political participation of coloured Capetonians and semisegregated transportation, he wryly noted that the city "keeps a dignified silence on the shantytowns of Windermere and African Locations [townships] of Langa and Nyanga 30 miles from [Cape Town's white] sacred precincts."[4] Rive further identified specific racial demographics and segregationist practices that characterized South Africa's three principal urban centers—Cape Town, Johannesburg, and Durban—enumerating how each city's set of practices restricted the mobility and access of residents according to racial classification: European, Coloured, Indian, and African. But the abundance of geographic references alone in his snapshot of Cape Town reveals a local landscape riven by racial stratification.

Hughes, in turn, offered his own reflections on the regionally specific terms of racialized 1950s America. In an October 1954 letter, he commented that "[l]ife [in South Africa] for colored people sounds just like it is for us in most Middle Western American cities. The East (New York and New England) is much better, the South much worse—we have such a variety of regional attitudes here. And none of it is perfect, most [of] it confusing to travellers, so I can imagine what happens to you when you venture further into your own hinterlands."[5] Hughes's focus on the particularity of place stressed white supremacy's local color. Although such particularity might seem to lock Hughes into an indelibly national frame, his appreciation of municipal and regional singularities, rather, facilitated a studied transnational comparison. Hughes oscillated between his experience of a variegated racial geography and Rive's description in a way that permitted an easily imagined relation: "*so I can imagine* what happens to you."

In a letter three months earlier referring to the impending U.S. publication of South African Peter Abrahams's autobiography *Tell Freedom*, he noted:

> Your racial situation seems about like ours in the Deep South. In talking with Alan Paton, he says he thinks Atlanta, Georgia, is our nearest city to Johannesburg in race attitudes—but with more hopeful things happening [in the American South]—as I gather from *Tell Freedom*. At least here there are some legal changes for the better, even if they take a long time to turn into everyday realities everywhere in our country. Here there's an enormous variation in race attitudes from one section to another. New York is like London, but Baltimore, only four hours away by train to the South, is like Johannesburg in some ways.[6]

Orienting by municipal or regional proxy, Hughes offered a descriptive map by which Rive might be better able to conceive of the American terrain.

In return, Rive sent Hughes an actual visual map to continue orienting his interlocutor to his local geography (see Figure 2). In his hand-drawn rendering of the Cape Peninsula, Rive sketched out sites (where other writers lived and where Rive lived, studied, and leisured) he earlier identified for Hughes. Rive's cartography of Cape Town highlights approximate distances between various locales—"1"=5 miles"—and the writers and artists who reside therein "so that you know relatively where we live from one another."[7] The local map quietly bespeaks an apartheid geography that only intensified in the coming years as the prospect of forced removals threatened to remake Cape Town's social landscape. For instance, the "X" that marks the place of Rive's birth, District Six—a predominantly coloured-classified, working-class enclave located in the City Bowl—designates what would become a demolition zone after city officials declared it a slum to be leveled and reclassified as a whites-only area in 1966. Years later, the notorious clearing of his beloved childhood landscape resurfaced as the subject of Rive's spatially attentive fiction.

In short, references to geography and race saturate the Hughes-Rive letters. As they shared their respective racial conditions, Rive and Hughes cast the contours of their lives in strikingly spatial terms. The writers, neither of whom had yet visited each other's country, aimed to reflect their worlds to one another, and their visual and verbal maps conveyed a South Africa and United States bearing the stamp of their racial orders. Their maps reveal both authors actively defining the structures, textures, and meanings of their worlds for one another. Making their worlds intelligible through comparison and other engagements of the imagination, the authors reveal how profoundly the spatial and racial predeterminations of their lives shaped their consciousness and their conscious expression. Through that conscious expression, Hughes and Rive

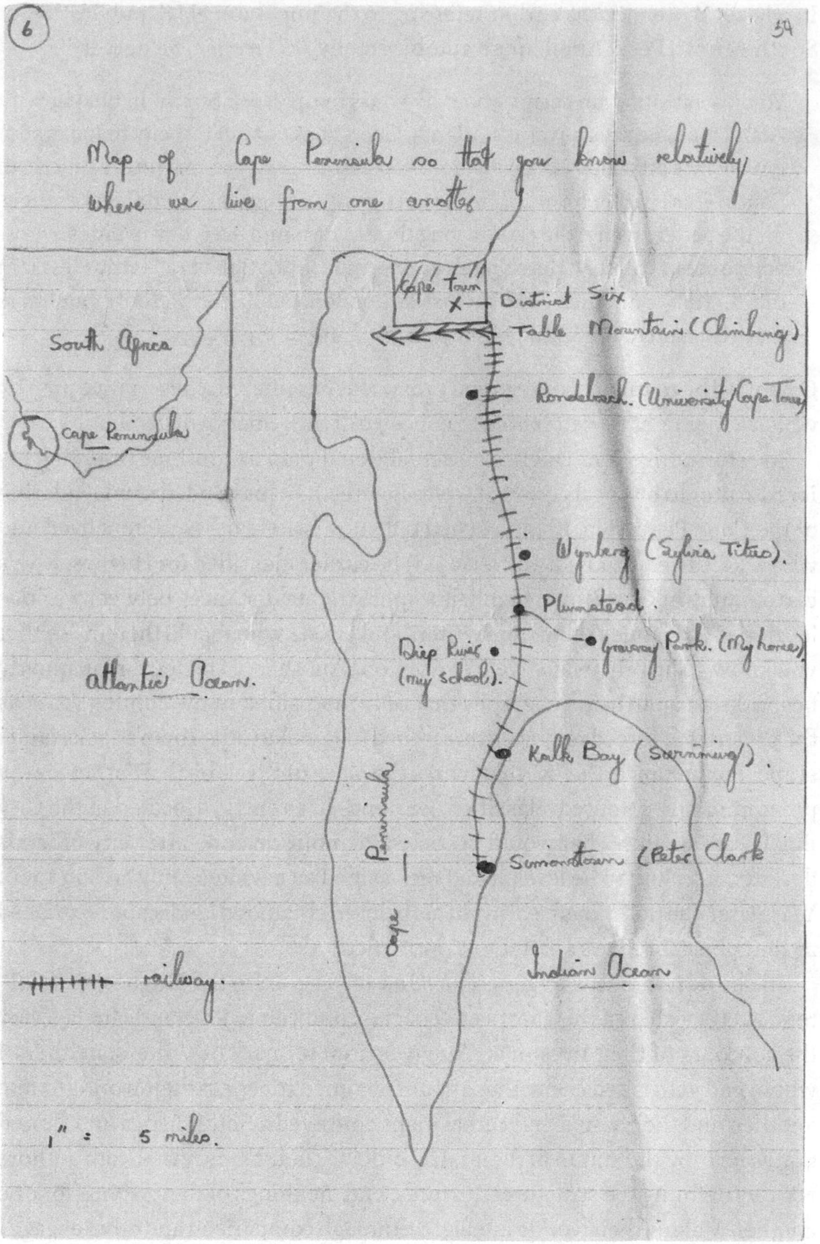

Figure 2. Hand-drawn map of Cape Peninsula from Richard Rive to Langston Hughes, circa 1954. The map charts key locales and residences Rive mentions in his letters (Langston Hughes Collection, JWJ MSS 26, Beinecke Library, 54).

not only depicted their distinct environs, but also delineated the shared ground between them.

Mapping the Territory

The exchange between Hughes and Rive illustrates in microcosm the scope and chief concerns of this book. *Grounds of Engagement* explores the literary relationships between black South Africans and African Americans during the years of South African apartheid (formally, 1948–1994), a period of heightened racial struggle and transnational solidarity. American and South African contexts gave rise to two of the most renowned—indeed, archetypal—struggles for racial justice in the twentieth century. Both countries' histories of entrenched, violently maintained racial segregation—and of the campaigns against it—have inspired constant comparison across the twentieth century, not only because their patterns of race-based oppression and resistance are at times strikingly resonant, but also because these national histories have long been intertwined with one another. This study takes up the literary dimensions of this intertwined history, as black people subject to the tyranny of racial domination in both lands frequently found the utility of imaginatively reaching out beyond their national boundaries and engaging one another in their battles for social justice. Their counteracting transnational practices helped black subjects on either side of the Atlantic reframe their experiences and exchange new ways of thinking, creating, and belonging.

By *transnationalism*, I mean to emphasize those engagements, transactions, exchanges, circulations, migrations, and practices that exceed the boundaries of nation-states. Other terms certainly evoke similar phenomena. *Internationalism*, in particular, conveys the relations among nation-states or among their constituents, and it does so in ways that either leave the sovereignty of nation-states intact, along with their boundaries, or maintain them as key components of wider cultural processes. Internationalism would include efforts to redress national grievances through international alliances or structures as well as efforts directly or indirectly aligned with the goals of the Communist International. As a historically specific black radical formation of the 1920s and '30s, *black internationalism* certainly challenged the terms of western nation-states and envisioned nonwestern political formations more conducive to black liberation. The black transnationalism I have in mind is very much heir to these extranational efforts and is entangled with them, especially when it comes to globally linked coalitions organized to resist nationally based political projects. In the eyes of those taken up in this study, the American and South African states represented the legal, economic, social, and philosophical apparatuses of racial domination, so black transnationalism names the efforts to navigate around, subvert, or directly confront the oppressive terms of the nation-state through strategic relationships that exceed it. Thus, I understand transnationalism to be sometimes compatible with, but not reducible to, some forms of black nationalism, internationalism, and Pan-Africanism. I use *black transnationalism* as a capacious umbrella term that can encompass these explicitly political projects, in part to distinguish it from earlier periods of extranational engagement, but also to denote a sometimes stronger challenge to the category of the nation-state. The term, here, does not so much aim to de-territorialize, ignore, or float above national politics as it does alternatively re-territorialize configurations of power—which is to say, it imagines arrangements of space and place that articulate modes of belonging not siphoned through the rubric of the nation-state.

To be sure, black investments in transnationalism well exceed the South African–U.S. dyad,[8] but my focus rests on this cross-cultural relationship due to its unique terms. My particular interest lies in tracing out literary relationships that developed between black communities in South Africa and the United States across the most dramatic phase of their freedom struggles. They provide us with an opportunity to study, in retrospect, the terms of black cross-cultural relation organized not so much through the nexus of ancestry or extended lineal bonds but through active contemporaneous engagement. Culturally speaking, as Hughes's and Rive's letters remind us, those engagements were fundamentally bound up with racialized land, social space, spatial arrangement, and physical geography.

This book foregrounds the significance of social and physical geography in black South African and African American imaginaries because nowhere is the entanglement of race and space more elemental or pervasive than in these segregated societies. Centuries of white supremacist rule yielded modern racial geographies that cardinally ordered twentieth-century (and twenty-first–century) South African and American life. In both contexts, space continues to be a key modality through which race is experienced, defined, produced, and reproduced. Since philosopher Henri Lefebvre theorized the social production of space, geographers have critiqued constructions of social space as a "passive receptacle" or as mere "field or container, inherent emptiness, within which the location of all objects and events can be fixed," and much research has stressed how space functions as an active constituent of social dynamics.[9] Contrary to serving as a mere stage upon which racial dramas have played out, geography and spatial arrangement have served as indispensible means through which societies define and revise racial meaning (which, in turn, redefines the terms of social space).

The histories of both countries, indeed, lay bare—at times, in blatant ways—the interconstitutionality of race and social space, or what Edward Soja (following Lefebvre) has called the "socio-spatial dialectic." In *Postmodern Geographies*, Soja declares that, at bottom, "social and spatial relations are dialectically inter-reactive, interdependent; that social relations of production are both space-forming and space-contingent (at least insofar as we maintain, to begin with, a view of organized space as socially constructed)."[10] By seizing and partitioning landscapes, dispossessing indigenous and black landholders, reorganizing and segregating cityscapes, displacing racially categorized peoples to assigned, correspondingly classified areas, curtailing the mobility of people of color, and policing black bodies in white and black spaces, both racial states violently etched their desired social orders into the lands they presumed to own. The spatial practices and social codes of the segregationist order, to use Grace Elizabeth Hale's terms, essentially "produc[ed] the ground of difference."[11] After all, *which* social spaces one can enter and on what terms—*how* one enters them—are markers by which race is performed, made salient, and reified. As South African and American societies persisted in making race matter in political, economic, cultural, and epistemic ways, they upheld their racial hierarchies by organizing and reorganizing racialized space. Invariably, these racial hierarchies relied upon and were animated by other categories of social difference (from gender and class to ethnicity and religion), categories that were themselves equally articulated through spatial relations. Scholars have long exposed, for example, the ways white supremacy has rested on normative conceptions of masculinity and femininity, and vice versa, and is experienced differently by men and women. It, accordingly, becomes impossible to think of race-making in America without realizing the co-constitutive constructions of gender, just as it remains necessary to recognize how heterosexuality structured black mobility and immobility in apartheid South Africa.[12] Appreciating the complex permutations between multiple categories of social difference, while also understanding the dialectical relationship between social identities and sociogeographic space in both countries, necessarily propels us toward Katherine McKittrick's concise but weighty observation that—as with other racial identities—"[b]lack matters are spatial matters."[13]

If spatial arrangement remains integral to modern racial meaning, it does so by shaping the contours of racial subjectivity in still underappreciated ways. The color line, as W. E. B. Du Bois noted over a century ago, worked its way into the psyches and imaginations of its residents by organizing their material and social worlds—residential areas, workspaces, leisure spots, and passageways—according to race.[14] Because the vast majority of public and private spaces in racially segregated countries were designed for white citizens who could more often than not take for granted freer access to privileged spaces, an acute spatial consciousness was more frequently the province of black subjects who could ill afford to be indifferent to the layout of their surrounding environments. Finely tuned geographic knowledge and spatial literacy in a segregated land served as essential tools for black subjects, whose well-being and survival depended upon distinguishing relatively safer spaces from evident danger zones. Spatial consciousness grew in accordance with the physical contours of the social world, and its reach was extensive. For example, discussing Du Bois, Peter Abrahams, and Frantz Fanon, Laura Chrisman notes that segregation had become "so integral to racism and colonialism that their imagination[s were] profoundly conditioned by spatial ideology."[15] It is worth adding that black "spatialized sensibility" preceded segregation proper as racialized, geographic configurations of power also emerged on colonially expropriated African territory and "New World" plantations, but segregation did much to intensify it.[16] As South African and American spaces reflected increasingly segregationist designs, a thoroughgoing spatial sensibility became more than a means by which to orient oneself on hostile terrain; it became for black people in these countries an essential way of knowing and interpreting the world.

The first claim of this study, then, is that spatial sensibility permeated black cultural expression and interpretation in both countries. South African and American racial geographies touched every aspect of black life—thus well exceeding the domain of human geography per se to fall additionally within the purview of sociology, psychology, philosophy, religion, as well as the expressive arts, literature not least among them. Black writers, indeed, have long enunciated a spatial sensibility, even before formal periods of segregation. Rive's and Hughes's visual and verbal maps index a preoccupation, evinced widely in African American and South African writing, with the significance of space and place, during a period when state-sanctioned or -mandated racial repression was most sharply contested. Across the twentieth century, writers charted the material terms of their social relations—and, indeed, the social dimensions of their material worlds—through representations of space and place in order to orient themselves in starkly racialized environments. These geographically attuned depictions mark a variety of objectives: Through them, the authors indict the material, social, and psychological terms of their racial geographies; (re)define their environments and, thereby, exercise some relative control over them; or furnish an imaginative alternative to their current social worlds altogether. They denote, in other words, the writer's active engagement with the conditions of possibility. And as rich records of desires about present and future social arrangements, representations of place and space are always charged representations of social relation, vertical (across social stratifications) and horizontal (within stratifications).

My second, larger claim is that we better understand black spatial expression when we locate it within a dynamic transnational framework. The spatial representations examined here were not only *about relation*, but were also necessarily *in relation*. Two principal forms of material traffic brought members of both racially stratified societies into real and imagined relation with one another. First, the circulation of texts: black South Africans reading African American writing (letters and publications, legally available or circulated underground) encountered unique yet recognizable geographies and experiences born of another segregated land; the same obtained for African Americans reading South African texts. Second, black writers themselves journeying from one country to the other frequently facilitated cultural cross-fertilization and translated the terrains they moved across. The shuttling of people and texts—novels, autobiographies, essays, poems, and personal letters—across national boundaries initiated cross-cultural engagements as those on one side of the Atlantic began to read about, think about, and dialogue with counterparts on the other side. The wide-ranging circulations altered individual imaginations and cultural imaginaries in their wake, leaving open the possibility of continued comparison and the forging of social ties. Simply put, if spatial sensibility independently infused black literary expression and interpretation in South Africa and the United States, it also inevitably formed part of the foundation of the black transnational relationships at the center of this study.

Grounds of Engagement, then, situates geography as central to the processes of black transnational relation. It examines more than literature's capacity to reflect the production and contestation of racial geographies. This study shows that literary representations of place and space became key grounds of engagement that facilitated cross-cultural legibility and set some of the terms for important black South African–African American relationships. In short, these representations served as imaginative means by which African American and black South African writers communicated their common experiences, mutual affinities, and differences. This fact helps illuminate the first, more literal meaning of this study's title.[17] Here, "ground" as topographical surface signals how instrumental physical and social geographies were to the ways that black Americans and South Africans expressed and understood one another. To be sure, writers did communicate to one another about their social and political conditions without mediating spatial metaphors or illustrations, but because geography was so critically constitutive of their sociopolitical conditions, space frequently figured into their communication to powerful imaginative effect. Thus, spatially dense writing that primarily addressed an author's singular context, when read cross-culturally, could call readers of another country to reflect on the relation between their own social and physical landscapes and those of the author's. The mid-twentieth-century autobiographies of Richard Wright and Peter Abrahams, for example, painstakingly charted the racist terms of their own singular environments, but as we will see, they would nevertheless fire readers' comparative imaginations. Other black writing—including the poetry of Hughes, Keorapetse Kgositsile, and Michelle Cliff—aimed to ignite an imaginative rethinking by explicitly associating American and South African spaces. And even when reality and representation appear mismatched—for example, when South African journalist Nat Nakasa's first encounter of Harlem does not gel with his mental image formed by reading James Baldwin's writing[18]—we nonetheless witness the forceful hold of these literary mappings or remappings of racialized space. These maps, then, help shape or reconfigure what Edward Said called "imaginative geography,"[19] whose contours are dictated no longer by the restrictive precepts of nation-states but by the utility of transnational black belonging.

Positioning cultural relation in a transnational frame necessarily places varying forms of engagement—dialogues, affiliative acts, gestures of affinity, expressions of solidarity, comparative interpretations, and assertions of commonality—center stage. And it is worth noting that transnational engagement signifies a common desire but not a single school of thought; while politically motivated, the spatial representations in question do not adhere to any one ideological position. Taken as a whole, figurations of space and place outline a general tropological mode that cuts across different ideological frameworks, from liberalism to black radicalism, as authors of different political persuasions employ them to ponder or express alternate forms of belonging. My approach, thus, also makes geographically rich South African–U.S. comparisons of various sorts, motivations, and objectives the subject of analysis. The force of these comparisons is most readily illustrated in the cross-invocation of black urban spaces that emerged in the popular culture of both countries, wherein Chicago was dubbed "Joburg by the Lake," the Bronx the "New York Johannesburg," Harlem the "Soweto of America," Birmingham the "Johannesburg of the South," and Sophiatown the "Harlem of South Africa" or "Little Harlem."[20]

More literarily, this approach zeroes in on the role of writers in effecting transnational reimaginings through spatial representation. The Rive-Hughes letters, for example, compare South African and American geographies, but the fact that they shuttle between South Africa and the United States reveals the outlines of a wider, transnational relation-in-process. "Traveling" to and within another country, these representations compel readers to envision places well beyond their own national boundaries. Note how, in one of his letters to Rive, Hughes compares South African and U.S. cities based on an earlier encounter with Peter Abrahams's depiction of Johannesburg in his autobiography: the municipalities are alike, he writes, "as I gather from *Tell Freedom*."[21] These representations become the basis of knowledge that enables and inspires more transnational comparison. Guiding readers through places well beyond their shores, geographic descriptions ask readers to comparatively reflect upon their surrounding environment and their relations.

In cases where texts explicitly associate South African and U.S. contexts, they provoke readers to deliberate on the relationship between them. Let us take Langston Hughes's 1966 poem "Question and Answer," reproduced here in full, as a case in point:

> Durban, Birmingham,
> Cape Town, Atlanta,
> Johannesburg, Watts,
> The earth around
> Struggling, fighting
> Dying—for what?
>
> *A world to gain.*
>
> Groping, hoping
> Waiting—for what?
>
> *A world to gain.*
>
> Dreams kicked asunder,
> Why not go under?
>
> *There's a world to gain.*
>
> But suppose I don't want it,
> Why take it?
>
> *To remake it.*[22]

Hughes's dialogue poem features a revolutionary persona (in italics) who offers his despondent interlocutor a transformative vision to galvanize political struggle against injustice. The concerted efforts to "gain" and "remake" the world into one worthy of reclamation are coded, for the poem juxtaposes South African and American cities that, by 1966, figured worldwide as infamous sites of racial repression and resistance. Recalling Hughes's analysis of American and South African racial geographies in his earlier letters to Rive, the pairing of municipalities draws attention to the significance of the local, while also forcing readers to contemplate the relationship between the two countries, or between their six representative locales, whose black populations are "[s]truggling, fighting, / [d]ying" and "[g]roping, hoping, / [w]aiting." The poem attests to the ways that Hughes's prior transatlantic *correspondence* as epistolary *exchange* informs his own creative work. It brings into clearer view the literary fruits of his relationships to South African writers and writing, which have fueled or shaped his comparative view of black transnational relation.[23] "Question and Answer" also highlights *correspondence* as social and political *symmetry* drawn between the two countries represented by the enumerated sites of struggle. By pairing symbolic locales from two seemingly independent movements almost halfway around the world from one another, Hughes de-individualizes insurgent black self-assertion, transnationalizes it, and thus frames local instances of opposition to racial subjugation as part of a larger, interconnected phenomenon. Itself the product of previously circulating verbal and visual maps, the poem becomes a map of relation and of action.

Hughes's poem also speaks to the second meaning of "ground" in *Grounds of Engagement*: the basis for—or, conceptual ground of—black South African and African American comparison. Hughes's poem and earlier exchanges with Rive elucidate how black American and South African texts have simultaneously reflected, asserted, and created a discursive ground of engagement between their constituencies. The relationships explored in this study were textually mediated—not merely textually expressed, but also textually produced.[24] "Produced" refers not to the writing and publication of a literary text, but rather to literature's generative role in shaping the imaginaries and perceptions of black South Africans and African Americans. That is, they were not just written about, but also written into being. A crucial part of this production involves a "remaking" akin to the one Hughes invokes in his poem, but the remaking explored here is an ongoing reworking of the individual imagination and collective imaginary that precedes or accompanies the explicitly material and political refashioning addressed in Hughes's verse. This other remaking is effectively generated by his reorienting text, which is to say that it outlines a new cultural cartography.

It is worth noting that a focus on textual production and the role of literature inevitably raises questions of readership, language, and literacy—questions magnified in multilinguistic contexts. This study takes up Anglophone literary relations because it was, among Britain's former colonies, the primary medium of transnational communication. However central it was to the colonization of southern Africa, English provided a vital alternative to Afrikaans for black South Africans, as the Soweto Uprising made apparent. But precisely because English-language literacy was possible for a select minority of indigenous language speakers under white rule, it considerably restricted who could be part of the transnational conversation. The language of communication, furthermore, overdetermined the kinds of conversation and identification that could form. We, thus, skew to the well-educated few and the literati, to boot. This does not foreclose transnational imaginings or interactions for (generally multilingual) speakers of Zulu, Tswana, and other indigenous languages, because English-literate and -nonliterate practices are hardly unbridgeable, but it does mean that their engagements with the English-speaking world involved another layer of translation and remove.[25]

Invocations of cartography, particularly in a colonial context, inevitably raise specters of epistemic violence and the hegemonic forms of knowledge that underwrote grand narratives of imperial European violence, domination, and exploitation. As Said argued, "[I]f there is anything that radically distinguishes the imagination of anti-imperialism it is the primacy of the geographical in it. Imperialism after all is an act of geographical violence through which virtually every space in the world is explored, charted, and finally brought under control."[26] The black American and South African authors examined throughout this study, however, demonstrate that the art of mapping is not the exclusive prerogative of the dominant culture. Reminding us that the way in which the world is conceptualized is a fundamental terrain of contestation, they engage in cultural counter-cartography by redrawing received cognitive maps and provoking a rearrangement of their readership's imaginative geographies.[27] This possibility implies an interconnectedness between geographic and conceptual orders beyond mere metaphor; broadly understood, maps are textual instruments that organize geographic and cognitive orders, making the world around us intelligible and investing it with particular arrangements of knowledge. As J. B. Harley argued, maps are more than pragmatic tools that inertly reflect "the way it is"; rather, they actively intervene in our ways of knowing to construct how we understand the existing world and (re)configure what it comes to mean.[28] Precisely because they operate as jointly creative and pedagogical instruments, maps—literary ones, at least—reorient us and reorder the world we presume to know.[29]

Figurations of social space sit at the convergence of the discursive and the material domains. For all their discursive work, the authors and texts studied here were also subject to very concrete facts, facts that remind us of an additional unavoidably spatial dimension to the South African–African American relationship. Circulation across vast distances, or the traversal of continents and oceans, is an inherently geographic process that facilitates the mutually transformative global exchanges taken up herein. The material nature of transnational traffic points to the investments, aspirations, and dangers that propel texts and people from one locale to another thousands of miles away, but it also underlines the tangible limitations on extensive mobility: limited economic resources, immigration laws, bans, censorship, and so on. The fact of distance not only has a considerable effect on when and how these exchanges take place; it also impresses itself on what may be transmitted—in turn, shaping both utterance and reception. As the following chapters bear out, nowhere is this more apparent than in the lives of exiles either yearning to go home or immobilized by legal limbo. In some of these cases, geographic remove also presents a challenge to ongoing interpersonal relationships conducted across continents and oceans. Texts and people are, thus, shaped by the distance as well as the movement between places in different hemispheres that are at once unique and yet recognizable to one another.

Histories of Engagement

Students and scholars of transnationalism inevitably run up against a range of conceptual challenges when comparing twentieth-century black South African and African American experiences. Searches for simple alignments between South Africa and the United States invariably run up against their significant social, historical, linguistic, legal, and demographic differences. Efforts to distinguish the countries in absolute terms likewise falter on the evidence of longstanding ties and the widely-embraced resonance between them. Approaches that presume either wholesale equivalence of black South African and African American situations or their radical singularity invariably miss the mark, as the uniqueness and parallels of black experiences in these countries lie in constant tension. This tension magnifies crucial methodological problems that bedevil any transnational study. What are the conceptual grounds for comparative analysis? How do we soundly and effectively frame this transatlantic relationship? The first step in establishing a firm foundation requires exploring the cultural differences and similarities between South African and U.S. contexts and evaluating their limitations.

Claims of cross-cultural commonality are frequently based on the perceived semianalogous histories of South Africa and the United States. From the outset, the histories of both countries appear to be strikingly resonant in many respects. Most obviously, both South Africa and the United States began as European settler colonies and ultimately emerged as multicultural societies structured by systems of racial dominance. Both countries have also undergone relatively recent transformations resulting from powerful campaigns for racial equality. These wide-angle resemblances go beyond broad initial impressions. Both nation-states share early histories tied to Dutch ventures—the settlement of New Amsterdam (later, New York City) in 1609 and, forty-three years later under the watch of Jan van Riebeeck, the settlement near Kaap de Goede Hoop (ultimately, the colony of Kaapstad, or Cape Town)—that were later appropriated by the British and ultimately agitated for their own autonomous rule. These early settler colonies were predicated on Calvinist proclamations of God-ordained supremacy conjoined with visions of free, self-determined futures in new lands of opportunity. Integral to these political and social visions were racist ideological apparatuses that variously rationalized colonial hierarchies in both South African and American contexts.

Born of early global flows of colonization, imperial rule, and racial capitalism, both countries rose as hegemons whose power rested upon land expropriation and the extraction of indigenous and imported labor.[30] Their histories of colonization set into motion material and social conditions that gave rise to powerful "racial states."[31] Both colonial formations began with various economic ventures, religiously sanctioned annexation of land, and violent expansion of white settlement. The displacement of indigenous populations—San, Khoi, and Bantu-speaking African populations, on the one hand, and Native Americans, on the other—accompanied elaborate mechanisms to ensure their legal exclusion from and geographic containment within the nascent body politic. Systematic labor exploitation in the form of slavery, peonage, pressed labor, and engineered economic bondage extended the legacy of each colonial formation.[32] Protracted periods of racially overdetermined chattel slavery—the importation of captive Africans in the New World and of a variously racialized bound workforce (from 1658 to 1834) in the Western Cape—embedded racial stratification into the political economy in ways that persisted well after formal emancipation in both countries and continue today. Those legacies structured subsequent and continuing patterns of conscripted labor (from Chinese workers in the United States to Indian laborers in South Africa). Both state projects required extraordinary feats of radical social engineering to racialize identities and segregate social spaces, achieved through an accretion of legal enactments of the white state and de facto practices of a racist civil society over centuries.

In *White Supremacy*, historian George Fredrickson outlined several comparable phases in the development of South Africa and the United States: namely, frontier history, racial slavery, miscegenation, white nationalism, and modern racial segregation.[33] But any comparative examination must acknowledge, as Fredrickson did,[34] the differences that nevertheless mitigate these striking parallels and the implications of those differences. Indeed, notwithstanding this shared foundational imperial enterprise of "self-realization through dominance" and exclusion, distinct circumstances produced two unmistakably different societies.[35] Certainly, if both countries share easily identifiable tenets and outcomes of white supremacy, their particular iterations and effects vary from context to context. Such differences manifest themselves at national and, as Hughes's and Rive's letters make clear, regional and local levels. Stuart Hall rightly warned against "extrapolating a common and universal structure to racism, which remains essentially the same, outside of its specific historical location,"[36] for to posit a single, uniform theory of race and racism is to vastly oversimplify the place-specific historical conditions, economic structures, social relations, attendant ideological forces, and geographic and climactic particularities that influence the process of race-making. Indeed, presenting the emergence and form of racism across space and time as invariable or universal is to yield to the dehistoricizing and naturalizing logic of racism, which obscures its own contingent historical production.

Basic demographic differences between South African and U.S. populations further illustrate the complications of transnational comparison. The origins and social status of indigenous, enslaved, and settler communities in the two countries do not easily align. Furthermore, unfolding histories on separate continents, privileged mechanisms of racial segregation, and dominant terms of social identity have yielded varying racial hierarchical systems and lexicons. Deviations in the two countries' racial schemas become readily apparent: the American binary racial system, based on the "one-drop rule" of hypodescent with a black population in the numerical minority, and South Africa's tertiary racial system, which positions a variegated coloured-classified population (sometimes including the category of Indian) buffering the white minority from a black majority (itself subdivided by apartheid law into ethnic identities). These disjunctive schemes are hardly representative of either country's actual demographic complexities—the overpowering nature of the binary, black-white sociological model in the United States, for example, has obscured the intricacies of a multiracial society as well as the fact that U.S. law has targeted and excluded a range of other racial and ethnic groups—but they nevertheless point to significant national asymmetries. This is especially the case when we consider which racialized populations were indigenous and which were imported as coerced labor or what colored/coloured came to mean in each national context. How, then, do we define blackness? Which bodies, communities, and histories fit within this appellation? And how do we conceive of and address black transnationalism in the face of these disjunctions?

Beyond the states themselves, then, the people and populations being examined pose challenges for the comparative enterprise. While this particular black transnational relationship takes place within the broader sociological frame of the African diaspora, it was not predicated on lines of descent traceable back to either the transatlantic slave trade or other past dispersals. A fusion of racial identity and heredity does not hold here, nor, therefore, does the traditional, lineal construction of the African diaspora account for this history of transnational engagement. Relation, rather than roots, predominate in this instance; as Édouard Glissant provocatively declared, "The root is not important. Movement is."[37] The South African–African American connections studied here result from an accruing set of movements, cultural interactions, and political commitments. In contrast to disaporic lines of filiation, in other words, this black transnational relationship rests upon active, freely chosen, and contemporaneous affiliation. It is the product of deliberate exchanges and efforts to forge connections across oceans, without the ineluctable consequence of received lineage or a putatively inevitable shared racial bond. It is made possible through an extensive history of transnationally circulating capital, ideas, people, practices, and texts, on the one hand, and an attendant tradition of cross-cultural comparison, on the other.

From as early as the late 1700s, a transatlantic network of commercial exchange and industrial trade formed between the white settler colonies that would become South Africa and the United States, establishing lucrative business relations for centuries to come.[38] Political support soon followed commerce as the Cape Colony assisted both Union and Confederate forces during the American Civil War,[39] and South Africa's late-1800s mineral revolution was well supported by American investors and the U.S. industrial sector. Their governments' mutually studied and deployed segregationist policies in the early twentieth century constitute some of the more sinister international exchanges between the two countries. And by the 1980s, as the United States prosecuted the Cold War battle for geopolitical supremacy, the United States would help shore up its strategic, mineral-rich ally, the Nationalist-led apartheid government, by means of a duplicitous foreign policy toward South Africa euphemistically termed "constructive engagement." The policy, to which we will return in the final chapter, encouraged significant trade with South Africa that extended the apartheid regime's lifeline amid a growing international embargo and divestment movement. Along with these exchanges, both countries were commonly linked for their relatively late, notoriously recalcitrant, and widely broadcast violent efforts, by government and white citizenry, to suppress bids for racial justice.[40]

If the two racially stratified societies were premised on the dispossession of manufactured racial underclasses, they also precipitated the emergence of countervailing traditions of resistance. Anthony Marx has argued that, despite variances in the two countries' constructions of racial hierarchy, juridical codifications of race figured centrally in their nation-formation.[41] The legal formalization of race in both contexts—unlike with Brazil, where racial hierarchy was socially operative yet neither legislatively enshrined nor administratively acknowledged—unwittingly provided a structure that ushered in racial consciousness and, thus, racially defined collective opposition. South African and U.S. dissident cultures' analogous and intersecting confrontations with white supremacy gave rise to networks of resistance stretching across the Atlantic. Thus, what began as a state and corporate network of capitalist advancement prompted a competing web of liberationist visions and practices between dissident black South Africans and African Americans. Starting from the second half of the nineteenth century, a transatlantic circuitry of people and cultural production sustained a range of black liberation ideologies, including redemptive missionary movements, black elite modernism (New Negroism/New Africanism), Pan-Africanism, black populism, black Marxist thought, liberal nonviolent resistance, and nationalist Black Power and Black Consciousness Movements. These shared ideologies fostered critical transnational flows, some of which took the form of key texts (manifestos, treatises, testimonies, and the like) that would substantially help forge solidarities between communities of resistance across the ocean.

The absence of simple social, governmental, or demographic correspondence between South Africa and America, thus, never prevented black, coloured, and Indian South Africans (to employ apartheid-era categories) from engaging African Americans, and vice versa, across the latter half of the twentieth century. In South Africa, while the state's racial classifications aimed to fracture the majority population, members of this majority nevertheless understood their political status as a function of exclusion from the circle of white government and civil society. Whatever their substantive cultural, linguistic, and phenotypic differences, they were also bound together by the logic of white supremacy—i.e., negatively and binarily defined against the white citizens of the South African state as "non-white" or "non-European" (as in Rive's reference to ubiquitous "Whites Only" signs). This more relational definition of racial identity found its fullest expression in the reformulation of blackness advanced by the Black Consciousness Movement (BCM) in the 1960s and '70s.[42] It underscores the plasticity and malleability of identities in the face of white racial power, and it highlights how subjugated communities conceive of themselves in relations of power—in ways not wholly dictated by the fragmenting nomenclature of the state (as in the case of blackness in Britain). I should add that a mutable definition of race does not mean to overlook the fact that certain identifications and claims of connection between South Africans and African Americans were often expressed in essentialist or familial terms. This study, however, understands the underlying discursive work that naturalized conceptions of race invariably perform, even if they mask it or encode it as shorthand. Accordingly, it aims to account for what assertions of af/filiation—be they framed as blood ties and brotherhood or not—aim to achieve. Indeed, this study seeks to render visible the considerable labor—imaginative, intellectual, and material—that transnational engagements rest upon, including efforts to diminish or bridge the differences between transoceanic counterparts.

A politically functional conception of racial identity (pronounced or not) in South Africa certainly helped facilitate transatlantic identifications with black Americans, whose own social identities underwent repeated revision and renaming. Subordinated political status gave many South Africans impetus to seek out and connect with marginalized communities in search of sustenance, symbols, or solidarity. In black Americans, racially oppressed South Africans found a community struggling for rights and recognition also denied on the basis of race. While some South Africans stressed an uncomplicated communality with U.S. counterparts, others were less likely to overlook differences. For the purposes of this study, blackness (like its counterpart, whiteness) is to be understood as a constructed, politically inflected category—an umbrella term subject to regular reshaping and redefinition to suit the needs of those who claimed this designation or found it imposed on them—a designation that admits its substantial intra- and transnational differences. As a category deployed and remade by South African and American governments and cultural formations, black is no neat, hermetically sealed moniker. Here, it broadly signifies an inclusive category that encompasses people of African descent in the United States, despite variations in ethnicity, language, nationality, and migration pattern. In the South African context, it will refer to African Bantu-language communities and their coloured and Indian compatriots, who shared a subordinated political status (albeit to varying degrees) under white minority rule.

If social and political power framed the interface between South African and American blacks, that relation to power, in both segregated societies,

materialized and was thus legible in the built environment. Spatial arrangements and geographies played a considerable role in the very processes of racial
identification, cross-cultural comparison, and the means by which intraracial
black differences were reworked or kept at bay. Rather than stages upon which
racial dramas might play out, geography and spatial arrangement on every level
served as principal mechanisms for defining modern racial meaning, which, in
turn, significantly colored the terms of social and geographic space. Certainly,
the apartheid state's strategy of dividing and conquering different constituencies was achieved through spatial manipulation, not least of which was systemic
segregation of ethnic groups across the South African countryside through
the Bantustan system and across each cityscape through the Group Areas Act
and Population Registration Act, both of 1950; the Reservation of Separate
Amenities Act of 1953; and preceding legislation, the Natives Land Act of 1913
and Natives (Urban Areas) Act of 1923. Despite their segmentation, various
constituencies shared quotidian experiences defined by a racialized "geography of exclusion"[43] made manifest daily through material arrangements and
spatial practices devised by the state to restrict black mobility, circumscribe
black access to white areas and facilities, and sever black claims to the land. In
the United States, as well, the divisions within the black communities (along
lines of class, gender, sexuality, nationality, region, ideology, etc.) were often
nevertheless held in relative check by segregation's ubiquitous spatial practices,
from living on the "other side of the tracks"—literally and figuratively—from
exclusive white areas to daily encounters with "Colored Only" signs to being
roped into the proliferating ghettos of the urban American North, Midwest,
and West. The negotiations of and struggles against racial geographies in both
countries laid the groundwork for black transnational identifications and solidarities. As with intraracial difference and segmentation within either country,
experiential proximity and continuity, even at a transnational scale, could at
times trump geographic contiguity.

Transaction and the Terms of Relation

Any inquiry into the grounds of black transnationalism would do well to clarify the terms of its own foundations. *Grounds of Engagement* engages several
approaches to form its own analytical lens, but this book's argument must be
situated primarily within the context of South African and American comparative scholarship, by which I broadly mean studies that explore the (dis)
similarities or (dis)continuities between at least two objects or phenomena.
Under the wide umbrella of comparative methodologies, we can (following

Rita Barnard and James Campbell) distinguish between two models: the parallel and the transactional.[44] These are methodologically unique, although their distinction sometimes blurs in practice, as one often conditions or highlights the other.

Generally speaking, parallel comparative projects position their two (or more) objects of study alongside one another in order to highlight revealing alignments or divergences between them. Parallel studies of black South African and African American literature examine recurring thematic patterns, authorial preoccupations, or literary tropes that point to symmetries in the countries' social structure or political unconscious. Frequently premised upon both countries' legacies of colonialism and entrenched racism, such studies underscore similar sociopolitical conditions, existential dimensions of everyday life, and/or resonant responses to either. For example, Mary Elizabeth Pope's essay, "'I am NOT just like one of the family,'" explores South African and American texts that identify a "family ideology" in both countries' popular constructions of domestic help. Isolating cross-cultural correspondence, Pope brings together narratives from both sides of the Atlantic that critique a tenacious family romance, which dubiously masks exploitative interracial domestic servant relationships. Sheila Smith McKoy's *When Whites Riot* analyzes the ways that historic South African and U.S. race riots, from the Wilmington Race Riot to the Soweto Uprising, were (mis)represented in twentieth-century popular media, literature, and film. Drawing upon contemporaneous fiction and journalism from both countries, Smith McKoy turns conventional constructions of race riots on their head: while popularly construed as instigated by black people, she demonstrates, riots in fact originated with white actors seeking to uphold political and social dominance. Smith McKoy zeroes in on cultural processes of racialization and subordination, and by isolating this parallel erasure of white racial assault in both countries, she identifies congruent forms of racial control and representational distortions as ties that bind the contexts together.[45]

Parallel comparative studies stressing similarities are not without their risks or their critics. Rita Barnard, for example, has challenged abstracted, reductionist tendencies in comparative inquiries. In her review of *When Whites Riot*, Barnard charges that the study obscures historical and rhetorical differences in order to draw uniform conclusions about U.S. and South African instances of racial violence.[46] More generally, Barnard warns against parallel studies that "lapse into an inert tabulation of samenesses and differences" and often privilege similarities at the expense of overlooking crucial distinctions.[47] She argues, instead, for inquiries sensitive to "the distances and disjunctions that must be traversed, or at least acknowledged, in any comparative enterprise."[48] Stephan

Meyer likewise raises concerns over the risks of other parallel studies, suggesting that they frequently trade in "assumption[s] of similarity" that skew the analysis before the fact.[49] These challenges, rooted in the logic of particularity and specificity, tease out some of the pitfalls of this comparative approach. At their best, parallel projects can both illuminate significant patterns and points of convergence across varied geographies and lead to conclusions we might not otherwise arrive at. Still, they often presume or beg the question of history, not in the sense that they necessarily ignore the historical contexts they compare, but rather in the sense that synchronically identifying similarities alone leaves unexamined the underlying background responsible for cross-cultural resonances. Without some diachronic angle, parallel studies overlook or take for granted extended periods of engagement as histories of relation—histories we must revisit and account for with deliberation. Shu-mei Shih has usefully reframed comparative studies as studies of relation, urging literary scholars to rethink comparison "not in terms of juxtapositions but in terms of a network of horizontal and vertical relations, which comparativists have so far consistently ignored due to various vested interests."[50] Challenging the Eurocentric foundations of classic comparative literary methodology, Walter Mignolo likewise argues that an approach that *relates*, rather than *compares*, two or more texts would constitute a beneficial shift from a distinguishing "ontology of essence to a relational ontology."[51] Shih's and Mignolo's emphasis on relation helps, as well, to outline relation as something with a history, a development, and a set of effects. My work, then, is not so much to advance claims of South African– African American comparison as much as it is to historicize them, to reckon with their formation and cultural significance.

Embracing a relational ontology, as this study does, commits us to the second analytical model of comparative studies: the transactional, a mode that deploys literary history or archeology to trace cultural networks, flows of influence, and the movement of people, cultural materials, and ideas across regional, national, or continental boundaries. Detecting stylistic or structural parallels, thematic echoes, homages, and other significations between South African and African American texts or writers may be an entry to a generative set of critical questions: What dynamics, conditions, and forms of traffic are responsible for the very ground of comparison that facilitates comparative literary study in the first place? What makes a comparative approach seem so commonsensical or self-evident? How have repeated cases of circulation, exchange, and connection yielded discernible "patterns of influence and cross-fertilization" across the black literary world?[52] These questions animate *Grounds of Engagement* in its quest to identify some of the cultural infrastructure undergirding black transnationalism and, in so doing, foreground the promise of transactional models that remain attentive to more planetary literary traffic.

Scholars have importantly addressed twentieth-century cultural transactions between black communities in South Africa and the United States,[53] but, to date, there is no sustained book-length study of literary exchanges between the two communities. In the current range of transactional scholarship, many pieces help articulate how or why black constituencies in both countries sought to bridge the physical and cultural gaps between them. Most comparative studies of the early twentieth century address intellectuals' efforts to articulate a new or alternative modernity capable of granting full subjectivity, rights, and freedoms to black peoples.[54] As studies of the later twentieth century indicate, by the late-1960s and the 1970s, exchanges between (U.S.) Black Power and (South African) Black Consciousness movements more or less eclipsed questions of an inclusive modernity and focused instead on projects of cultural self-definition and political self-determination.[55]

Taken as a whole, however, most of these transactional approaches, inadvertently or not, have elucidated only one dimension of dynamic transnational traffic between black writers in South Africa and the United States. Over the last twenty-five years, scholars have carefully documented the impact of (African) American cultural production on black South Africa to remarkable effect. Charting South Africa's cultural relationships to the wider world and marshaling evidence of South Africans' ingenuity through local adaptation of outside influences have become commonplace. As a result, we know a considerable amount about how South Africa has taken up black American cultural and intellectual work. We know, for example, that New Negro cosmopolitanism of early-twentieth-century America contributed greatly to the rise of urban-centered New Africanism that surged through black South African cityscapes, as iconized in the bustling culture of Sophiatown.[56] Widely circulated cultural texts and political treatises by African Americans were studied by the black urban South African intelligentsia from the dawn of the twentieth century. Booker T. Washington's *Up from Slavery*—one of the most popular African American texts in early-twentieth-century South Africa—in addition to W. E. B. Du Bois's *The Souls of Black Folk*, Marcus Garvey's writing, and Alain Locke's *The New Negro*, are all widely credited with profoundly influencing black South African thinkers who negotiated the modernist quagmires of their own white power structure.[57] Decades later, South Africa's black urban literati and cosmopolites of the 1950s actively drew upon and refashioned American literary, musical, commercial, and filmic representations for their own local purposes, or as Es'kia Mphahlele might put it, "hammer[ed] them out on the anvil of South African experience."[58]

Forging his philosophy of Black Consciousness in the 1960s and '70s, Steve Biko drew upon the milieu of African American thought that included that of Malcolm X, Martin Luther King Jr., and American Black Power advocates like Stokely Carmichael/Kwame Ture, James Cone, and Eldridge Cleaver.[59] Other proponents of Biko's philosophy sometimes accepted and other times rejected or modified the insights of black Americans—Du Bois, Langston Hughes, and James Baldwin, but also Lance Jeffers, Desiree Barnwell, and other Black Power authors—in order to begin redefining the terms of South African blackness central to the Black Consciousness project.[60]

More explicitly imaginative African American writing—autobiography, fiction, and poetry—likewise shaped the contours of the cultural imaginary across the Atlantic, particularly during the early phases of apartheid. From the 1940s onward, black American literature of the Harlem Renaissance and the post-Renaissance protest tradition captured black South Africans' interests by uncompromisingly addressing the conundrums of the color line. In a retrospective *New York Times* piece, Richard Rive would assert that "[a]lthough trailing from the Harlem Renaissance by two decades, [the 1940s and 1950s black South African literature] ran parallel to the literature of that movement. In an indirect way Richard Wright and Langston Hughes can be seen as the progenitors of the black South African literature which flourished from the later [19]40s."[61] Indeed, Wright's work made a widely acknowledged impact upon the imaginations (if not always the aesthetics) of various South African authors, including Peter Abrahams, Keorapetse Kgositsile, Alex La Guma, Es'kia Mphahlele, and Richard Rive.[62] Hughes loomed just as large. Of Wright's short story collection *Uncle Tom's Children*, Mphahlele explained that "the agony told me how to use the short story as a way of dealing with my anger and indignation"; he quickly added that the "gentle and almost unobtrusive manner of Langston's short fiction and poetry did things to me. I realized later that I needed them both—those two antithetical idioms of black American expression, Wright's and Langston's."[63] Rive attested to the influence of both writers, along with Countee Cullen and Jean Toomer, on his own authorial development. In "The Ethics of an Anti–Jim Crow," an autobiographical essay that explicitly signifies on the works of Wright and Hughes, he found that, upon reading black American literature in his formative years, "a new world with which I could identify opened up to me. I knew that there were others who felt the way I did and, what was more, articulated it in a way I had never realized possible. I was now able to analyze my own situation through theirs, rationalize my own feeling through theirs. I could break with my literary dependence on descriptions by White folks and the Ways of White Folks. Native Son had come of age."[64] In comparable fashion, Lewis Nkosi and Bessie Head, among others, noted their profound appreciation for James Baldwin's work.[65] At least according to the male writers, Wright, Hughes, and Baldwin stood as a virtual holy trinity of literary influence. But if black women seem consciously underrepresented in this panoply of writers at midcentury, it is largely due to an almost exclusively male literary culture—not just within black South African circles, but also in the black American texts that circulated in southern Africa. The question of an equivalent black women's transnational literary culture prior to the 1970s merits much more attention—especially, its less visible formation and impediments across the early- to mid–twentieth century.

For all the rich evidence of black America's imprint on black South Africa's literary production, scholars have been much slower in tracking the flows of cultural or literary influence in the opposite direction. By collectively framing popular, intellectual, and/or literary cultures in the United States as the generative source of influence acting upon—or engaged by—a South African audience, much of the scholarship threatens to reinforce a diffusionist perspective. As geographer J. M. Blaut has contended, diffusionism presupposes a geographic epicenter (in this case, the United States) out of which all things cultural emanate unidirectionally toward less culturally saturated regions of the earth.[66] Diffusionist approaches typically rest on at least two problematic assumptions under scrutiny in this study: The first assumption is that a "culturally deficient" recipient group merely absorbs incoming influence indiscriminately. This assumption is ratcheted back in the studies of black transnationalism referenced earlier, as most stress South African refashioning of American cultural and intellectual productions.[67] A second assumption is the inverse of the first: the notion that the disseminating culture remains unaffected or unaltered by transnational transaction. This assumption risks positioning African Americans as the default progenitors of twentieth-century black radical traditions or, in Laura Chrisman's critique, the "vanguard global class" and black South Africans appreciative, if adaptive, recipients.[68] Although no studies explicitly advocate this position, the striking paucity of scholarship that considers the influence of black South African cultures on black America could very well lead one to this conclusion. The danger here is not that it propagates an imbalanced model, for there is really no way to quantify a qualitative relationship, but that it effectively obscures the ways black South African thought, art, and political developments have shaped black American intellectual and artistic traditions.[69]

There are, of course, understandable reasons for the asymmetrical treatment of black South African and African American cultural relations. The uneven standing of the United States and South Africa in the Cold War global economy—coupled with the appropriation and mass exportation of black culture by a hegemonic American commercial-entertainment industry—significantly contributes to this asymmetry. So, too, does South Africa's increasing isolation under a heavily entrenched apartheid regime facing cultural and economic sanctions across the 1970s and '80s. Another factor involves black South Africans' historically more restricted access to capital, cultural products, and presses within the country (although exiles operated outside its borders). These dynamics certainly make black South African influence on black America less evident. To be sure, projects carefully exploring the manufacturing of nonwestern desire for western commodities in an age of intensive global capitalism are quite valuable. But without considerable attention to the mutually constitutive nature of the transaction, unidirectional transnational cultural studies between "West" and "East," or "North" and "South," risk running along disturbing, well-worn grooves.[70]

There is, then, a great need for more complex, polyvalent analyses of black cross-cultural relation. Without abandoning future scholarship that traces the impact of black transnationalism on South African writing and culture, it is nevertheless imperative to consider the *mutuality* of black cultural transformations that took place on both shores of the Atlantic over the twentieth century. Shih has rightly claimed that "[r]elational comparison is not a center-periphery model, as the texts form a network of relations from wherever the texts are written, read, and circulated."[71] Holding networks of relation in mind aids in elucidating how South Africans and African Americans have conceived of and fashioned themselves in relation to one another. Such an effort outlines the literary dimensions of James Campbell's claim that "African and African American identities are and have always been mutually constituted."[72] To demonstrate how African Americans and black South Africans have partially constituted each other's imaginaries and identities, *Grounds of Engagement* helps address the general lopsided trend by tracing out more multidirectional and dialectical forms of engagement than are generally acknowledged. Exposing the crisscrossing flows of South African–African American influence involves raising some of the effects black South African writers' physical and textual presence in the United States have had on their American counterparts' imaginations, self-understandings, and worldviews.

My effort to plot out where and how several exemplary literary texts are written, read, and circulated also provokes a reevaluation of what we mean by "primary text." This approach has required that I reread well-known published autobiographies, novels, poetry collections, and short stories in light of their author's spatial sensibilities and transnational engagements. But it has also sent me to archives in South Africa, Botswana, and across the United States in search of unpublished material in order to articulate a more capacious view of literary and cultural transactions between writers featured here. These materials (letters, drawings, magazines, pamphlets, cards, etc.) reveal a larger field of interaction, inspiration, and thus literary consequence for which approaches restricted to published texts alone cannot properly account. Archival materials force us to rethink what we take to be primary materials, not only because the unpublished words of authors often precede their published work, but also because, when shared between writers, they can shape the literary field as much as published works can.

In addition to the kinds of texts I take up in this study, there is also the question of how those texts can be read. Insofar as it involves coming to terms with the importance of the geography in black life and writing in segregated societies, a wide range of spatially attentive literary and cultural studies have inspired this study's approach. Geography (and its representation) as a culturally relevant matter has been the explicit subject of South African literary and cultural criticism for over the last thirty years. Rita Barnard, Lindsay Bremner, David Bunn, J. M. Coetzee, Hilton Judin and Ivan Vladislavić, Achille Mbembe, Sarah Nuttall, Abdoumaliq Simone, and Itala Vivan have variously detailed the geographic and spatial dimensions of South African literature and culture.[73] Louise Bethlehem's "The Drift to the Map" even takes up the prevalence of cartographic language in literary criticism to importantly remind us of the material conditions and imperial histories on which such language is often unconsciously predicated.[74] Critical attention to spatial dimensions of African American literature has been comparatively less prominent, but recent scholarship suggests a more concerted focus on the geographic in literary analysis. Early and continuing contributions by Melvin Dixon, Farah Jasmine Griffin, Houston Baker, Katherine McKittrick, and Thadious Davis importantly examine geography and mobility as defining features of black American life.[75] *Grounds of Engagement* draws fruitfully from these insightful analyses, but its espoused transactional approach means not comparing or contrasting the geographic foci of these studies (one set focused on South Africa, another focused on black America) so much as placing them into conversation with one another. By using racial geography as a principal basis of relation between black South Africans and African Americans, this study bridges the two nationally based bodies of scholarship I feature here via their common analyses of the geographic. Bringing these two heretofore separate pools of criticism into conversation not only permits us to reimagine their relation to one another; it also provides us with a broader horizon according to which we may study black transnational relation.

Chapter Overview

This book offers a literary history informed by spatial and cultural theory. On the one hand, it advances a mode of cultural analysis that foregrounds the geographic in black lives and cultural imaginaries and, in doing so, models a way of reading black South African and African American writing attuned to the relevance of race, space, and place. On the other hand, this study interprets the two literary traditions in relation to one another. Bringing attention to underaccounted-for cultural traffic that has shaped both traditions in the latter half of the twentieth century, it develops a literary history based on defining moments of cross-cultural engagement. The chapters that follow roughly correspond to different decades across the period of formal apartheid that allow us to chronicle some shifts in transnational literary relationships over this period, but they figure more as bearings than as strong historical claims about neatly segmented decades.

The chapters are also organized around formative encounters between black writers from South Africa and the United States—episodes that, over the course of this book, prove to be intertwined and relevant for subsequent interactions. An episodic format seems apt for several reasons. Rather than a comprehensive history that stresses unbroken continuity, it shows that transnational engagement is ongoing but also uneven, interrupted, and sometimes rearticulated. This approach to literary history also acknowledges that tracing traditions of contemporary cross-cultural exchange is itself a process of ongoing recovery and reassessment. Furthermore, Michael Titlestad has noted the knotty dilemmas of abstraction that often bedevil transnational approaches. The necessarily enormous magnitude of scale to which such studies are gauged frequently puts them at risk of "becoming teleological, channeling analysis along predetermined and limited paths" with the possible effect of "regulating countless local stories of contest and cultural emergence."[76] Organizing this inquiry around a focused set of engagements helps minimize, though not wholly avert, such dangers. It also leaves room for more detailed readings of texts and interactions between writers that too often get whittled down or relegated to the footnotes in more sweeping, comprehensive histories.

Despite the ambitious breadth of this transnational study, I wish to underscore several points about the ultimately modest nature of its claims. First, my emphasis on the literary does not and cannot successfully claim exclusive rights for literature over individual imaginations or whole cultural imaginaries. Rather, literature must be understood here to operate within a larger cultural milieu and thus coexist synergistically with other equally consequential artistic and discursive forms—including visual art, performance, and arguably above all, music. Indeed, relationships among musicians and intellectuals perhaps most clearly shaped black transnational relation in the popular imagination, particularly as exiled South African musicians spent years in the United States. One thinks of the powerful collaborations between Miriam Makeba and Harry Belafonte, Abdullah Ibrahim/Dollar Brand and Archie Shepp, as well as Sathima Bea Benjamin and Duke Ellington, plus the iconic marriage of Makeba and Stokely Carmichael/Kwame Ture. The scope of this study permits only limited engagement with these other art forms, but they should be understood as part of the same cultural matrix as the literature I examine.

Second, while I gesture toward black transnationalism generally, I consciously restrict my discussion to one constitutive and emblematic strand within a global web of variously inflected cross-cultural engagements. By focusing predominantly on literary transactions and comparisons between black South Africans and African Americans during the apartheid era, I mean to draw attention to a dynamic relationship that might otherwise get diluted if we adopt a wider scope. Although there are risks in isolating one strand from a wider array of networks, institutions, and trajectories that originate in or connect to other parts of the world (for example, Russia, Cuba, India, England, Algeria, Zimbabwe, or Ghana, among others), my approach is calculated to recover what falls away when we adopt too distant or global a perspective. It is offered to encourage more studied foci on other transnational relationships rather than to claim any comprehensive purview. Even within this singular literary strand, my study is far from exhaustive; other candidates merit more attention, including South Africans writers and intellectuals in the United States—Phyllis Ntantla, Duma Ndlovu, Lewis Nkosi, Dennis Brutus, Sindiwe Magona, Mazisi Kunene, Njabulo Ndebele, Es'kia Mphahlele, Mbulelo Mzamane—as well as black American sojourners in apartheid South Africa, such as Michael Harper and Frank Wilderson, III.[77] The wide array of still undiscussed U.S.–South African literary relations is testimony to this subject's ripeness for future consideration.

Third, a focus on transnational black relation, in part, foregrounds the role of racial consciousness in transnational contexts, but it does not suggest an absence of interracial interactions among writers, either intranationally or transnationally. Black intellectuals, activists, and artists primarily waged struggles for racial justice in both contexts, yet many efforts involved coalition or collaboration with white South Africans and Americans. Literary relationships rarely abided by the logic racial boundaries alone, and writers forged affiliations across the color line according to shared literary networks, aesthetic interests, or social visions. These would bring writers like Langston Hughes and Alan

Paton, as Hughes's letters attest, as well as authors such as Toni Morrison and Nadine Gordimer into literary relation.[78] It is also worth adding that, while white authors historically have not, by necessity or obligation, been compelled to confront or address racial geographies in their work—or have enjoyed the privilege to ignore them in the ways that black writers have not—a minority of white writers, including J. M. Coetzee, William Faulkner, and Gordimer, have been notably explicit about racialized space in their writing, as well.

Finally, I understand the texts and authors I study to operate within the contours of other intellectual, political, and imaginative geographies—for example, Cold War, feminist, working-class, Pan-Africanist, or Third-Worldist geographies. The authors and the relationships they cultivate, in other words, function in conjunction with other sets of commitments and engagements. That they do so points to the enmeshments between different political interests, aesthetic commitments, and social agendas across the black world. The concept of "grounds of engagement," with its explicit plurality, however, provides a useful heuristic for grasping a range of (black) transnational relations, affiliations, and solidarities.

I begin the subsequent chapters with the ways racial geographies profoundly shape the texture and meaning of black South African and American literature. Chapter 2, "Race, Place, and the Geography of Exile," takes up the early writing of Richard Wright and Peter Abrahams that starkly traces out the caustic terms of race and place in their formative years. The unmistakable similarities between Wright's and Abrahams's famed autobiographies, *Black Boy* and *Tell Freedom*, highlight the significant impact of their respective racial landscapes. This chapter reads both texts for the central role that racialized place played in forming the consciousness of these young men. Moreover, I argue that place also prominently affected the stylistic and aesthetic modes of the two autobiographies. This approach draws our attention to rather different locales: for Wright, the American South from which he fled and, for Abrahams, the exilic space of Europe to which he fled. Indeed, I suggest that their texts' resonances result from intersecting, rather than merely parallel, lives. As both writers fled the racism of their native lands, they crossed paths in 1940s Europe, a key locus of black transnational engagement. It was during their short-lived but generative friendship that Abrahams wrote and revised *Tell Freedom*, a process with which Wright was involved.

This chapter lays out the primacy of the geographic, an analytic that runs throughout the course of this study, but it also sets up some terms that subsequent chapters complicate. The chapter partially upholds the dominant tendency in scholarship to emphasize American cultural influence and South

African reworking. In this case, the American expatriate helped shape Abrahams's account of his racially riven land, but as a gesture to antidiffusionist dynamics in the remaining chapters, I also point to the ways that Abrahams helped Wright settle into a life of exile. In addition, the second chapter's emphasis on the power of place permits us to read these autobiographies as mappings of their social and physical geographies. The boundaries that both writers traverse to escape their native lands leave their national frames intact. But as remaining chapters bear out, artists also redrew these maps to formulate alternative forms of belonging.

By the 1960s and '70s, a growing number of exiled black South African writers had moved to the United States, where Pan-Africanism and black nationalism reemerged as discourses through which black American and South African artists consciously recast their transnational relationships. Chapter 3, "Remapping the (Black) Nation," traces the migration of a later South African exile, Keorapetse Kgositsile, who emigrated to the United States in 1962. I argue that Kgositsile labored to reconfigure how readers understood the world to be arranged, and his repeated explicitly geographic references throughout his 1971 poetry collection *My Name Is Afrika* played a large role in this process. Guided by the principles of the burgeoning Black Arts Movement he engaged upon arriving in the United States, his poems sutured together South African and American sites of black revolutionary struggle. By insistently coupling South African and American places, his poetry militated against the segregationist logic encouraged by South African and U.S. states to keep liberation efforts on either shore separate. Kgositsile's approach was based in a dynamic cultural milieu, and occasional turns to his ideological foils and counterparts—from Nat Nakasa to Gil Scott-Heron—help to put his artistic project into relief.

Transnationalism is not the exclusive province of globe-trotting authors, but also includes the practices of those who could not access the means of transatlantic mobility explored in earlier chapters. Chapter 4, "Cultivating Correspondences; or, Other Gestures of Belonging," considers a "grounded transnationalism" expressed in the 1970s and '80s correspondence between Bessie Head, who remained an exile in rural Botswana, and four black American women writers: Nikki Giovanni, Toni Morrison, Alice Walker, and Michelle Cliff. Head's epistolary exchanges with the latter two authors reveals proliferating figures of the garden, a black feminist geography that imbues their writing. This microgeography, I argue, outlines a type of relation that parts ways with the expansive territoriality advanced by nationalisms of the racial state and its opponents. Indeed, the garden directs attention to simultaneously sub- and extranational forms of belonging. Head's, Walker's, and Cliff's widely circulating gardens also elucidate the ways that letter writing functions as a cultivation of transnational relation. The letters, however, also alert us to the limitations of epistolary cultivation tested by the challenges of long-distance empathy.

The fifth and final chapter, "Constructive Engagements," considers the outcomes of some interactions among black South African and African American writers discussed in preceding chapters, but "updated" here in the context of the 1980s. It explores how earlier transnational engagements led to a series of subsequent texts and interpersonal relationships as the global antiapartheid movement began to reach its apex. Those works—by Rive, Cliff, Audre Lorde, and Gwendolyn Brooks—attest to the impress of earlier writers (Hughes, Wright, Kgositsile, and Head) and, by returning us to the matter of cultural influence, point to the considerable role South Africa and its writers played in shaping African American writerly imaginations. Furthermore, I argue, Cliff's poem "Constructive Engagement" plays with the name of the Reagan-era U.S. foreign policy toward South Africa to powerful effect. In a way that recalls the advice of Hughes's revolutionary in "Question and Answer," Cliff "take[s]" the name of U.S. foreign policy "to remake it" and, in the process, reflects precisely the discursive work that the literature of the 1980s (and before) sought to accomplish. Beyond this, the phrase captures the imaginative labor that literature on both sides of the Atlantic across the apartheid years, more broadly, exemplified and invested in: the development of a transnational(izing) worldview that accompanies cross-cultural relation and renders it imaginable.

CHAPTER 2

Race, Place, and the Geography of Exile

I n early August 1947, Richard Wright and his family disembarked the *SS America* onto a pier in Southampton, England.[1] As symbolically loaded as any moment in his widely celebrated writing, this event definitively marked Wright's quitting of the United States. Having abandoned his repeatedly frustrated attempts to live in peace in the segregated country of his birth, he was bound for Paris, France, which he had visited six months earlier but would now adopt as his new home. Upon concluding the longest leg of this journey across the Atlantic Ocean, he and his family left the ship to prepare for a quick trip across the English Channel the following day to their final destination. Waiting on the wharf to welcome Wright into his new life abroad was a 28-year-old South African writer-in-exile, Peter Abrahams.[2]

Abrahams had himself disembarked in England almost seven years earlier in October 1940. Born in Johannesburg, he left his South African home at the age of nineteen, taking a far more prolonged and circuitous route aboard various ships—first journeying up the eastern coast of Africa and edging along to the Bay of Bengal from Durban, then reversing course, and eventually traveling northward up Africa's western coast toward his European destination, after over a year at sea.[3] Abrahams sought in his ultimate destination the same object Wright desired: a freedom that long eluded him under the racial regime of his native land. Both authors desperately sought to find refuge from the structured inequalities and routine indignities rooted in their respective countries and long desired to practice their craft under more viable conditions.

Both internationally acclaimed black fiction writers, Wright and Abrahams were in a veritable league of their own in the mid-1940s. Having written two chapbooks of verse during his adolescence in South Africa,[4] Abrahams's first years in his adopted England were particularly fruitful ones, yielding a collection of vignettes (*Dark Testament* in 1942) and two novels, *Song of the City* (1945) and *Mine Boy* (1946). His early success inaugurated a milestone career, making Abrahams a key figure in early modern African literature—the second black South African to publish novels in English and a major influence on subsequent generations of aspiring black South African writers and African writers more broadly.[5] Not long before Abrahams, Wright shot to literary stardom to become "the most successful black writer of his generation."[6] With the publication of *Uncle Tom's Children* (1938), *Native Son* (1940), *12 Million Black Voices* (1941), and *Black Boy* (1945), he became arguably the most globally read black fiction writer of his time.[7] By midcentury, his stature beyond the United States was considerable, particularly in the black Anglophone world.

Wright and Abrahams were not strangers at their Southampton encounter.[8] They had first met in Paris, during Wright's earlier short stay in the French capital, which coincided with Abrahams's visit for the months-long 1946 Paris Peace Conference.[9] They began writing one another shortly thereafter; their letters crisscrossed the Atlantic and, later, the English Channel, as the writers traded work and reflections on both writing and the political issues of their day. While returning to the United States after their eight-month European sojourn in December 1946, the Wrights briefly reunited with Abrahams in his adopted London.[10] The friendship that formed between them was not especially long-lived, but it spanned across critical periods in both Wright's and Abrahams's lives: from Wright's first stay in France, his brief U.S. return, and his definitive emigration back to Paris all the way through Abrahams's own move to Paris in 1948.

Their early epistolary exchanges occasionally accompanied parcels of published books (their own and others') as well as works-in-progress.[11] On his ten-day transatlantic passage into exile, when he was not working on his own manuscript (which would become *The Outsider*), Wright read a partial manuscript that Abrahams had sent him—an early chunk of what would eventually become the latter's popular autobiography, *Tell Freedom*, which chronicled his fraught childhood and youth in a deeply segregated pre-apartheid South Africa.[12] Wright considered the section he received "very good" and wanted to tell Abrahams "how swell I think his book is."[13] The narrative reminded Wright "of his own childhood in Mississippi. He had wired Pete[r], and hoped he would be in Southampton to meet them."[14] Both Abrahams's expatriate circumstances and writing had impressed Wright. In an interview shortly after their meeting, Wright noted the South African author's experiences, referring to Abrahams as "brilliant" and added that South Africa had "a lulu of a situation down there, comparable only to the situation of the Negro on the plantation in the deepest South."[15] Later, Wright offered glowing words of salutation in a blurb for *The Path of Thunder*, Abrahams's 1948 novel: "To read Abrahams," he avers, "is to be haunted by the feeling that he is writing about our own problems. His art is powerful enough to bridge the gap of oceans and cultures."[16]

Southampton, Paris, London, Johannesburg, Durban, New York, Mississippi. These points of departure and arrival figure as regular coordinates along extensive trajectories for two very mobile expatriates. The locales that fill Wright's and Abrahams's texts and lives speak to a profound particularity of place, indeed. This chapter focuses upon the imprint of place in the writing of Wright and Abrahams, by which I mean both the primacy of place in and on their writing: on the one hand, its deeply textured representation in their work and, on the other, the ways in which place shapes the very production of writing itself. Yi-Fu Tuan defines place as "the concretion of value" through which abstract space is particularized, domesticated, recognized, and more clearly understood.[17] Place, then, is the site-specific arrangement of qualities and characteristics rendered unique through an accumulated effect of physical geography, built environment, and social formation in a given moment in time. Rather than generic way stations the writers passed through or resided in, the locales represent accreted layers of historical processes, dynamic social and cultural configurations, economic flows, architectural designs, and people—all of which are fundamentally imbricated in the individual and collective memories, associations, and symbolic charges that manifest in both writers' work.

A keen attentiveness to place cannot be wholly surprising in the writing of exiles, for exiles' lives are, by definition, structured by the geographic fact of displacement, by the physical and experiential disparities (or symmetries) between point of departure and point of arrival. Abrahams's and Wright's displacements, of course, originated from another equally geographic fact: the racial segregation that saturated each author's everyday childhood experiences in South Africa and the American South, respectively. Their refusal to accept the terms of segregation or bear its consequences led to their expatriations. Wright's and Abrahams's acute attention to the racial contours of place prove exceedingly evident in each author's acclaimed autobiography: *Black Boy* (1945) and *Tell Freedom* (1954), respectively.[18] Each narrative charts the author's early experiences of his racial geography, by which I mean both his defining incidents *in* a specific location and, more literally, his sensation *of* racialized spatiality— sociogeographic arrangement that harbors, reflects, and produces racialized experience and consciousness. As such, both autobiographies illustrate for us the mutually constitutive nature of race and space that is the basis of, not the exception to, early-twentieth-century modernity, and how that very fact so crucially shapes the author's writing. The modern entanglement of race and space, indeed, greatly informs the narrative modes of the two authors' autobiographies, whose geographically dense expressivity showcases a racial-spatial literacy—the reading (and writing) of one's physical and social landscapes that registers its racially hierarchical structures.

Aside from acutely geographic dimensions and narrative structures that arc toward the young personas' climactic flights from alienating "homes," both autobiographies share strikingly parallel themes and formal devices: from the traumatizing onset of their racial consciousness, the stunting effects of their racist societies, defining scenes of formative violence, and life-altering encounters with literacy all the way to unconventional narrative strategies. The list of similarities is too extensive and detailed to be coincidental, especially for autobiographical narratives that presumably hew close to the reality of past experience.[19] Despite the particularities of place they name, the similarities across both narratives are enough to make black U.S. readers feel "haunted by the feeling" that Abrahams is addressing "our own [American] problems."

Wright's assessment of Abrahams's writing implicitly frames their work in terms of the men's parallel contexts. Their literary congruences reflect their sociopolitical ones, Wright's words imply, because comparable conditions of racial segregation produce similar experiences and, thus, parallel expressions of protest. Intimate, quotidian familiarity with a racist social order—its forms of exploitation, exclusion, inequity, and alienation, along with the range of emotions and actions they prompt—certainly gives rise to resonant scenarios figured in literature, and the common goal of eradicating them can provide some basis for black transnational engagement. Indeed, they are the singular precondition of black transnationalism. But this alone cannot fully account for the formal and stylistic parallels evident in the authors' autobiographies. Wright's and Abrahams's intersecting trajectories noted earlier suggest a more complex process that includes but exceeds their echoing social contexts.

What conditions, then, lead to such overt textual resonances? In a rare analysis of the two autobiographies, Chinosole astutely casts *Tell Freedom* as a telling analogue of *Black Boy*. She positions Abrahams's autobiography as a rewriting of Wright's and attributes their textual similarities to the matter of influence, to Wright's "centrality as a Black biographer."[20] Wright was, indeed, a dominant figure in the world of black letters. In South Africa alone, his impact upon black writers was considerable, as his work helped shape the black literary scene there across the twentieth century. Wright's *Native Son*, for example, proved instrumental in shaping Abrahams's *Mine Boy*, and his short story collection, *Uncle Tom's Children*, would likewise exert its influence on the writing of Abrahams's *Dark Testament*, Alex La Guma's work, and Ezekiel (Es'kia) Mphahlele's *Man Must Live*.[21] Mphahlele averred that an encounter with Wright's *Uncle Tom's Children* helped him recognize key cross-cultural correspondences and mold his own aesthetic style. In the late 1940s, Mphahlele received the volume "through an American book club with an agency in Johannesburg," and upon reading it, he found an immediate connection:

> Here was a man who spoke my language. I saw the South African black in Big Boy ("Big Boy Leaves Home"). I smelled our poverty in this Southern setting; the smell of burning was symbolically the smell of the heat and dust and sweat of farm labor we knew in white man's territory. The searing long black song of Wright's people was ours. The stories hit me in the pit of my stomach. The agony told me how to use the short story—as a way of dealing with my anger and indignation. It was the ideal medium. I fed on the fury and poured more and more vitriol into my words until I could almost taste them.[22]

Richard Rive likewise acknowledged Wright's powerful prose and would go so far as to credit Wright, along with Langston Hughes, with indirectly being one of "the progenitors of the black South African literature which flourished from the later [19]40s."[23] Wright's influence extends to later generations of South African writers, as well. *Black Boy*, in particular, was a towering achievement whose wake was felt across the globe. Poet Keorapetse Kgositsile credits a widely circulating contraband copy of Wright's *Black Boy*—passed along from an African American sailor who anchored in Cape Town—with setting his imagination alight and modeling for him a new representational approach. "That book," he notes, "travelled all over [South Africa] among those of us who were interested in writing. What was interesting, too, was that nobody got selfish enough to keep it. You got it, read it, reread it, etc., and maybe kept it for two or three weeks and passed it on. When it got to me, it was then that I realized I didn't have to have European models to write."[24]

The testimonies of Mphahlele and Kgositsile do more than outline Wright's general influence. In identifying the material trajectories of their books, they point to a history of less visible but crucial underlying transactions—the deeper transnational cultural infrastructure that yields, among other things, textual resonances and thematic correspondences—which this chapter seeks to out-line. Andrew van der Vlies's concept of the "textual Atlantic," or a transatlantic "*text*scape," helps highlight the material dimensions of a cultural circuitry that underwrites influence and resonance across vast geographic distances.[25] The movement of texts—from published books to works-in-progress to personal letters (all of which figure in Wright's and Abrahams's relationship)—across a wider Atlantic world, among other oceanic basins, has profoundly shaped black expressive cultures in ways still underappreciated. As Kgositsile's example bears out in the scenario above and in the next chapter, the corollary oceanic crossings of people, from seamen to writers, drive and reshape this *text*scape. For Wright and Abrahams, too, circulation involves the writers themselves, who met, moved in overlapping circles, and exchanged ideas. If we take seri-ously material geography—the concrete terms of place and the movement of texts and people between locations—we can productively clarify the literary relevance of place and trace the impact of the two writers' relationship on black literary expression for generations to follow. In the case of Wright and Abra-hams, I argue, both authors' experiences of place play a fundamental role in how they wrote their widely celebrated autobiographical narratives. A geographi-cally attentive approach enables us to connect the kind of aesthetic approach Wright adopted back to his early sense of the American South's racial geogra-phy. Moreover, accounting for Wright's and Abrahams's intersecting expatri-ate lives in England and France permits us to better appreciate the crafting of Abrahams's own autobiographical narrative. While much of this chapter will consider Wright's significant influence on Abrahams, revisiting this period of their overlapping lives nevertheless provides a slightly clearer sense of what Abrahams offered Wright, in turn—a point frequently obscured by a routine focus on Wright's influence, generally.

I begin this chapter by examining the topographical dimensions of Wright's *Black Boy* and follow this with a reading of "I Choose Exile," Wright's damning essay that articulates his rationale for expatriation from the United States and whose depiction of American racial geography is even more explicit than in his autobiography. From there, we move to a reading of the places of *Tell Freedom*, rendered all the more visible because of Abrahams's own geographic repre-sentations, which are partially born of the African American literature Abra-hams encounters. The teleology of flight that structures both authors' autobio-graphical texts leads us to consider the literary consequences of Wright's and Abrahams's relocations to their respective European capitals. Zeroing in on the writers' relationship in Europe enables us to more fully appreciate the role these locations play in the production of *Tell Freedom* and, furthermore, helps throw into fuller relief the places of black transnational engagement as incubators of cultural production.

Black Boy and the Place of Race

The childhood and adolescence that Wright depicts in *Black Boy* coincides with unprecedented regional and national changes across the United States as historic shifts took place. Between the 1890s and 1940s, the South underwent rapid transformation as it was being reintegrated economically with the North after a postbellum period of relative marginalization. In what ultimately led to the rise of a national consumer culture, a tide of increasing industrialization, technological innovation, capitalist expansion, and accompanying new social practices sent old ways into disarray. As historian Grace Elizabeth Hale explains, "[t]o make order within the seeming fragmentation of their world, some Americans elaborated spatial mediations of modernity—ways of attaching identities to physical moorings, from bodies to buildings to larger geographies like region and nation. They produced new grounds of difference to mediate the ruptures of modernity."[26] Racial distinctions proved paramount in helping to facilitate an emergent modern American identity. Across regions, economic classes, and ideological camps race offered a fundamental stabilizing ground for the turbulent period of a rapidly modernizing American life. Multiple constituencies across the country, argues Hale, "simultaneously but for different reasons, found race useful in creating new collective identities to replace older, more individual, and local groundings of self."[27]

Race, of course, could matter only if distinctions were starkly drawn. The emergence of the twentieth century saw the solidification of the color line, but W. E. B. Du Bois's now classic metaphor for racial segregation was more than just a metaphor; the color line, as James Tyner reminds us, was "the literal inscription of social injustice and inequality on the American landscape."[28] This period was marked by an intensified spatialization of race, a process legal geographer David Delaney dubs "fanatical hyper-territoriality." He explains: "The spatiality of Jim Crow involved the assignment of legal meaning to determinable segments of the physical world. . . . It presupposed the creation of more or less durable lines and spaces or the addition of an increment of meaning to existing lines and spaces. It entailed the assignment of consequences to the crossing of lines. It was constituted by ensembles of stationary space, such as rooms, toilets, buildings, parks, cemeteries, and by moveable spaces such as streetcars, trains, and later buses and airplanes."[29] Under this regime, racial distinctions and hierarchies were *spatially productive*—that is, by way of white

supremacist laws and customs, social and physical space was arranged, segregated, and inequitably apportioned according to specific categories of racial
difference (white and black/colored). In turn, racial difference and hierarchies
were simultaneously *spatially produced*—that is, the continuous etching of categories of racial difference into the landscape and built environment made
them socially salient, meaningful conceptions that were rendered concrete and
thus materially, tangibly determinative of everyday experience. If the racialized
spatial orders, or the arrangements of sociogeographic space and of the marked
bodies within them, have adhered to a deeply segregationist vision, they have
done so by redefining each other in an ever-adaptive racial geography. This
mutually constitutive and reinforcing relationship has followed what critical
geographer Edward Soja calls the socio-spatial dialectic.[30] Put differently, in the
era of intensive modern American segregation (as in periods before and since),
race-making and space-making have been inextricable, coterminous processes,
such that spatiality and racial identity mutually provided the necessary conditions for one another. It must also be stressed that this entanglement centrally
implicates gender and sexual identities as well, given their integral roles in the
production and reproduction of social bodies, categories of dominance and
subjection, and social spaces; gender has structured the codes of conduct across
racial geographies, so precariously principled on racial purity and white fears
of miscegenation.

As anchoring racial identities were spatially embedded, race was rendered
even more overtly registerable in the new social and geographic designs that
modernity wrought, most notoriously through legislation, demarcation, and
violent enforcement. The processes of spatially defining race and racially
marking geographic space—devising a spatial order to support an envisioned
social order—were precisely goals of the literal and figurative architects of white
supremacy. Maintaining these racial-spatial boundaries precipitated a panoply
of practices, from the most spectacular, violent means of lynching and white
rioting to far less obvious mechanisms that nevertheless amounted to a highly
structured sense of segregated place.[31]

Marked by his own effort to quit the land of his birth, the writing of the
Mississippi-born Wright reflects his geographic movement across this segregated landscape. Desperate attempts at life-preserving flight developed into a
leitmotif across his oeuvre, as numerous scholars, including Farah Jasmine Griffin, Melvin Dixon, Houston Baker, and Thadious Davis, have noted.[32] Casting
Black Boy as a modern revision of the classic slave narrative structure predicated
upon the illicit acquisition of literacy that facilitates a northward escape into
freedom, for example, Robert Stepto highlights the autobiography's vitalizing

arc toward flight. Despite a textualist focus on Wright's "sustained effort to gain authorial control of the text of his environment," Stepto notes that mobility in Wright's writing is "very much a physical matter as well. . . . [H]e wanted to get the hell out of Dixie."[33]

As Wright expresses his own growing compulsion to leave the South, *Black Boy* becomes, among other things, a narrative about the primacy of place. Quite literally a topography (a written description of place),[34] it presents a detailed account of his surrounding social and physical environment; in the process, Thadious Davis observes, Wright "map[s] his physical and psychological body in the landscape of privation and want."[35] While his whole oeuvre renders African American life in acutely geographic terms, the autobiography lays bare a caustic southern landscape not only by charting the overtly racial demarcations of social space, but also by conveying the more intimate textures of place.[36] The texture of Wright's southern places emphasizes the experience of a rigidly segregated world, particularly that world's deep impact upon black psyches and cultural imaginaries. In effect, it registers the ways in which the arrangement of Wright's external world structures black interiority. Accordingly, *Black Boy* emerges as a narrative of experience, but not exclusively an episodic record of formative events; it is also a concomitant chronicling of Wright's phenomenological experience of place itself, the invidious social formation that constitutes it, as well as its consequential interpellating properties. Within this scheme, Wright plots his persona's developing consciousness stamped with a growing sense of Jim Crow spatiality.

Wright's geographic acuity figures most prominently in his representation of movement, and most scholars have justly stressed Wright's flight from the South. I draw on those critical insights to consider a set of other movements that help us better outline the pressures and motivations for his regional "movement out of the deforming southern environment."[37] Two related movements precede and help catalyze Wright's climactic departure: a physical movement across the South and an imaginative movement beyond it. Tracing out these two types of movements not only helps frame Wright's final choice to flee the "southern night" of his childhood and adolescence as consistent with earlier patterns of mobility, but it also lets us assess the mutually constitutive machinations of race and place that underpin Wright's psychic development, thought, and aesthetic mode.

Movement across the southern landscape by Wright's persona deserves particular attention, as it is the least noted. *Black Boy* conveys the incessant internal migration that the segregationist political economy imposes upon his family. By the age of seventeen, Wright reports, he relocates from Natchez, Mississippi, to

Memphis, Tennessee, then briefly to Jackson, Mississippi, to Elaine, Arkansas, back to Jackson, then to West Helena, Arkansas, then to Greenwood, Mississippi, back once more to Jackson, and finally back to Memphis; and between these intraregional moves, Richard repeatedly changes domiciles within a given town. All this before he strikes out for imagined opportunities "up North." The Wright family's recursive shuttling from one southern location to another—a pre-Ellisonian form of "moving without moving" spurred by a potent combination of racial terror and destitution—marks their ever-frustrated search for safety and sustenance. The condition of African Americans in the Jim Crow South is frequently figured as static suppression, an engineered state of social and geographic immobility—a trope that Wright also incorporates in his text, most viscerally through the representation of his stroke-stricken mother.[38] But here, caught within the circuitry of lateral mobility across a landscape of black dispossession no less pernicious than physical stasis, the Wrights are not so much physically contained as they are subject to the vortices of the South's financial and physical economies of violence. The conditions of black hypermobility and immobility ultimately exist as two sides of the same segregationist coin that foists black bodies into regimented geographic relations.

Young Richard's experience of continuous relocation produces a deep social and existential dislocation that initiates in him a clear sense of differentiation from his peers at an early age. By twelve, Richard contrasts himself to fellow black pupils at his Aunt Addie's religious school. He asserts an "objectivity" not possessed by those who were "*claimed wholly by their environment* and could imagine no other, whereas I had come from *another plane of living*, from the swinging doors of saloons, the railroad yard, the roundhouses, the street gangs, the river levees, an orphan home; had shifted from town to town and home to home."[39] Giving him an alternative set of coordinates by which to orient himself, his experience of different locales unmoors him from a fixed, monologic point of reference. Wright's repeated uprooting develops into an irreversible estrangement that sets him apart from those around him.

During Wright's recursive childhood movement, the other, equally significant movement begins. This second, less physical form of mobility stems from young Richard's experience with stories and books, which transforms his relationship to the world around him, often supplanting it or transporting him imaginatively beyond it. His initial encounter with storytelling—via Ella, the schoolteacher boarding at his grandmother's house who whispers to him the story of *Bluebeard and His Seven Wives*—produces an indelible effect. As Wright listens to the story, "reality changed, the look of things altered, and the world became peopled with magical presences. My sense of life deepened and the feel of things was different, somehow."[40] This world-altering moment triggers his first sensation of "a total emotional response," leading to a passion for language and words, which form "the gateway to a forbidden and enchanting land."[41] Wright's subsequent enchantment with reading and, eventually, writing widens the already discernible distance—"this apartness, this eternal difference"[42]—between himself and surrounding white and black communities begun by his cyclical regional relocation. Predicated on a renewed imaginative and knowledge hunger, this "sense of distance was increasing each day."[43]

Young Richard's physical and imaginative dislocations effectively rescue him from being place-bound—a debilitating inability to venture physically, intellectually, or imaginatively—and he resists the curtailments that manifest in the sedentary life to which so many of his family members and companions are condemned. But these dislocations create a dangerous predicament: Wright's immersion in the literary world produces an irrepressible autonomous imaginative interiority. He euphorically and ominously reports that "I was beginning to dream the dreams that the state had said were wrong."[44] Because these heretical dreams doom him to either a physical death for his refusal to stay in his racial "place" or an imaginative death for not pursuing the possibilities the dreams inspire, these outlaw dreams effectively force Wright into a state of fugitivity, as the only living way out he imagines is *out*, to a "land where I could live with a little less fear."[45] Wright unambiguously yokes his drive toward greater knowledge and a literary life to his escape to the North.

Well before his departure, Wright regularly reads the lines of demarcation etched deeply into his surrounding geography. Initially, Wright's text presents a rather understated gloss on his environment. For example, the idyllic anaphoric passages on Wright's early childhood—the "Whitmanesque catalog of sensual remembrances"[46]—detail his youthful impressions of summertime in his native Natchez. Consider the following:

> There was the wonder I felt when I first saw a brace of mountainlike, spotted, black-and-white horses clopping down a dusty road through clouds of powdered clay.
>
> There was the delight I caught in seeing long straight rows of red and green vegetables stretching away in the sun to the bright horizon.
>
> There was the faint, cool kiss of sensuality when dew came on to my cheeks and shins as I ran down the wet green garden paths in the early morning.
>
> There was the vague sense of the infinite as I looked down upon the yellow, dreaming waters of the Mississippi River from the verdant bluffs of Natchez.[47]

These lines render an extraordinary sense of openness and spaciousness, aspects that, as social geographer Yi-Fu Tuan reminds us, speak directly to the experience of freedom: "Spaciousness is closely associated with the sense of being free. Freedom implies space; it means having the power and enough room in which to act. Being free has several levels of meaning. Fundamental is the ability to transcend the present condition, and this transcendence is most simply manifest as the elementary power to move. In the act of moving, space and its attributes are directly experienced."[48] Tuan's reflections revolve around physical conditions more than political ones (but in light of this observation, Wright's own temporary immobility in a later instance of white racist hostility nevertheless denotes a clear absence of freedom[49]). But what emerges as Wright's anaphoric lines continue is a nebulous sense of gathering fear and desire for something out of reach. It builds to a more complicated sense of attenuated freedom, developing into a discernible antipastoral strain in *Black Boy*:[50]

> There was the hint of cosmic cruelty that I felt when I saw the curved timbers of a wooden shack that had been warped in the summer sun.
> There was the saliva that formed in my mouth whenever I smelt the clay dust potted with fresh rain.
> There was the cloudy notion of hunger when I breathed the odor of new-cut, bleeding grass.
> And there was the quiet terror that suffused my senses when vast hazes of gold washed earthward from star-heavy skies on silent nights.[51]

These latter lines convey a more strained psychological and emotional existence, and they do so by signaling the strictures of Wright's surrounding social world through physical and geographic description. Wright's attention to the "cosmic cruelty," "quiet terror," "cloudy notion of hunger," "curved timbers of a wooden shack," and "odor of new-cut, bleeding grass" defines a texture of place steeped in subtle yet keen intimations of poverty, privation, and violence that speak to the spatial-racial dimensions of his life. Wright, here, formally interweaves the social and physical landscape, giving credence to Tuan's view that "[a] function of literary art is to give visibility to intimate experiences . . . of place."[52]

Young Richard's sense of place sharpens as he gets older: his coded expressions yield to a far more explicit and palpable racial geography. His first experience queuing for tickets at a Mississippi train station booth reveal to him sharply segregated lines with differentiated bodies occupying differentiated physical space, and as this realization permanently seeps into his powers of perception, a racial consciousness is "born in me with a sharp concreteness that would never die until I died."[53] He later details the process of boundary maintenance upheld through brutal forms of socialization among neighboring boys. Both white and black boys play their

> traditional racial roles as though we had been born to them, as though it was in our blood, as though we were being guided by instinct. All the frightful descriptions we had heard about each other, all the violent expressions of hate and hostility that had seeped into us from our surroundings, came now to the surface to guide our actions. The roundhouse was the racial boundary of the neighborhood, and it had been tacitly agreed between the white boys and the black boys that the whites were to keep to the far side of the roundhouse and we blacks were to keep to our side. Whenever we caught a white boy on our side we stoned him; if we strayed to their side, they stoned us.[54]

What interests Wright are not the imbricated spatial and social processes alone, important as they are. He devotes most of his attention to charting the imaginative, intellectual, and emotional violence of his racial geography: "I began to marvel at how smoothly the black boys acted out the roles that the white race had *mapped out for them*. Most of them were not conscious of living a special, separate, stunted way of life. Yet I knew that in some period of their growing up . . . there had been developed in them a delicate, sensitive controlling mechanism that shut off their minds and emotions from all that the white race had said was taboo."[55] As Wright articulates it, the received map of constricted black possibility is adhered to in order to keep the peace and secure black life through a self-policing accommodation of white rule, but the process exacts an extraordinary cost. Wright regards this imposed and accepted map of subordinated existence with tragic contempt, for its required emaciation of the mind and spirit is precisely part of the terror that inheres in the land.

Much of the power of racially segregated place that Wright charts, then, lies in its ability to "claim" the many black southerners who accede (consciously or not) to the white supremacist order or remain dangerously oblivious to their own naïveté and ignorance. None represent the latter as clearly as his Beale Street landlady and her daughter, Bess, both of whom exemplify what he calls a "peasant mentality," a worldview with "no tensions, unappeasable longings, no desire to do something to redeem themselves."[56] His incredulity is summoned by the fact of place itself: "Had I met Bess upon a Mississippi plantation, I would have expected her to act as she had. But in Memphis, on Beale Street, how could there be such hope, belief, faith in others?"[57] For Wright, "peasant mentality" is the height of ignorance, the exemplary effect of naively "being claimed wholly by [one's] environment"; Bess and her mother operate as if place-bound to the stultifying locus of the southern plantation itself. Despite inhabiting a small city, they fall prey to the grasp of a rural landscape, and the power relations it represents, and so remain trapped in a corresponding mentality of subjection.

Fusing mentality to place, worldview to environment, Wright deterministically articulates one of the most pernicious powers of segregated racial geography: its capacity to interpellate and produce deforming place-bound subjectivities and psychologies. Wright's depiction of black life allows little possibility, beyond physical escape, of contesting the terms of southern life, characterized by a veritably totalizing dominance over the wretched of the earth that forecloses the possibility of complex, agential lives. Where he admits the creation of shelter from the machinations of white power, he renders his surrounding black southern community inept, effete, superstitious, ignorant, and leached of any political will—in a word, defeated. Reductive as it may be, Wright's rendering conveys precisely the terms of his chosen aesthetic mode: a broad naturalism, infused with social realism and environmental determinism that harness the grave damage wrought across the southern region.[58] As a mode of representation that underscores the puissance of social and physical environment and its tenacious hold on the individual's imagination, for Wright, naturalism is the aesthetic of place and place-boundedness par excellence.

In *Black Boy*, Wright bends the frequently urban-based aesthetic toward a more rural, southern experience. More than this, he demonstrates the fact that naturalism not only conveys the profound primacy of place; at least in Wright's case, it is also an aesthetic response to place itself. He explains in *American Hunger* that his purpose in writing is "to capture a physical state or movement that carried a strong subjective impression,"[59] and it most obviously figures in his representation of his journey across Jim Crow geographies. Such an inclination makes sense: Wright notes in *Black Boy* that he devoured the potent mixture of civics, English, and geography books in school. While fastidiously studying the novels of Zola, Maupassant, Lewis, Dreiser, Norris, and Gorky that he gorges himself on, Wright comprehends that "[a]ll my life had shaped me for the realism, the naturalism of the modern novel."[60] Most striking about the latter point is Wright's implication that experience of southern place fashioned his gravitation toward a particular aesthetic mode as both reader and writer. His predisposition of aesthetically attending to environment—to place and the people who shape and are shaped by it—is an effect of his own experience of it. Born of his early years, Wright's consequent spatial sensibility saturates his literary production, in which his habitual recourse to geographic language variously helps set the scene or image, delineate a specific frame of mind, or render a vivid metaphor. But it also extends beyond setting, imagery, mood, metaphor, or symbolism.

Black Boy's prolific references to social space and physical geography register a necessary preoccupation with place that reveals how the racial order is grounded, made concrete, and apprehended via the spatial order. In so doing, Wright's autobiography strikes a tone similar to that of his naturalistic predecessor texts: being "defensively critical of the straitened American environment" in the hopes that "America could be reshaped nearer to the hearts of those who lived in it."[61] But, here, Wright makes equally clear that his environment, the formative social space of his younger years, has also shaped his writing and, by extension, his autobiography.[62]

Theorists from Henri Lefebvre and Michel Foucault to Edward Soja and Katherine McKittrick have asserted that social space is the material manifestation of social and political power.[63] The configuration of the built environment, the racialized allotment of land, and the regulation of black presence and behavior within a given sociogeographical space all relay a complex, often conflicting and contested assemblage of social designs and effects. In addition to the spectacular episodes of racial conflict, the stratified social order is writ large and small across Wright's landscape. Well before spatial theorists' elaborations, Wright's classic work illustrates the fact that the political is, at the level of routine quotidian life, experienced materially, bodily, and phenomenologically, all of which are inevitably tied to spatiality. If the scale of the body is distinguishable from wider geographic scales, it is also wholly encompassed by and produced by them.[64] And if the powers of the state and of the dominant white class are legible in laws and social customs, they are also fundamentally intimated through the kinds of space and place they evolve and, thus, the experience of such spatial arrangements. Yi-Fu Tuan's approach is instructive here, as he argues that one's sense of space and place—one's interpretation of one's world (from the very narrowly physical to the broadly cosmological) and of one's position within it—is unconsciously absorbed through different modes of mutually reinforcing experience: sensorimotor, tactile, visual, and conceptual.[65] Wright's work elucidates the manner in which place-specific segregationist power relations continually operate upon *and through* his senses and psyche. His understanding of racialized power is gained viscerally, sensorially—taken in not only through conversation and fraught social interaction, but also through the nonverbal experience of an environment conveying a barrage of hostile messages, overt or subtle, about his status and his proper social "place."

How this occurs crucially involves heavy doses of conditioning, the normalized fashioning of orientation, preference, value, and action through the layout of place and the social meaning assigned to it. In societies where racial power is most materially manifest through segregation, this conditioning rests upon the pedagogical and disciplinary dimensions of place. The exclusive separation and varying quality of public spaces (bathrooms, parks, restaurants, etc.) and residential areas according to race; which places racially classified people can own, occupy, or work in; how those individuals may do so (as servants or managers in an office, as residents or cleaners of a home, as unskilled labor or bosses in a factory, as overseers or hands on a farm)—all are racially instructive experiences of place, crafted in accordance with white supremacist designs that masquerade as the natural order of things but all the while amassing into modern racial meaning.

The social and geographic arrangement of a place, in other words, "grounds" and teaches black and white subjects their positioning in the social hierarchy and geographic terrain and subsequently naturalizes it "*as though* it was in [their] blood."[66] Wright's passage describing the black and white boys' reinscription of the racial boundary illustrates precisely this dynamic. It elucidates processes of socialization under Jim Crow that often elude critical attention. Imbibing both fear and hate, the boys quickly apprehend the racialized codes of conduct and spatial differentiation, and as either a means of perceived empowerment or a protective resistance against it, they dutifully reproduce the racial order—a reproduction that necessarily also involves mastering the performance of southern masculinities. All of this complex knowledge is learned, but only some of it is done so consciously; some is absorbed phenomenologically through experience and attentive observation of a racially riven Mississippi landscape.[67] Some, in other words, is learned through the spatial arrangement and reproduction of place itself—through the implicating pedagogy of place.

The Geographies of Exile

In *Black Boy*, Richard Wright's explicit association between worldview and environment is predicated upon a bifurcated mythical geography of American life that sets a premodern folk South devoid of rationality against a hypermodern northern sophistication defined by critical self-awareness.[68] Wright grounds this schema in an abiding faith in the fruits of modernity, progressive possibility, rigorous innovation, intellectual movement, and critical literacy, all of which Wright seeks beyond the boundaries of the South, as his southern "environment contained nothing more alien than writing or the desire to express one's self in writing."[69] Powerfully operative but admittedly fictive, this mythical geography framed young Richard's aspirations: "The North symbolized to me all that I had not felt and seen; it had no relation whatever to what actually existed," Wright acknowledges. "Yet, by imagining a place where everything was possible, I kept hope alive in me."[70]

As Thadious Davis has argued, his northward migration gave Wright access to critical institutions necessary for his professional development and self-fashioning.[71] For all the professional advancement it made possible, the urban North hardly freed Wright from the confining power and pedagogy of racial place. Although Jim Crow's forms of spatiality and codes of conduct no longer held sway, Wright encountered in his new environment forms of segregation that had evolved their own types of immobility, hypermobility, economic exploitation, entrenched poverty under a different guise, and coercive forms of spatiality that would saturate his fiction, most famously in *Native Son*.[72] Although he crucially found in Chicago and New York settings in which to write, neither sheltered him from racism or anti-intellectualism. Persistent racial discrimination—including his inability to purchase property in the Northeast and his trouble buying a Charles Street apartment in Manhattan's Greenwich Village—precipitated Wright's initial sojourn to Europe. Unwilling to cope with the continuing indignities and exclusions under American racism, from which neither growing fame, wealth, nor geographic location could shield him or his family, Wright sought an alternative geography. Not long after his widely distributed autobiography was published to great acclaim, with Paris in his sights, he would repeat the gesture of flight, on a global scale, that defined his late youth.

Wright's recourse to permanent exile had various rationales. His biographers cite the challenges of reacclimating to 1940s America—a general devaluation of writers across American culture, Wright's distaste for a rising "Americanism" and materialism, a challenging return to their West Village apartment, and most of all, the racist hostilities regularly encountered throughout New York City[73]—as the impetus for his permanent relocation. Wright outlined his decision with considerable detail in "I Choose Exile," a caustic unpublished essay he penned in 1950 that extends and intensifies the dense topography in *Black Boy*.[74] Wright's ascerbic *apologia* represents the move in terms of a need for personal peace and artistic freedom. Comparing each country's relative freedom in explicitly geographic, qualitative, and quantitative terms, he declares that "I live in exile because I love freedom, and I've found more freedom in one square block of Paris than there is in the entire United States!"—adding that he must be "free to question and probe my environment."[75]

What follows this declaration is an account of his failed effort to buy property that drives home the ubiquity of racial discrimination. Worn out by city life, Wright seeks a quieter, more peaceful existence, but he ponders the dilemma of location, for the pristine bucolic splendor of rural America is too frequently marred by racist terror and exclusive territoriality. He explains:

> [W]hen an American Negro harbors a yearning for a landscape, it wisely behooves him to choose with care, for, for him, most American landscapes have been robbed of the innocence of their sylvan beauty by the fact that almost every lynching in American history has taken place in such an Arcadian setting.[76]

In ways that recall Hughes's regional map of American racism, Wright's yoking of violent racial histories to rural landscapes exemplifies the racial-spatial literacy Wright developed as a young man. Wright rules out the South and the West Coast, but instead settles upon New England, the mythic progenitor of the American liberal tradition: "Had not the dauntless Abolitionists risen in that transcendalistic atmosphere? Had not Hawthorne, Emerson, and Thoreau sprung from that stubborn but free Yankee soil?"[77] Upon locating some property for sale, he beholds a "holy hush [that] hung in the tranquil valleys" and discovers the essential existential elements he requires: "this immense neutrality of nature, this indifference."[78]

Wright's quest for highly prized neutrality and indifference, however, devolves into the discovery of typical "racial muck."[79] Wright makes an offer on the home, but his haunting suspicion that "the dreadful issue of 'race' was lurking somewhere amidst those lovely, snow-clad New England hills" is eventually confirmed: the white seller refuses to sell to a black buyer.[80] If he momentarily bought into the pastoral association of the visually open, sylvan vistas with freedom untainted by a rigged social world, Wright is reminded (and reminds readers) that the social world has not only mapped out this landscape, but it has so capaciously done so that it has foreclosed his prospects of proprietorship. He cannot own this land available on the "free" market, only visit or rent it. Denied the basic terms of ownership and belonging, he is once again rendered a stranger in a terribly familiar land. In the closing pages of *Black Boy*, Wright employs horticultural language to cast his flight from the South as a social experiment: "[I]n leaving, I was taking a part of the South to transplant in alien soil, to see if it could grow differently, if it could drink of new and cool rains, bend in strange winds, respond to the warmth of other suns, and, perhaps, to bloom."[81] Five years after the publication of those lines, "I Choose Exile" announces that that migratory experiment, loaded with fragile hope, definitively failed. Incapable of finding the nurturing elements in either the rural and urban South or the urban and rural North, he would seek more accommodating soil, rain, and sun on another continent. In the face of an early alienation that has only intensified across time and space, an exasperated Wright elects expatriation.

The thoroughly geographic dimensions of "I Choose Exile" demonstrate a continuing acute sensibility to race, place, and environment in Wright's writing, and as such, it offers up several "geography lessons." It chiefly underscores the absence of racism-free territory in the New World, gesturing to the fact that race-making and place-making have comfortably coexisted from the early phases of European colonization to the later mass-scale expropriation and "development" of a continent to modern-day property laws. Wright's denied attempt at securing a home reveals a thin slice of a dense, multilayered history of privileged white proprietorship.[82]

Facing the fact that a racially neutral U.S. ground is a contradiction in terms, that all American land seethes with exclusion, Wright also implicitly engages in national myth-busting, with a particular emphasis on America's incarnation as the "Land of the Free." He exposes the racist practices that thrive under patriotic appeals to liberatory and liberal traditions, thereby denouncing the stories America tells itself in bad faith. Chief among these is the regional dichotomy between an illiberal racist South and a benign, color-blind North. Wright's account contrarily places New England's veneer of liberalism on a smooth, unbroken continuum with the brashest of southern injustices. If the 1945 edition of *Black Boy* ends with Wright's departure from the South, "I Choose Exile" sketches out an inescapably "wider South" rendered visible even when seeking out America's putatively progressive nooks and crannies. Effectively redrawing the U.S. map, including his own earlier mythical geography, Wright anticipates Malcolm X's damning 1964 denunciation that frames the United States as an enlarged South and thereby jettisons any schema of regionally differentiated racism: "America is Mississippi. There's no such thing as the Mason-Dixon line—it's America. There's no such thing as the South—it's America."[83] Both intellectuals ultimately work to broaden the scales of America's regional racial geography.

The similarities between both intellectuals end there, however. Whereas Malcolm X used scale in an effort to radically transform American social space, Wright sought to escape its tyrannical reach; his works and trajectories of flight suggest a ceding of space—and the ability to define and control it—to a violent white America. In *The Geography of Malcolm X*, James Tyner makes clear that Malcolm X's political battle against American white supremacy involved a complex scalar politics that led him to imaginatively reach out to international spaces, especially regions of anticolonial Africa, as conceptual fulcrums to dislodge the spatial and racial formations of the United States.[84] But his efforts concentrated on wholly transforming America—how it operates politically, economically, socially, and spiritually. Wright, too, turned his attention to the space beyond

U.S. boundaries but primarily to find a place of respite from the racism of his home. In neither his fiction nor his nonfiction would he represent the successful contestation of racialized space; social and political resistance in Wright's work is frequently narrowly constructed as fleeing segregationist social and spatial orders, as opposed to working individually or collectively to alter their terms.[85] (We might, nevertheless, read Wright's representation of U.S. racial geography and his discursive resistance to racial dominance as an effort to contest the terms of the American state.) In some ways, then, Wright's expatriation from the United States can be understood as a repetition of his regional flight—first from the American South, now from America.

Wright's alienation produced by the ubiquity of racial exclusion across the American territory undergirds the least explicit but most obvious of all geographical lessons in Wright's *apologia*: exile always begins at home. Estrangement is no consequence of relocation to a newfound land; on the contrary, expatriation attempts to resolve, or at least negotiate, one's condition of natal alienation that precedes and prompts the physical move abroad in the first place.

Unfree Landscapes of *Tell Freedom*

Exile always begins at home. This "lesson" also plays out gradually across *Tell Freedom*, whose 1954 publication was met with critical acclaim. Abrahams's autobiography became the first black text to be banned by the apartheid regime's censorship board in 1957, but its publication in England and the United States ensured that it, along with other works including Alan Paton's *Cry, the Beloved Country*, would draw critical international attention to South Africa during the early portion of the apartheid years.[86] Abrahams's writing had already invited comparison to Wright's work, but, given the resonances between their two autobiographies, such comparisons were unsurprising.[87] Published nine years after Wright's, Abrahams's autobiography recalls the narrative arc, defining tropes and themes, and many formal devices that structure *Black Boy*. Most obviously, the autobiographies chart the rising alienation of youth that crescendos into the damning, mournful, and triumphant departures from the lands of their birth in search of freer terrain. As several critics have noted, this arc toward flight has its own history in the black American autobiographical tradition, which both twentieth-century narratives participate in—that of the slave narrative, which (a) couples literacy to psychic and physical freedom and (b) highlights the evolution of racial alienation into flight toward freedom.[88] Both narratives share key thematic patterns, including the authors' traumatic encounters with racism; their negotiations of violence visited upon, but also enacted through, their own communities and families;[89] bouts with hunger and poverty; the corrosive effects of their stratified societies; and their transformative experiences with books that offered vivid imaginative alternatives to their dreary environments.

Most prominent among the formal strategies, for example, are the long ana-phoric passages capturing the feel of idyllic youthful summers that help con-struct very particular places in both texts. Echoing Wright's imagistic snapshots of his early years in Natchez, Abrahams offers this rendition that captures scenes of his brief stay in rural South Africa with his aunt and uncle:

> There was the hot sun to comfort us. . . .
> There was the green grass to dry our bodies. . . .
> There was the soft clay with which to build. . . .
> There was the fine sand with which to fight. . . .
> There were our giant grasshoppers to race. . . .
> There were the locust swarms when the skies turned black and we caught them by the hundreds. . . .
> There was the rare taste of crisp, brown backed, salted locusts. . . .
> There was the voice of the wind in the willows. . . .
> There was the voice of the heaven in thunderstorms. . . .
> There were the voices of two children in laughter, ours. . . .
> There were [Abrahams's friend] Joseph's tales of black kings who lived in days before the white man. . . .[90]

Chinosole's framing of Abrahams's autobiography as an analogue of Wright's offers valuable insight. If Abrahams patterns his narrative after Wright's, she notes, it is not to blindly mimic his predecessor's epic autobiography. Abrahams showcases his own distinctive qualities as a writer, at times, via his narrative's divergences from *Black Boy*; as the anaphoric passages convey, Abrahams sought a smoother, simpler line than Wright's wrought evocations. Beyond the authors' unique stylistic modes, Chinosole identifies a key difference in each protago-nist's relationship to his surrounding collective: young Richard is portrayed as the solitary figure, sharply critical of the white world and black community alike, whereas young Abrahams seeks the company and solace of his family and friends, without whom he withers; indeed, the passage just quoted incor-porates the presence of his black companion, Joseph.[91] This distinction lends Abrahams's narrative a more communal, encompassing tone that pushes past the strident, lone individualism of *Black Boy*. However, Abrahams's nurturing ties to family and friends gradually erode as the narrative continues. After the familial distancing brought on by Abrahams's early educational opportunities, the faltering of interracial relationships, and his rejection of Marxist political organizing in Cape Town, Abrahams finds himself a solitary individual(ist), a stranger in his own land, by the close of the autobiography and quits South Africa as lonely and determined to escape his world as Wright was.

The juxtaposition of Abrahams and Wright also highlights their distinct but overlapping representations of place. In some respects, their narratives appear as mirror images of one another. Whereas Wright's early life unfolds in rural areas and small southern towns, peppered by episodes in larger cities, Abrahams hails from one of South Africa's largest cities and occasionally ventures into the countryside. Such relationships across the urban-rural divide, at times, make each author susceptible to romanticizing life in locales that are not primarily their own. As the anaphoric descriptions suggest, Abrahams was prone to romantic flourishes about the bucolic splendor of rural life, which stand in sharp contrast to the gritty urbanity of segregated Johannesburg that Abrahams couches in bleak realist terms. When Lee (as young Abrahams is called) leaves the city to attend Grace Dieu, the rural Transvaal mission school outside Pietersburg, the grateful youth offers scenes of pastoral idyll: "Vrededorp, the market, the dark places and those past hurts were forgotten. There was peace here, and I was happy. I was among the people who were brothers one unto another, and there were books and the land was beautiful. Almost, I was in another land. A land free of hurt, insult, colour and poverty."[92]

Unlike Wright's autobiography, Abrahams's depicts religious spaces as zones of liberality and relative openmindedness, at least initially. But after a violently racist episode ruptures the emotional bond to his adopted paradise, his faith in religion falters, and Lee returns to the "slumland,"[93] well aware of the city's defining exclusions. The romantic language of the "peaceful valley"[94] ultimately transitions back to hardened urban realism as Lee later arrives in Cape Town, where he describes the sprawling township geography:

> Entering the Cape Flats was stepping into a new Dark Age.
> The earth, here, is barren of all but the hardiest shrub. It is a dirty white, sandy earth. The sea had once been here. In its retreat it had left a white, unyielding sand, grown dirty with time. Almost, it had left a desert. And in this desert strip, on the fringe of a beautiful garden city, men had made their homes. . . . They had lain with their women. And their women had brought forth children. And the children grew, stunted as the shrubs on this desert strip.[95]

Michael Wade's observation that *Tell Freedom* successfully achieves the imaginative aims of realism—indeed, more so than in most of his novels—is born out in this passage.[96] Like Wright, Abrahams employs an aesthetic mode designed to denounce the pernicious forces that structure people's lives, and he does so by recourse to the natural forces of an indifferent, desolate landscape that claims the lives of those condemned to occupy it. Both seize the geographic elements of their local environment—one, the persistent plantation; the other, the barren flats—to convey society's most relentless conditions.

However unique the two youths' specific landscapes may be, what both young men share is a growing racial-spatial literacy to navigate their environments. In *Tell Freedom*, the social and psychological relevance of place intensifies for Lee as the young boy's consciousness of the spatial predeterminations of race grows. As if to hammer home the geographic dimensions of Abrahams's story, the cover of *Tell Freedom*'s Faber and Faber paperback edition features a multi-colored portrait of Abrahams overlaid across a partial map of southern Africa; so tightly does the cover associate Abrahams with his environment, he literally

Figure 3. Cover of *Tell Freedom* by Peter Abrahams, with cartographic imagery (Faber & Faber paperback edition).

becomes part of the map (see Figure 3). Growing up in the rundown, working-class coloured suburb of Vrededorp, located on the western edge of downtown Johannesburg, Lee finds few comforts beyond the lively company of his family. Because schooling is not compulsory for coloured children, he comes late to formal education, but an enterprising and passionate Lee, driven by a thirst for the literary, quickly makes up for lost time. As with Wright, what initiates his voracious search for knowledge is pivotal with literature, in this case, the story of Othello read to him by a young Jewish woman: "The story of Othello jumped at me and invaded my heart and mind as the young woman read. I was transported to the land where the brave Moor lived and loved and destroyed his love."[97] Transfixed, and after learning to read at breakneck speed, he loyally carries with him everywhere *Lamb's Tales from Shakespeare*, Palgrave's *Golden Treasury*, and a volume of John Keats's poetry. "With Shakespeare and poetry," he reports, "a new world was born. New dreams, new desires, a new self-consciousness, was born. . . . I lived in two worlds, the world of Vrededorp and the world of these books. And somehow both were equally real."[98] Unlike Wright, Lee does not seek escape from his surrounding tangible world via this imaginative realm but, rather, remains content to have them coexist simultaneously.

Another, oft-noted literary encounter in the Johannesburg's Bantu Men's Social Centre even more intensively redefines Lee's worldview. A product of transnational support from the American Board Mission and, indirectly, the Carnegie Corporation of New York—both of which, Tim Couzens has argued, promoted white liberal strategies to quell black labor organizing among black mine workers[99]—the Centre offered patrons recreational activities, including access to American and African American cultural texts. In the Centre, Lee hears the voice of Paul Robeson singing "Ole Man River," then turns to find bookshelves, the epicenter of his ground-shifting discovery of black American literature:

> I reached up and took out a fat black book. *The Souls of Black Folk* by W. E. B. Du Bois. I turned the pages. It spoke about a people in a valley. And they were black, and dispossessed, and denied. I skimmed through the pages, anxious to take it all in. I read:
> "For this much all men know: despite compromise, war, struggle, the Negro is not free."
> The Negro is not free. . . . I remembered those "Reserved for Europeans Only" signs; . . . I remembered my long walks in the white sections of the city, and the lavatories, and the pack benches, and the tea rooms; . . . I remembered Aunt Mattie going to jail; I remembered spittle on my face. . . . The Negro is not free.
> . . . Du Bois's words had the impact of a revelation.
> . . . For all the thousands of miles, for all the ocean, between the land and people of whom he wrote and my land, Du Bois might have been writing about

my land and people. The mood and feeling he described was *native to me*. I recognized the people as those among whom I lived. The only difference was there
was no laughter in this book. . . . Du Bois had given me *a key to the understanding
of my world.*[100]

Lee then finds Booker T. Washington's *Up from Slavery*, James Weldon Johnson's *Along This Way*, Countee Cullen's *The Black Christ and Other Poems*, and Alain
Locke's *The New Negro* anthology, which, along with works by Langston Hughes,
Sterling Brown, Claude McKay, Georgia Douglas Johnson, and Jean Toomer,
set his political consciousness ablaze. "I became a nationalist," he writes, "a
colour nationalist through the writings of men and women who lived a world
away from me. To them I owe a great debt for crystallizing my vague yearnings
to write and for showing me the long dream was attainable."[101]

The transnationally circulating British classics, channeled through colonial
and missionary curricula, quite evidently fuel Lee's dreams, desires, and aesthetic sensibilities by providing him new worlds to envision. But the newfound
canon of black American literature offers him (a) a way of making sense of his
everyday social world, and (b) a model for how to express both his experience
and sense of racial solidarity. The Centre's available literature and activities
were designed to stanch radical activism, but Lee's experience—his euphoric
encounter with *The Souls of Black Folk*, in particular—does catalyze a more holis-
tic reevaluation of his own and others' experiences of racial exclusion as such.
Du Bois's "key," here, signifies doubly. While an instrument that unlocks a way
of thinking heretofore inaccessible to Lee, Du Bois's diagnosis of American
racism also operates as a legend to help him decipher his rigidly segregated
environment, which although obviously present, lacked sufficient legibility up
until this moment.

Not incidentally, he brings this newly acquired key to decode his own territory and his positioning within it shortly after his literary encounter with
Du Bois and other African American writers. One night, Lee climbs atop a hill
in Mayfair—a predominantly coloured Johannesburg suburb where he has relocated as a teenager—and detects a now-conspicuous pattern in the nocturnal
landscape before him: the clear correspondence between the racial classification
of varying Greater Johannesburg neighborhoods and their degree of access to
electricity. From this hilltop,

> I could map the city by its lights.
>
> That was the heart of it. There, where it was almost as light as day. I could see
> cars and trams clearly. And the outlines of people moving. White people. To the
> left, and a little towards me, was Malay Camp, an inky black spot in the sea of
> light. Couldn't see anything there. Dark folk move in darkness: white folk move

in light. Well, Malay Camp wouldn't be a slum if it were as light as the city. Slum is darkness. Dark folk live in darkness.

Beyond Malay Camp, a little to the left again, was white Fordsburg. White: lights. Black: darkness. A strip of darkness ran through black Fordsburg and became a big black blob. Vrededorp. And to the left of it, that world of light was Mayfair. And the patch of light to the right of it was Upper, white, Vrededorp.

To the right of me, beyond the heart of the city, lights moved away in waves. Those were the white suburbs: there was Hospital Hill; beyond it, out of sight, was Parktown and the other suburbs of light. Light is white: dark is black.[102]

Lee's voracious literary engagement brings him literacy of a different sort: racial-spatial literacy. Now reading race as materially and spatially manifest, he registers his country's racial Manichaeism writ across the Witwatersrand according to the presence/absence of technological amenities.[103]

Gifted with "second sight"—though not yet the kind that Du Bois defines in *The Souls of Black Folk*—Lee, who clearly identified instances of racist discrimination before his literary encounter, now perceives the arrangement of race and space as systemically structured. By means of its transnational circulation, Du Bois's *The Souls of Black Folk* and its assertion of unfree American space becomes the means by which Abrahams now identifies the racialized denial of freedom as "native" to him and his country. In effect, Abrahams can recognize the similarities between the two countries only by simultaneously undergoing a *re*cognition, or rethinking, of his own environment.

Lee's rethinking extends to a burgeoning understanding of the planetary dimensions of racial subordination. Drawing from the evidence found in African American literature, Lee confronts the facts that he shares with African Americans (with or without their less evident humor) the condition of unfreedom, despite being "thousands of miles away," and that that similarly denied freedom is the consequence of his racial identity. He sees at once locally and translocally to assess the shared state of being subject to white supremacist designs. Understanding himself now affiliated with others subject to the same designs in and beyond South Africa, he espouses "colour nationalism," which will inform his worldview for years to come. In search of radical (transnationalized) struggle, Lee is initially attracted to Marxism, although, like Wright and numerous other black intellectuals,[104] ultimately rejects what he takes to be communism's narrow focus, inattention to racism, and suppression of creative expression. Lee's rethinking also recalls another Pan-Africanist's illumination of a global color line. Although he only briefly broaches the expansive reach of racial segregation in his classic *The Souls of Black Folk*, Du Bois accentuates its transnational scope in later work, including his analysis of the West's imperial extension of global capitalism in his 1925 essay, "The Negro Mind Reaches Out."[105] Du Bois's title captures precisely Lee's newly acquired literary and political imagination that shaped his personal aspirations toward flight to escape the increasingly unviable terms of the country of his birth.

Lee's experiences at the Bantu Men's Social Centre permit him to further refine his sense of the world beyond South African borders with an increased sense of purpose and destination. Fueled by racist prohibitions and an irreversible sense of constriction in pre-apartheid South Africa, his increasing alienation ultimately propels Lee abroad, but thanks to J. R. Rathebe, the Centre's secretary who had visited both Harlem and England, Lee sets his compass well in advance of his departure. Rathebe regales his young black male interlocutors with the details of each; his "words gave us some slight yardstick with which to attempt an understanding of the meaning of freedom."[106] While all other young men listening select Harlem as their imagined destination, Lee's mind is "divided. The call of America's limitless opportunities was strong. The call of Harlem, Negro colleges, and the 'New Negro' writers, was compelling."[107] Nevertheless, Lee admits, "England, holding out no offer, not even the comfort of being among my own kind, could counter that call because men now dead [i.e., poets including Charles Lamb, Keats, and Shelley] had once crossed its heaths and walked its lanes, quietly, unhurriedly, and had sung, with such beauty that their songs pierced the heart of a *black boy*, a world away, and in another time."[108] Like Grace Dieu, the Bantu Men's Social Centre is an all-male venue whose social terms expose Lee to an almost all-male literary canon, black or white, according to which he shapes his aesthetic values. Lee's rather masculine list of forebears, like Wright's, is a ledger of literary giants who not only help Lee hone his sensibilities, but also draw him imaginatively toward other lands, as do world travelers he encounters. A persistent focus on literature's imaginative geographies drives Lee toward a destination rather than simply fleeing South Africa. And while his British models ultimately win the day, Lee's identification as a black boy bespeaks a continued use of African American literature as his frame of reference. As his allusion to Wright's autobiography indicates, Abrahams's affinity for African American culture continues well after he leaves South Africa.

The Locations of Cultural Production

The geography of exile is constituted not only by the place from which the exile flees; it is equally defined by the place to which the exile relocates. Wright's and Abrahams's efforts to escape their respective national geographies effectively catapulted them into a wider global racial geography. They arrived in Europe's two chief seats of imperial power during an especially fecund period of black transnational intellectual and cultural revolt. From the interwar period on, Paris and London boomed with the converging presence of international students, expatriate communities, local intellectuals and dissidents, artists-in-exile, laborers cheaply recruited from the colonies, and World War I veterans choosing to stay put after having been conscripted into Europe's theaters of war from far-flung territories. An unprecedented cultural mélange and intellectual exchange took root in both capitals and had an irreversible effect on international politics and literary modernism alike. Paris and London became key destinations for what Edward Said called the "voyage in," in which intellectuals and artists from across the colonized world could converge, engage one another, and think cross-colonially in the very heart of European imperialism.[109] Seats of colonial power and Eurocentric chauvinism though they were, both imperial metropoles at midcentury simultaneously, if inadvertently, formed the staging ground where black intellectuals could articulate and strategize a transnational resistance to western imperial power.

Black transnational engagement in these paradoxical locales also raised the prospect of disjunction and mistranslation. As Brent Hayes Edwards notes, interactions on the page and in person resulted in cultures of black internationalism being "characterized by unavoidable misapprehensions and misreadings, persistent blindnesses and solipsisms, self-defeating and abortive collaborations, a failure to translate even a basic grammar of blackness."[110] As we will see, this would hold for Wright and Abrahams. Initially drawn together by the thrills and trepidations of exile and by jointly imagining a wider transnational unity, Wright and Abrahams ultimately parted ways as they elected different ideological paths. Nevertheless, both sites initially filled Abrahams and Wright with a hopeful sense of possibilities as anticolonial foment mounted.

Abrahams came to England eager to extend the Du Boisian process of reaching out via "colour nationalism" he had discovered years earlier and put it into practice. Upon his arrival in 1940, Abrahams found London awash with intensive black intellectual engagement. Along with Harlem, London became the epicenter of the Anglophone world's black radical activity during the 1930s and '40s as intellectuals from across the black world gathered to found new organizations, presses, publications, and other institutions.[111] London would serve as home or resting place for a wide variety of black activists and thinkers from across Britain's colonies—not only for Abrahams but also George Padmore, Kwame Nkrumah, Jomo Kenyatta, Amy Ashwood Garvey, T. Ras Makonnen, and at other times, C. L. R. James and Paul Robeson—who helped set the terms of the black

Anglophone world's political modernity.[112] And while the fifth Pan-African Congress convened in Manchester in 1945, its staging ground was London, where its chief organizer, Padmore, lived. Self-identifying as black and forswearing his South African designation as coloured, Abrahams actively participated in this milieu of intellectual production committed to the demise of European colonial rule. He joined in leftist and Pan-Africanist causes and, under the tutelage of Padmore, helped organize the 1945 Congress, which gave succor to what became the midcentury wave of African independence movements. Abrahams's work with Padmore and other members of the London-based black intellectual and political circles significantly defined his worldview for the period of his residence there. Moreover, the engaged black writing community in the British metropole sustained his literary life. The ardent cross-cultural engagement was exemplified by groups of artists like the Colored Writers' Association, of which Abrahams was a member along with Makonnen, Peter Blackman, Mohammed Maghoub, Cedric Dover, Birman Maung Ohn, and Malcolm Joseph Mitchell, among others.[113]

Wright turned to Europe in search of intellectual and artistic freedoms he likewise could not find at "home." Wright's trajectory from the rural South to Europe would not ultimately resolve his problems. Davis notes that, in the end, flight lent Wright no comfortable terminus:

> The projection from Mississippi to Illinois to New York can be traced as repetition that paradoxically cannot be duplicated. Each space presents the same and yet different antagonists with identifiable markers traceable back to preceding incidents. Racism, enacted differently but perceived similarly, remains constant in a shifting environment. A disillusioned Wright can move from New York to France, but once there, he cannot catapult himself into a new place. . . . France becomes the end point on the map of transformation and migration. Once the reality of his inability to actuate a new space for either his professional or personal life descends, Wright seemingly settles into despair.[114]

Wright could not escape the long reach of American racism; his efforts to relocate to London shortly before his untimely death would be rebuffed by the British, spurred on by an invidiously surveilling U.S. government.[115] However, before despair set in, when he first moved to Paris, Wright enmeshed himself into its active intellectual culture. Much has been made of his friendships with Jean-Paul Sartre and Simone de Beauvoir, but Wright also very quickly ensconced himself in Paris's black literary world. The birthplace of Négritude and the Francophone world's Pan-Africanist projects, Paris had long been the meeting ground of black intellectuals originating from the French colonies, from the

Nardal sisters, Aimé Césaire, Léopold Sédar Senghor, and René Marin to Paul Hazoumé and Alioune Diop. But, perhaps due to an active English-speaking community, Paris's black intelligentsia also served to bridge the Francophone and Anglophone worlds, as is evident in the bilingual Pan-African journal, *Présence Africaine*, founded in 1947 by Diop and actively supported by Wright. As supporter, organizer, and participant, Wright also shored up one of the journal's defining cultural events, the First Congress of Black Writers and Artists convened at Paris's Sorbonne in 1956. Furthermore, Tyler Stovall argues, as the paradigmatic figure of Paris's expatriate African American community, Wright "stood at the center of this community," frequently helping arriving black Americans connect to the wider Parisian intelligentsia composed of overlapping expatriate, African, Antillean, and white French circles.[116]

Their dynamic social geographies in exile, then, played a crucial role in the development of Abrahams's and Wright's professional and personal lives. Far from static places to which the authors simply relocated or mere containers that held residents of all types, Paris and London (as any other locale) were dynamic places-in-perpetual-remaking, continually shaped and reshaped by those who passed through them, and they, in turn, shaped and reshaped the transformative individuals who redefined the meaning of Paris and London.[117] Neither Abrahams nor Wright operated in an exilic vacuum upon arriving on European shores; they immersed themselves in occasionally overlapping political, cultural, and intellectual circles and, well beyond that, helped craft them. The intellectual dimensions of place had an inestimable effect on their outlooks, engagements, and ultimately, cultural production.

This is particularly the case with Paris, where Abrahams and Wright initially met and where they repeatedly encountered one another in subsequent years. Paris became, in many ways, the setting of their "intimate political and intellectual friendship."[118] The epistolary correspondence that followed their initial encounter was intermittently punctuated by in-person meetings, some of which happened in England but most of which took place in Paris. In the first few years of Wright's exile, when they lived in different capital cities, the two men intermittently shuttled across the English Channel—Abrahams when vacationing in France and Wright when attending events in England—and reunited as each made arrangements for the other.[119] In June 1948, however, Abrahams and his future second wife, Daphne, made a much more substantial journey across the Channel to take up residence in Paris for more than a year, only blocks away from Wright's own Left Bank apartment. Wright would reciprocate Abrahams's personal reception in Southampton, almost a year earlier, by welcoming Abrahams at the Gare du Nord to help him resettle.[120] Their correspondence ended at this point, as they were within walking distance of one another, and so most documentary evidence falls away. But, in his second autobiography, *The Black Experience in the 20th Century*, Abrahams recounts ongoing contact between them; he recalls Wright's disputes, affairs, and his visitations, when he "sometimes came to visit us at Rue Servandoni" to feast with Abrahams and his wife at their home.[121]

Their Parisian setting, then, fostered a rich intellectual engagement between the authors. Their letters (from 1946 to 1948) register a warm, generous, and jovial connection. According to Ntongela Masilela, their deep affinity for one another rested on a similar search for an alternative to Marxism as a transformative political philosophy, a search they also shared with their mutual friend, George Padmore.[122] As intellectuals who, like Padmore, ended up disillusioned with Communist Party politics while retaining an appreciation for Marxist analysis, Abrahams and Wright shared a mixture of skepticism, critique, and distant but informed interest in the party's ultimate aims. Framed by an interest in Cold War politics and 1940s and '50s glimmers of African decolonization, they sought to define the significance of race in modern life, "the nature of African modernity," and "the meaning of Pan-Africanism in the African diaspora."[123] Their personal engagements, indeed, took place while both writers explored the changing political conditions across Africa and the Third World: Abrahams traveled to South and eastern Africa, Wright to the 1955 Bandung Conference, and both to the Gold Coast as Kwame Nkrumah began to assume power.[124]

In addition to specifically political matters, their friendship primarily revolved around their métier as writers. Their correspondence testifies to two artists devoted to their craft—often indicating productivity on a project, which publishers had been in touch to discuss what publication, whether or not a given text or draft worked successfully, etc. As an early fan of Abrahams's work, Wright lent Abrahams inestimable professional advice and had a strong hand in the publication of his early work in the United States. He offered Abrahams his feedback on published and unpublished work. While briefly back in New York in 1947, Wright personally delivered the manuscript of what would become *The Path of Thunder* to his editor at Harper, strongly recommending it for publication, and writing a glowing blurb for its 1948 release.[125] He even facilitated a change in the novel's name from "Quiet Valley" to the eventual title, after a Countee Cullen poem, once more showing the impress of black American literary production—Wright's as much as Cullen's—on Abrahams's own work.[126]

Most interesting for our purposes is Wright's ongoing influence on Abrahams's work, including the initial writing of *Tell Freedom*. Wright read an early chunk of the autobiography's manuscript during his transatlantic passage into expatriation and continued reading portions as he and Abrahams connected in Paris.[127] He also forwarded a portion to his literary agent for review, and Abrahams consulted with Wright about early publishing feedback in 1948.[128] Just months before resettling in Paris, Abrahams wrote Wright to inform him of Harper's lukewarm response to an early "Tell Freedom" draft. His editor suggested considerable revision after temporarily setting aside the manuscript to devote his time to a next book of fiction. The recommendations included beefing up the geographic description of places mentioned in the manuscript; in contrast to the richness of his prior work, the feeling of and relation between places required more development, his editor noted, primarily to familiarize his American readership with South African places. The editorial suggestions raised an imaginative gap that the South African's writing was required to close, and Abrahams sought advise from his mentor about how best to proceed.[129]

Archival evidence does not reveal Wright's answer or how Abrahams resolved the matter. Although Abrahams's letters indicate some dialogue on this, Wright's letters to Abrahams are unavailable; moreover, Wright and Abrahams would have subsequently discussed this in person.[130] More to the point, in the absence of Abrahams's early manuscript, it remains unclear how much and what kind of geographic description was initially present. Was the evidence of racialized place already present in the manuscript but not yet explicitly named, illegible to non–South African eyes or to white eyes unfamiliar with reading race spatially? Did the editor instead prompt Abrahams to render explicit what he knew intimately about his South African cityscape but had taken for granted? If, in fact, he did not initially render the same kind of description as was present in his earlier work (or in the published version), did it stem from an altered sense of geography after eight years of exile that made South Africa more difficult to apprehend or represent? We cannot, should not, draw firm conclusions here.

We know definitively, however, that the final, published version of *Tell Freedom* six years later burst with topographical detail. We know, further, that the most successful model yet for black autobiography, *Black Boy*, was well within Abrahams's reach. So was its author, whose person and advice were only blocks away from the South African writer. We also know that, after over a year in Paris, Abrahams relocated to the hamlet of Paley for another year with the explicit mission of revising *Tell Freedom*.[131] The interval of time between Abrahams's editorial feedback and his year in Paley was spent in Paris with evidence pointing to Abrahams's and Wright's ongoing interactions. Although we cannot know the extent or full nature of their interactions, it seems clear that his mentor's influence continued during the Parisian interval in which Abrahams weighed the feedback and rethought his autobiography before typing it out.

In light of Wright's prior assistance with this and earlier work, and in light of Abrahams's continued gravitation toward African American culture, as his autobiography attests, it seems particularly difficult to dismiss the strong patterns of resemblance between their narratives as coincidental. In the intervening years between Abrahams's Parisian period and the publication of *Tell Freedom*, Abrahams would produce both *Wild Conquest* (1951) and his report on visiting his former South Africa, *Return to Goli* (1953), but it seems clear that his autobiography bears more than the exclusive imprint of his native land. It also bears the traces of his social relations developed in the French capital.

Wright's and Abrahams's relationship was not wholly a one-way street. During the same period, Abrahams reported to Wright the terms of his own writing and intellectual life. In the early years of their friendship, before he moved to Paris, Abrahams kept Wright apprised of people and events on the British cultural scene that might interest him. For example, he referenced people Wright should be in touch with and alerted him to cultural events, including the London opening of a play based on *Native Son*.[132] Documentary evidence makes clear that Abrahams was a significant conduit of information for Wright about British life and politics and that Abrahams was not only an intellectual among Wright's fairly wide circle, but also a friend, for some time at least. Abrahams proved to be a confidante who quite literally ushered Wright into his life in exile. Even before then, he discussed with his interlocutor the sense of deracination and homelessness that Wright must have been feeling on the precipice of expatriation. Stressing his identification with these emotions, in this same letter, he noted his working title for the manuscript of the autobiography he shared with Wright: "Long Way from Home."[133]

It is worth noting that Abrahams's temporary title, taken from the Negro spiritual "Sometimes I Feel like a Motherless Child," frames his narrative in terms of alienation in ways that extend Abrahams's affiliation with Wright on multiple levels. Abrahams, here, appropriates the narrative of cultural orphanhood and displacement at the core of collective African American experience to name his own sense of estrangement. He aligns his and African Americans' (including Wright's) existential sense of alienation resulting from the political, economic, and intellectual dispossession in their respective racially segregated lands.[134] This marks once more the way that, throughout this period, Abrahams refracted his experience through the prism of African American culture, from the title of *The Path of Thunder* to the eventual narrative of *Tell Freedom*. The use of the spiritual also recalls an earlier history of African American cultural circulation through South Africa—where the Virginia Jubilee Singers led by Orpheus McAdoo undertook two extended tours in the 1890s, performing spirituals and vaudeville classics—that formed part of the expressive lexicon of South Africans in its wake.[135] More contemporaneously, it stakes out more direct common ground with Wright: their soon-to-be-shared experience of being geographically far from home as "aliens" outside their natal lands. In Europe, Abrahams and Wright would literalize their prior conditions of estrangement in their quests for greater freedom, effectively understanding themselves as orphans from the very societies that disowned them.

Abrahams's commiseration denotes his empathy as he shepherds his mentor into Europe's fraternity of exiles. Such an exchange offers a passing glimpse into what too often has been obscured: what Abrahams offered Wright in their relationship. The general scholarly focus rests on what the relatively empowered Wright offered a less established Abrahams, and for good reasons, reasons that this chapter has also taken up: Wright's generosity to Abrahams—the expertise, advice, and extensive network—are more literarily evident and legible than the inverse. In part to provide an exemplar against which subsequent chapters of this study will work, much of this chapter does lean toward reinforcing a diffusionist model of influence, whereby South Africans engage dominant American cultural production, rather than vice versa. But, here, we have an indication of some mutuality in their engagements—not only in the form of political and cultural knowledge Abrahams shared with Wright, but also in the way he helped Wright face the challenges of expatriation and extended him the hand of transnational fellowship. It would be a gesture that Wright himself reproduced as other exiles arrived in Paris after him.

Even so, their relationship did not persevere for many years beyond their overlapping time in Paris. They parted ways as their own personal trajectories led them in different directions: Wright continued to live in Paris, focusing on travel writing that investigated key political shifts across the world and fiction steeped in existentialist explorations of modernity until his premature death in 1960. After moving to Paley in 1949, Abrahams returned to England in 1950 before permanently emigrating with his family to Jamaica in 1956 to continue his fiction writing and work as a journalist, contributor, and editor for local media outlets, including the *West Indian Economist*, Jamaica Broadcasting Corporation, and Radio Jamaica.

Their physical distance reflected an ideological and personal drift, as well. Carol Polsgrove argues that many of the tight-knit relationships among the Pan-Africanist intelligentsia in Europe during the 1940s and '50s fell apart due not only to the fraught politics of anticolonialism that sometimes led to various acts of betrayal, but also to the fiercely independent agendas of those intellectuals.[136] This certainly applies to Wright and Abrahams, both of whom sharply refused

political party affiliations after their initial interests in communism and maintained the primacy of the individualist writer. Ntongela Masilela characterizes
this difference in terms of the frameworks they espoused to supplant their earlier
interests in Marxism: "Abrahams embraced Pan-Africanism; Wright, resident
in Paris, aligned himself with Existentialism."[137] But Wright regularly supported,
albeit in sometimes strained ways, Pan-Africanist and Third-Worldist causes,
while Abrahams shifted away from African or more broadly global struggles to
zero in on the politics of Jamaica and the West Indian Federation.[138] Even while
in Europe, Abrahams eventually underscored his differences with Wright. In
"The Blacks," a 1953 essay that Hughes republished in his edited volume, *An
African Treasury*, Abrahams discusses meeting Wright in Accra, Ghana, while
the latter was researching for his study *Black Power*. There, he represents Wright
caught in the confounding grip of Puritanism and racialized assumptions.[139]
Perhaps not incidentally, the two authors' last encounter, which took place on
London's Charing Cross Road in 1955, was an icy one: "It was not one of our
usual friendly encounters. [Wright] was distant, almost aloof," reports Abrahams in his later autobiography.[140] Furthermore, he contrasts the personalities
of Wright and Langston Hughes by stressing Hughes's relative lack of psychic
weight around matters of race. Implicitly presenting Wright as hamstrung by
racism, Abrahams explains that, with Hughes, the question of color was not a
mainstay of their relationship but "part of the baggage we carried, part of the
obstacle we had to overcome. It made for an easier relationship. We did not
upset or hurt each other unnecessarily."[141] In his elegiac reminiscence of Wright,
Abrahams characterizes Wright's passing as though it were "a loss in the family" of "a dear, difficult, at times trying, member of the family. . . . What would
this man have been, what would he have done, if he did not carry the burden of
colour? He was not as polished, learned, wise as Du Bois. He was as sensitive,
as American, as damaged."[142]

The two writers' relatively brief literary and personal relationship reminds us
of the temporal nature of articulation that Stuart Hall stresses in his nonessen-
tialist conceptualization of identity and social structure. But the spatial terms
of Hall's concept-metaphor—the linking of two separate and distinguishable
entities, brought into relation to create a complex, nonnaturalizable structure
for a particular purpose[143]—should not be lost on us either. With regard to *Tell
Freedom*, in particular, both dimensions help us see the generative, if temporary,
nature of their literary engagement. Abrahams's and Wright's intersecting trajectories reveal how *Tell Freedom* was very much a product of its time—a period
after the publication of *Black Boy* broke the mold for black literary success when
protests (particularly those in the form of "authentic," first-person accounts)

could be heard more loudly, especially as the apartheid state was shifting into high gear in the late 1940s and early 1950s. I have argued that Abrahams's auto-biography was equally a product of its place. Replete with Abrahams's memories of South African racial and spatial orders, *Tell Freedom* conveys a deep locality he carried with him to England and France where, upon reflection, he recollected it. But Abrahams's representation of the past did not—indeed, could not—hap-pen within a vacuum. The exposure and access to particular texts, writers, and editors that Abrahams's presence in 1940s and '50s Europe made possible bore upon the production of his text, as well. Abrahams's residence in England and, later, France afforded the South African the opportunity to work out a formative relationship with Richard Wright, and, beyond the basic terms of his recorded youth, the authors' intersection ultimately impacted upon the way Abrahams represented space and place.

This is not to suggest that Abrahams blindly imbibed African American cul-ture or merely mimicked Wright to create his own autobiography. The aesthetic and stylistic differences between their autobiographies (including Abrahams's fusion of modernist and Romanticist aesthetics) suggest a far more complex dynamic[144]—as does the fact that it would take multiple years after his close connection with Wright to be published by a different press than Abrahams initially worked with (by Knopf and by Faber and Faber, not Harper). Wright's imprint, direct and indirect, is evident even if the precise degree is not. What seems more evident is how, notwithstanding a considerable trace of British authors, Abrahams's narrative is a fusion between his own experience in South Africa and a series of layered engagements with American literary culture: (a) his initial encounter with African American writers, Du Bois chief among them, who sparked his political consciousness; (b) his personal relationship with Wright, and his writing, especially his autobiography; and (c) the American editorial responses to his manuscript. That layered engagement was made pos-sible by the mobility of texts across an Atlantic *text*scape as well as the migra-tions of Abrahams and Wright, which led both of them to intersect in Europe. Abrahams, who was drawn to England because of its writers and eventually to France, produced there an autobiography that bears the marks of disparate places—soldering together as it does elements from South Africa, the United States, and his own exilic location in France and England. If Wright affirmed in 1948 that Abrahams's "art is powerful enough to bridge the gap of oceans and cultures,"[145] it is in no small part because both writers were themselves crossing oceans and cultures.

I have shown that place not only emerged as a key subject of Wright's and Abrahams's autobiographies. It also became a formative medium that shaped the very production of these classic texts. Wright's experience of the Jim Crow South led him to adopt a blend of naturalism and realism in order to work out human psychology in his work. Through this aesthetic approach, Wright mapped out his physical and social landscape in *Black Boy* to reveal a pernicious racial geography he felt compelled to flee. After fleeing his own country for similar reasons, Abrahams settled in Europe, where he found, along with the sufficient freedom, the connections and literary models through which he crafted his own autobiographical narrative. In that narrative, he would also chart his South African territory, or rather remap it according to a new consciousness brought on by his encounters with various writers in print and in person. Place mattered in definitively literary ways for Abrahams and Wright. The autobiographies' powerful mappings of racialized place helped give definition to the terms of life in South Africa and the United States in the mid–twentieth century. Those mappings forcefully pushed readers to come to terms with the conditions of the authors' separate countries under the rubric not of fiction but of artful personal attestation. In the generation to follow, however, the mapping of racial geographies in separate countries—*as* separate countries—underwent its own changes as artists began revising received geographies to reveal more explicitly transnational arrangements. In the following chapter, we continue to focus on the significance of place in literary production through the presence of a South African poet in the United States, although he and his contemporaries in the 1960s and '70s sought to remap place for their own revolutionary purposes.

CHAPTER 3

Remapping the (Black) Nation

> And my special geography too; the world made
> for my own use, not tinted by the arbitrary colors of
> scholars, but with the geometry of my spilled blood . . .
>
> —Aimé Césaire, *Notebook of a Return to the Native Land*

By the time the 23-year-old Keorapetse "Willie" Kgositsile left South Africa in 1961, the successive white minority regimes had profoundly reconfigured the country's social and physical landscape. In 1948, the Afrikaner-based National- ist Party had begun assembling its edifice of segregationist legislation, notori- ously dubbed *apartheid* ("apartness"), as the party and state platform. But, owing to its extensive history of colonization and land expropriation, South Africa was already intensely segregated, the consequence of numerous laws enacted prior to apartheid proper. Most evident among these was the bedrock 1913 Natives Land Act, passed by the Union government, which set aside "reserve" areas for blacks across the South African landscape that laid the groundwork for the Bantustan system decades later. In conjunction with other laws implemented by multiple white supremacist administrations, it effectively barred Africans from owning over 87 percent of the land across the country, which would be restricted for whites, roughly 15 percent of the population.[1] Sol Plaatje—the first secretary-general of the South African Native National Congress (later, renamed the African National Congress) and first black South African Anglo- phone novelist—opened his classic study of the effects of the Land Act, entitled *Native Life in South Africa*, with this sobering assessment: "Awakening on Friday morning, June 20, 1913, the South African native found himself, not actually a slave, but a pariah in the land of his birth."[2]

The Nationalist government would build on this and other preexisting legislation—such as the 1923 Natives (Urban Areas) Act that severely curtailed black residence in the country's cities (while permitting coloured and Indian residence)—to systematize and intensify the processes of land expropriation and black spatial regulation. It instituted a program of race-based social and spatial engineering as explicit state policy with an armament of additional legislative measures, including the notorious 1950 Population Registration Act, the 1952 Natives (Abolition of Passes and Coordination of Documents) Act (which, contrary to its name, mandated an elaborate pass system), and the Group Areas Acts of 1950 and 1957. The apartheid government's manipulation of race and social space—its use of one to redefine the other—that became the bedrock of South African life lays bare the extent to which geography was central to the state's project of race-making. Indeed, capitalizing on ways racial subjectivity coagulates around and through spatial dimensions of social life has been one of the cornerstones of modern racial statecraft. In the early 1960s, South Africa accelerated this racial state-craft with diligence.

By this account, the young Kgositsile was exiled well before his 1961 departure. As with Richard Wright and Peter Abrahams before him, Kgositsile's condition of exile began at home and prompted his exit. His efforts to politically remedy blacks' nationally codified alienation sent him abroad; under orders of the then-banned leadership of the African National Congress (ANC), Kgositsile left to wage battle against the apartheid regime outside the country. Relatively little ink has been dedicated to a rigorous consideration of Kgositsile's time in exile or the work he produced during the period between 1961 and his 1990 return to South Africa. The critics who have begun paying attention to his work concur with each other about the fact that both Kgositsile's writing and his U.S. presence highlight a powerful conjunction between Africans and African Americans at a pivotal historical moment.[3] Margo Natalie Crawford, for example, argues that Kgositsile played a crucial role in helping black American writers and readers refashion their identities during the Black Power era. She points to how the South African poet facilitated African American identification with the potent 1960s symbol of a more liberated and unifying Africa, while also "complicat[ing] the packaging of the core identity of the 1960s and '70s Black Arts Movement as African-American."[4]

Those familiar with Kgositsile's poetry also justly view his nine volumes of poetry through the prism of music. The poet's devotion to jazz and respect for its most innovative practitioners mark his entire oeuvre—most explicitly in *This Way I Salute You*, his award-winning 2004 volume devoted to past and present jazz singers, composers, and musicians. Staunchly adhering to the Black Arts Movement lauding of experimental black musical expression, Kgositsile has explicitly acknowledged the influence of black music on his oeuvre as he aims to fuse musical and literary arts, proclaiming that, "at its best, poetry is music."[5] Tsitsi Jaji's exploration of sonic synesthesia in Kgositsile's oeuvre highlights the artist's "poetics of distortion" in his own jazz prosody.[6] Jaji isolates the rhythmic layering, lyrical cross-referencing, and sonic bending as defining features of Kgositsile's cross-cultural work and positions synesthesia, the mingling of sensory responses, as an "aesthetic parallel of the search for solidarity between Black Americans and South Africans in exile."[7]

This compelling critical attention to Kgositsile's work is long overdue not only because of the often overlooked nuance of his poetry, but also because of the way in which his writing takes up transnational political struggle, exile, and identity. If, as Jaji makes clear, South Africa's second poet laureate invariably explores these and other themes through music, he also does so through an acutely spatial poetics that is the focus of this chapter. Geography saturates his work as both subject and mode of expression, from the matter of land ownership to the racialized arrangement of people across it. His oeuvre also bears strong traces of his trajectory of exile—his movements, encounters, and the influences in their wake—so a more sustained inquiry into the meaning of sociogeographic space in Kgositsile's work seems all the more pertinent. Several related factors shaped Kgositsile's spatial sensibility, but three stand out most prominently: the early exposure to the geographic violence of South African apartheid; his encounter with U.S. forms of racial segregation, which he recognized as intimately familiar; and the fact of exile that produced a sensitivity to distance between his South African point of departure and his subsequent global coordinates.

All three factors point to the global reach of white supremacist political projects, which have fueled Kgositsile's explicit antipathy toward the imperialist domination of people and place—thus, lending weight to Edward Said's assertion that "the primacy of the geographical" inheres in the anti-imperial imagination.[8] Said's observation rests upon a tight association between geography and the imagination—an association whose far-reaching political consequences Said draws out more explicitly in *Orientalism*. Pointing to the cultural practice of drawing geographic distinctions between "us" and "them" that form in the "mind's geography," he explains that this geography underwrites a set of narrative structures and lenses prevalent in Europe that ultimately "shape the language, perception, and form of the encounter between East and West."[9] His term "imaginative geography" accordingly names the mechanism by which

Europe discursively invents its Other as a far-off domain removed from itself and, in the process, creates its own object of study.[10]

Kgositsile's poetics shares in Said's link between the spatial and the imaginative, but Kgositsile extends the latter's insight by deploying his anti-imperialism in his own art to *re*work widely received and accepted imaginative geographies. Kgositsile's writing goes beyond detailing acts of cultural resistance to racism and imperialism; it also powerfully raises the exile's and the diasporic subject's overlapping problem of geography—posing existentially fraught questions of where and how Africans or diasporans belong in a world produced by racialized displacement. It calls our attention to specific locations, points to the primacy of space and place in social struggle, and puts these observations into cultural practice. As a result, the Pan-Africanist poet actively redefines spatial meaning so as to counteract debilitating forms of separation and isolation. In this way, Kgositsile's literary engagement invests in what we might call, after Fredric Jameson, a project of cognitive *re*mapping.[11] To lay out this claim more thoroughly below, I first consider Kgositsile's American period in exile in order to situate him as a key cultural bridge-builder. Then, I turn to his acclaimed 1971 volume of poetry, *My Name Is Afrika*, to explore the relevance of the specific places identified in the poems and parse out what and how they signify. Following this, I analyze the meaning of Kgositsile's literary "maps" and their reconceptualization of distance, all of which help us better appreciate the poetics of space at work in Kgositsile's oeuvre. In the process, I turn to the works of Nat Nakasa and Gil Scott-Heron as illustrative examples—one contrastive, the other analogous—that set into relief the contours of Kgositsile's artistic and intellectual endeavors.

Bridge-Building in Exile

Of his twenty-nine years in exile, Kgositsile spent thirteen (from 1962 to 1975) in the United States. After a brief period in Tanzania, he arrived in the United States as part of a wider South African exodus that began in earnest in the early 1960s, as the apartheid government cracked down on dissent with brutal force, banned black political organizations nationwide, and enacted a series of laws that turned it into an extensive security state. Opposition to the South African state accordingly evolved new strategies not only by turning to armed resistance to defeat the regime, but also by extending itself transnationally. As life under increasingly repressive measures became more difficult to bear, dissidents began to mobilize beyond South Africa's borders, and exiles fled to numerous other countries—Tanzania, Kenya, Ghana, Zambia, Botswana, Nigeria, England,

France, Germany, Canada, among others—in search of temporary havens, new homes, or strategic bases of operation.

The waves of South Africans arriving in the United States initiated a variety of cultural and intellectual exchanges—whether in popular culture, in academic settings, or on political frontlines—and these exchanges transformed parties on both sides of the encounter, far exceeding any unidirectional sense of cultural influence. Life in America enabled exiles and expatriates to access new social networks, amplifying institutions like publishing houses and airwaves, and wider audiences as a result. But far from merely reaping the presumed benefits of American society, relocated South Africans (among other Africans in the United States) played a part in reshaping their newfound country, particularly during the 1960s and '70s. While moving within and between different African American cultural circles, non-American black artists and writers made a profound impact upon those communities. South Africans helped sate the African American public's growing desire to extend political and cultural ties to the African continent, continue activism, and build a more broadly transnational perspective—catalyzed by a heady mixture of Pan-Africanism, revolutionary post-Bandung Third-Worldism, and cultural nationalism.[12] Such engagements between Africans and diasporans further resulted in an exchange of knowledge of local African affairs too often overlooked, obscured, or censored in America, and they fueled a strong current of American, particularly African American, interest in the South African struggle, in turn. Poet and critic Eugene Redmond has underscored how the productive cross-pollination attendant to black transnational encounters led to a refashioning of black American expressive culture across the mid- to late twentieth century. Noting that "[t]he atmosphere [of 1960s and '70s black American literary circles] was enhanced by a number of African thinkers, artists, poets, and novelists who arrived in America to teach, lecture, perform, and travel," Redmond asserts that "[t]he importance of this interaction among Blacks from various parts of the globe in America cannot be overemphasized."[13] This milieu, to borrow from Gwendolyn Brooks, would yield furious flowers in the fields of African American and African letters alike.

Kgositsile was neither the first nor the last South African writer to participate in this rich milieu. Authors made their way to North America under all kinds of circumstances and to different ends. Nat Nakasa, for example, had been a celebrated staff member of *Drum* magazine and founding editor of *The Classic* before being offered a one-year Nieman Fellowship for Journalism at Harvard University to advance his work in journalism. Following the South African government's seemingly arbitrary decision to deny him a passport with which he could return home, Nakasa warily left the country in 1964 under an exit visa, which effectively rendered him a stateless person.[14] He landed in New York City before promptly moving to Cambridge, Massachusetts, for the academic year and shared his initial impressions of the Big Apple. "I did not like New York—that is, those few parts of it that I saw," Nakasa reported, couching his discomfort in explicitly spatial, architectural, and comparative terms:

> The city has the looks of a great, modern slum. Too many of its tall, redbrick buildings reminded me of Durban's many-storeyed hostels where African men live. The difference is that New York buildings don't have high wire fencing around them like the "game reserves" (which is what we used to call them) in Durban. Instead they look more like giant filing cabinets. . . . Many of the structures, countless blocks of flats, are without paint on the outside. A lot of the passages and corridors are in a state of perpetual semi-darkness, and few people see the sun rise in the morning.[15]

New York bore few familiar traces of home, including its variety of segregation, but its cold concreteness proved far from inviting. From Cambridge, he would return to New York several months later and pen an extended piece reflecting on Harlem for the *New York Times* in a 1965 article entitled "Mr. Nakasa Goes to Harlem." He points out that he had already imagined the iconic district through earlier literary depictions long before his first visit; the stories of Hughes and essays of Baldwin, he explains, "often made Harlem sound like one of the townships in Johannesburg. When Baldwin spoke of the ghetto, I likened Harlem to Sophiatown."[16] In the Harlem of his mind, he had conjured private homes converted into shebeens (illegal drinking clubs) and being "welcomed like a long-missed cousin."[17] This was not what he encountered. Discombobulated and disappointed by the misalignment between his actual experience of Harlem and his literarily forged mental map of it, Nakasa wryly notes Harlem's "facade of respectability," and he laments his rather lukewarm reception there.[18] With an exile's nostalgia, however, Nakasa does identify some similarities between Harlem and his former home. In his view, whites enter both black communities "at their own peril,"[19] and black residents, despite their hardships, fiercely defend their country—or their exclusive right to criticize it—from outsiders. In a moment of solemnity, Nakasa observes, "A lot of Harlem's battles and preoccupations are no different from mine. The people here are still fighting for a place in the sun, just like me."[20] He goes on to chronicle Harlem as a place of contradictions, where the African immigrant is met with both attraction and repulsion, familiarity and exoticism.[21]

Nakasa's spatial analysis of his new urban American residence reveals the vast extent to which Hughes's and Baldwin's own geographic descriptions had captured the South African journalist's imagination. Grafting his own township environment onto the topographies of Hughes and Baldwin, Nakasa finds himself confounded by the Harlem before his very eyes. Still, his reflections offer us several insights. Firstly, Nakasa's disjunctive coordinates nevertheless affirm the potency of these literary mappings of place, whether or not they align with the material places. Secondly, his own representations of New York space bespeak how deeply geographic a thinker and writer Nakasa was—the result not only of being an outsider making sense of his encountered social and material landscape through comparison with what is familiar, but also of a spatial sensibility developed under apartheid before his departure. But outsider he would remain; not long after these reports, the young exile's life ended in an apparent suicide in 1965, as he struggled with the fate of being barred from returning home.

Former *Drum* editor Es'kia Mphahlele spent a more extensive period in the United States after sojourns in Nigeria, France, and Kenya.[22] David Attwell has argued that Mphahlele's twenty years of exile were marked by a set of gradual ideological shifts: the staunch nonracialism of his early years gave way to a more radical, race-conscious perspective that ultimately led him to fashion his signature African humanism, a shift evident in his 1974 revision of his original 1962 study, *The African Image*.[23] Much of Mphahlele's evolving position had to do with his transformative engagements across the African diaspora, some involving strong ties and others, disappointment or alienation. His eleven years in the United States stoked his desire to discover the connections between Africans and diasporans, a search that saturated his scholarship, and his location seemed to play a role in his changing vision:

> [T]he influence of those very streams of identitarian thinking that [Mphahlele] had earlier found so exclusive of his own, peculiar history, began to have an effect, especially since his circumstances in the United States were those of a member of a racial minority that has to look deep within itself to find the resources to survive. Indeed, there is ample evidence . . . of a sustained intellectual search on Mphahlele's part for points of contact between his own particular sense of racial identity and those of diasporic origin.[24]

Location mattered profoundly, but it was the formative place of his childhood that continued to grip him. Facing what he called the powerful "tyranny of place"—a "tyranny that gives me the base to write, the very reason to write"— Mphahlele made his way back in 1977, an option available to few exiles, indeed.[25]

Keorapetse Kgositsile's American period of exile partially coincided with both Mphahlele's and Nakasa's. Like his compatriots, Kgositsile undertook a vigilant search for connections between his South African home and his new American setting. He would share with Mphahlele a keen attention to place and space as well as a deep appreciation for music, as the titles and content of Mphahlele's two autobiographies, *Down Second Avenue* and *Afrika My Music*, attest.[26] But whereas Mphahlele slowly articulated a Pan-Africanism over the course of his years in exile, Kgositsile espoused a black revolutionary politics aligned with the mid-1960s rise of Black Power politics upon arrival and quickly felt "at home" in the black artistic community he joined.[27] Kgositsile's politics involved, among other things, urging black communities toward revolutionary struggle while advancing a trenchant critique of liberal solutions to racial oppression, from white or black proponents. For example, in his introduction to the 1971 American edition of Peter Abrahams's historical novel *Wild Conquest*, Kgositsile praised his fellow author's astute reconstruction of the Afrikaners' Great Trek and clash with the Matabele alongside Abrahams's development of characters' complex interiority, while inveighing against his embrace of a teleological sense of progress. Rebuffing Abrahams's "wishful dreams of racial harmony," he roundly rejects the novel's "desperate idealism" that remains "unsupported by anything real, neither by people, by events nor by any facts that Abrahams himself selects to share with the reader."[28]

Kgositsile's position was a foil to the liberalism that also characterized Nakasa's worldview. Biographer Ryan Brown portrays Nakasa near the end of his life as "mentally hobbled"—"desperate to commit to a more radical politics" yet nevertheless unable to renounce old ways of resisting apartheid through individual instances of social and intellectual subversion.[29] This was not Kgositsile's way, and their differences bore out in contrasting topographies. Rather than distantly assess or puzzle over the received social and political geographies he encountered, like Nakasa did, Kgositsile committed himself to the task of reconfiguring them in his own writing. To be sure, some South Africans were not received by African Americans as long-lost brothers and sisters or cousins as Nakasa had anticipated, but rather as exotic foreigners in cosmopolitan Harlem and elsewhere. A common black identity unified across the globe was certainly not a given, but rather than accept a miscellany of unrelated black communities, Kgositsile labored to forge a connectedness through political and literary engagement.

Kgositsile began his American years near Oxford, Pennsylvania, where he briefly enrolled at Lincoln University, but he transferred to the University of New Hampshire and eventually settled in New York City, where he studied at the New School and Columbia University and devoted himself to writing poetry. Like most other black South African writers-in-exile, Kgositsile was already acquainted with African American literature and music. He has credited, for instance, a transient copy of Richard Wright's banned *Black Boy*—surreptitiously passed to him, read, and handed off to another reader—with making him realize that "I didn't have to have European models to write."[30] Moreover, the U.S. Information Service's library in Johannesburg stocked works by Langston Hughes, James Baldwin, and Frank Yerby that attracted many aspiring writers, Kgositsile among them, in search of literary models.[31] Once in New York, Kgositsile found company within black artistic circles and moved among established and rising talent in African American letters: Hughes, Amiri Baraka, A. B. Spellman, David Henderson, Ishmael Reed, Askia Touré, Barbara Simmons, John O. Killens, and Paule Marshall.[32] By 1965, he was well aligned with a burgeoning Black Arts Movement (BAM) in the process of hammering out aesthetic principles rooted in black nationalism. Kgositsile drew inspiration from a wide orbit of sources, particularly Pablo Neruda and Aimé Césaire, but his newfound environment made Kgositsile's early U.S. years "comfortable" and "exciting," as it permitted him to hone his craft and collaborate with artists and intellectuals dedicated to the same principles of political liberation through cultural expression.[33]

The result of these literary engagements is that Kgositsile's Pan-Africanist and Third-Worldist vision abound in his poetry. His 1971 poetry collection, *My Name Is Afrika*, announces his plentitude of transnational cultural networks through a panoply of paeans, homages, and salutations to African and African American jazz musicians, writers, activists, and intellectuals alike. In addition to a glowing introduction by Gwendolyn Brooks and numerous references to family members and friends, the volume features dedications to *Black World* editor Hoyt Fuller, Nina Simone, Don Lee (now Haki Madhubuti), compatriot Mazisi Kunene, Ghanaian author Ayi Kwei Armah, Brooks, African Revolutionary Movement founder Max Stanford, Nqabeni Mthimkhulu, and more geographically, to "Afrika, Asia, South & Afroamerica."[34] Beyond these tributes, invocations of Césaire, Malcolm X, Patrice Lumumba, Charlie Parker, Billie Holiday, and Ray Charles pepper this volume. These names bespeak Kgositsile's active cultural engagement and political vision, which won him the respect of his newfound community, and his high standing found textual expression: Kgositsile was the only African-born contributor consistently collected in the defining BAM anthologies.[35]

His literary practices established Kgositsile as a transnational bridge builder who worked to span cultural and political gaps between Africa, the diaspora, and other parts of the world. Mphahlele identified in Kgositsile's rhetorical register one chief way he forged cultural ties, noting that Kgositsile "is the only [South African] poet in exile who has decided to take his chances with the Afro American idiom. Black American poets regard him as truly one of them. He can make the rhetorical connections between the two black worlds."[36] Kgositsile's bridge-building, indeed, operated on multiple levels within his host country. His participation in BAM extended beyond publications to include a stitching together of several BAM regions across the United States.[37] In addition to crisscrossing the country for cultural events, Kgositsile resided in a number of cities—in addition to New York City (where he taught at Columbia University), he resided in Greensboro, North Carolina (teaching at North Carolina A&T University), and Denver, Colorado (where he was an instructor at the University of Denver).[38] His movements helped facilitate the cultural webbing, or intranational cross-fertilization, of several U.S. regions that were generating their own local BAM variations in the 1960s and '70s.[39]

Not unlike Richard Wright, who welcomed African Americans in his adopted Paris decades earlier, Kgositsile served as a cultural mediator by introducing newly arrived South African exiles to existing black American artistic and intellectual circles. For example, Kgositsile played a critical role in helping to orient Mongane Wally Serote—writer, former Umkhonto we Sizwe (MK) soldier, and former ANC member of parliament—in his period in the United States.[40] Arriving in the United States in 1974 on a Fulbright Scholarship to study creative writing at Columbia University, Serote found New York City to be off-puttingly foreign, unlike other parts of the country he would visit. On the verge of switching from creative writing to African politics and literature as his subject of study, he met Kgositsile there as his new instructor. According to Serote, this chance encounter proved to be a generative one because his mentor was already well established, politically savvy, and quite familiar with the United States.[41] Keeping close to Kgositsile, who tutored him in revolutionary African thought and politics (including the writing of Amílcar Cabral and Kwame Nkrumah), Serote journeyed with Kgositsile across America, including the East Coast, the West Coast, and the South. Through this tutelage, travel, and the conversations that ensued—with Kgositsile, Nina Simone, Eldridge Cleaver, Angela Davis, James Baldwin, among others—Serote gained an understanding of the ongoing American post–Civil Rights struggle and better positioned himself for his own impending participation in the political struggle against the apartheid government—thus rendering Serote's American experience a very significant period in his own life.[42]

During his exile in the United States, then, Kgositsile assumed an important mediating role across interpersonal, national, and transnational registers by facilitating conversations and connections among a variety of constituencies he sought to bring into closer relation. Kgositsile's multidimensional bridging made for a variety of political and cultural (re)orientations, but it also meant that he was not restricted to specific cultural organizations or agendas. His work consistently validated the aims of black liberation, but it did so without being singularly bound to specific BAM tenets or to the imaginative horizons of a narrowly American landscape, for he maintained his transnational coordinates. As I detail below, Kgositsile's wide geographic scope is precisely what structures his poetics.

A Poetics of Race and Space

The anti-imperialist commitments of Kgositsile's writing imbue *My Name Is Afrika* and beyond. They are particularly apparent in "When Brown Is Black," a poem penned in the late 1960s that innovates upon traditional oral poetry, "southern Africa's most characteristic form of literary expression,"[43] to address his turbulent contemporary moment and setting. Indigenous language oral poems traditionally honor a people's past king or chief with exceptional leadership qualities frequently exhibited against competing surrounding kingdoms or European colonial forces, with the poem's ultimate consequence of providing a "focus of communal identity and solidarity."[44] Kgositsile revises and popularizes the venerated community-solidifying form to champion a contemporary leader in the pitched 1960s battle against racial oppression in America, thus maintaining focus on solidarity through the lens of black nationalism.[45] Dedicated to former SNCC chairman and Black Panther minister H. Rap Brown (now Jamil Abdullah Al-Amin), "When Brown Is Black" celebrates Brown's steadfast determination to ending the history of violence that "the white game" has dealt.[46] The poem's speaker references ongoing black urban rebellions across America—stressing, in particular, the youth's powerful rage that makes "obscene ghettos / go up in summertime flames."[47] Addressing Brown, one of the rebellions' defenders and attempted harnessers, in the second-person singular "you" common to oral poetry, the speaker opens with a set of laudatory rhetorical questions:

> Are you not the light
> that does not flicker
> when murderers threaten summertime
> passions of our time
> Are you not the searchlight
> in our red eyes with the dust
> from the slave's empty grave[48]

The sense of righteous resolve in this stanza alone contradicts skeptics who misguidedly dismiss the irrupting insurrections:

> Some say it's youthful
> adventure in the summertime
> for they have lost natural instinct
> which teaches a man to be free[49]

By the last third of the poem, the geographic scope, which has been implicitly focused on uprisings within the United States, assumes a much wider frame of reference that encompasses South Africa:

> For Malcolm,
> for the brothers in Robben Island
> for every drop of Black blood
> from every white whip
> from every white gun and bomb
> for us and again for us
> we shall burn
> and beat the drum
> resounding the bloodsong
> from Sharpeville to Watts[50]

The speaker's vow to continue the fiery resistance to racial oppression features self-sacrificing leaders on either side of the ocean, from the fallen Malcolm X to the ANC and Pan-Africanist Congress (PAC) leadership imprisoned on the notorious Robben Island. The poem also raises the matter of transnational relation: Kgositsile's association of Sharpeville and Watts compels readers to ponder their specific relationship. Resonating with characteristic inventive wordplay, his "bloodsong" conjoining the two locales at once evokes a shared racial (blood) bond and a common historical experience of brutal racial violence.

Sharpeville and Watts are, indeed, sites laden with infamous political strife and bloodshed. Sharpeville names the township twenty-eight miles southwest of Johannesburg where, in March 1960, over 5,000 black South Africans assembled to nonviolently demonstrate against restrictive pass laws, but upon whom police opened fire, killing 69 and wounding 180 protesters. The subsequent wave of repressive measures (arrests, bans, and targeted killings) instituted by a defensive but aggressive state government aimed to squelch political resistance of all kinds. The regime's violent crackdown sent the country reeling and scattered thousands of South Africans, Kgositsile among them, abroad. Only five years after Sharpeville, Kgositsile was in New York involved in Black

Arts programs when the Watts section of South-Central Los Angeles lit up in flames.[51] Watts residents protesting the arrest of three black citizens—and an incendiary mix of ongoing racial discrimination, police surveillance, and economic underdevelopment beneath it—set fire to the central business district and local shops. The uprising was met by the martial force of 16,000 activated National Guard troops and other law enforcement officials, which transformed Watts into a battlefield for over 5 days, leaving 34 dead, over 1,000 injured, and 4,000 arrested, the overwhelming majority of whom were black.[52] Both events indelibly marked Kgositsile's consciousness, moved as he and many others were by collective black rebellion against white authority. Since 1965, both the names "Watts" and "Sharpeville" carry the memory of costly black struggle, accruing what Stephen Henderson called "*a massive concentration of Black experiential energy*."[53] These proper nouns may not specifically qualify for the designation of the NASA-like term "mascon," which Henderson reserved for charged colloquial terms, but both references hum with cultural and political significance across the black world.

Appreciating Sharpeville and Watts as not merely location-named incidents but also as geographic sites whose conditions and contradictions gave rise to explosive events provides additional clarity about Kgositsile's poetic vision. It should not be lost on us that both of the South African and American protests took place in what Kgositsile calls in the poem "obscene ghettos," black residential zones carefully engineered through economic dispossession and geographic practices. In both cases, resistance coalesced to contest the particulars of the resulting black spatial circumscription. South African townships were the outcome of the government's dual desires to have at its disposal cheap, exploitable black labor that would power the economy and to maintain those cities as islands of white privilege and wealth. The national policy rested on a regime of visibility that required the expulsion of black residents from city centers, kept black residents out of white sight (as much as possible), and strictly patrolled their mobility.[54] The pass system—an instrument introduced during the colonial era and zealously implemented by the South African government in 1952—accomplished the latter by mandating that all blacks carry passbooks with which authorities could regulate and police their presence in any area. Numerous popular protests had been organized to condemn and reverse the racist legislation, whose juridical foundation was the 1913 Natives Land Act and the 1923 Native (Urban Areas) Act. But on March 21, 1960, a day the PAC coordinated peaceful protests around the country, protestors in Sharpeville burned their passbooks in front of the township's police station in an effort to trigger their arrests, jam up the jails, and exhaust the judicial system in defiance of their spatial regulation. Their costly resistance helped change the course of modern South African history.

The creation of an almost exclusively black Watts was born of a less centralized but no less nefarious convergence of marginalizing strategies. A product of the era of the American ghetto, the period stretching from the early- to mid-twentieth century marked by a nationwide spike in urbanized racial segregation, Watts was subject to a declining job market as black migration to southern California increased. But it was redlining, restrictive covenants, and other forms of racial discrimination in real estate, compounded by an attrition in city services including the rerouting of accessible public transportation, that hemmed black residents in. Within the span of three decades, Watts became the poorest black community in an already widely stratified Los Angeles.[55] Routinely abusive policing strategies exacerbated the economies of violence that residents faced and heightened the indignities of life under hypersegregation; police appeared to patrol the area not for the sake of its own residents, but for the sake of Angelinos beyond Watts's perimeter. The repressive social, economic, and spatial orders effected a system of containment, against which Watts residents ultimately exploded in fiery, but not indiscriminate, opposition. Indeed, Gerald Horne notes that, in the ensuing violence, "[f]ew homes, churches, or libraries were damaged, a fact that supports the contention that the Watts Uprising was no mindless riot but rather a conscious, though inchoate, insurrection."[56]

The politics of enforcement in both locales emblematize broader American and South African 1960s strategies to separate and contain black populations through mutually reinforcing forms of racially demarcated enclosure. Both states worked to isolate black populations to ensure against large-scale organized opposition to the racial order. At local and national levels, and to different degrees of design, South African and American racial states orchestrated the concentration and management of black bodies through manufactured geographies of containment. In this light, Kgositsile's inclusion of the third place name, Robben Island, in the poem "When Brown Is Black" damningly signifies upon the other two place names. Alongside the infamous island prison holding South African freedom fighters, the carceral qualities of Sharpeville and Watts come into even sharper relief.

The title of the poem, however, directs us to a different dynamic altogether that nonetheless works to tighten the connections that the bloodsong exemplifies, one that hails the redefinition of racial identity consistent with a wider ideological shift in its historical moment. The poem's title, "When Brown Is Black," puns on the subject's surname to champion, in the Black Power parlance of his day, a proud revolutionary *black* identity over and above a more quiescent or accommodationist *brown* or *negro* label—one that gels with what Kgositsile elsewhere called a "Black Revolution" to supplant "negro confusion."[57] Black nationalists proclaimed a more politicized identity to restore a nobler sense of self systematically obscured by the earlier appellation *negro*,[58] and the poem participates in altering the sense of self in multiple ways. The first is a matter of numbers: the poem's shift from a singular "you" to a focus on the plural "we" and "us" marks a pivot from the expression of an individual self (when and how H. Rap Brown demonstrates his *black*ness) to the articulation of collective Self (when African Americans fight for their freedoms *as blacks*). A focus on collectivity dovetails with the poem's widening geographic scope, as it taps into black nationalist interests in Africa and the "Third World" and gives expression to what Kgositsile called a "militant Black internationalism."[59] Forswearing a nationally circumscribed worldview, it imagines a wider black collectivity well beyond North American shores.

This latter point is particularly important because the changing terms of African American identity coincided with the Black Consciousness Movement's (BCM's) redefinition of race in South Africa. By the very late 1960s, Steve Biko and his colleagues began defying the social categories promulgated by the apartheid state as well as the terms of resistance that white liberalism set.[60] No longer willing to accept the white privilege that infused the antiapartheid movement once black political organizations were banned after Sharpeville, the BCM reconfigured the state's racial taxonomy, arguing that blackness should operate as an umbrella under which all people of color could gather and should collectively mobilize. Much like the BCM, then, Kgositsile rendered blackness in his poem a political designation premised far more on commitment and social action than on the predeterminations of descent.

The coterminous redefinitions of race had an additional appeal for a South African exiled in the United States who sought to make connections between both countries, each with its own unique national nomenclature. Well acquainted with the tertiary racial classification system (black-coloured-white) from his home country, Kgositsile now operated within the American binary racial structure of hypodescent (white-black). The revaluation of blackness among African Americans and South Africans across the 1960s and '70s enabled him to linguistically establish some form of transnational correspondence upon which to ground claims of similitude—even in the face of interpretations that construct the African American as more coloured than black in the South African schema.[61] Playing on this nomenclatural shift, then, Kgositsile could now

remap race transnationally and discursively align two discrete racial classificatory systems.

Kgositsile repeats his association between the two sites of racial and spatial struggle in his short poem, "Brother Malcolm's Echo" (quoted in full), also
published in *My Name Is Afrika*:

Translated furies ring
on the page not thoughts
about life
but what should be
real people and things
loving love
this is real
the human Spirit moves
what should be
grinning molotov cocktails
replenishing the fire
WATTS happening
SHARPEVILLE burning

much too damn talking
is not
what's happening[62]

Kgositsile's *ars poetica* not only is guided by Malcolm X's iconic pronouncement
"by any means necessary," but it also echoes Amiri Baraka's own "Black Art."[63]
Working out what black art should accomplish and how, Baraka's poem envisions poetry that performs violence, and Kgositsile's similarly demands an art
and a base of artists willing to take action—"replenishing the fire" of Watts and
Sharpeville—and change the terms of society.[64] The poem pushes back against
two prevailing trends, poetry full of vague or abstract "thoughts / about life"
and an absence of political action. He challenges the first by underscoring what
should be more central: "the human Spirit" that compels social action and the
basis of commitment to social action, "real people and things / loving love."
Indeed, his homophonic pun on "Watts/what's" sets up the central contrast
of the poem, with "much too damn talking" being the antithesis of acceptable
behavior (something that is "happening," in the black idiomatic sense) and of
political struggle (as in "WATTS happening").

What might initially seem like another of the poem's contrasts, the invocation of love and the fiery developments at Sharpeville and Watts, for Kgositsile,

actually operates on a very clear continuum. This is the reverberation of Malcolm X's charge of action in service of self-determination and self-defense, one that would resonate, as well, through the opening lines of a later poem "Red Song": "Need I remind / Anyone again that / Armed struggle / Is an act of love."[65] In this way, one fire begets another: the fires of interpersonal passion and communal love inspire precisely Kgositsile's Molotov cocktails and the burning at Sharpeville and Watts. Across his oeuvre, Kgositsile's Promethean fire doubles as a generative and destructive force, so that the passion for community, or need to bring about the conditions for that community to thrive, ignites a righteous rebellion against forms of black social, political, economic, and spatial containment. The fire motif of "Brother Malcolm's Echo" and "When Brown Is Black," accordingly, signifies a black agency destructively challenging its constraints and, in so doing, helps define Sharpeville and Watts as struggles over freedom, space, and mobility and as vehicles toward that future political arrangement. Kgositsile's selection of these two specific sites thus highlights the defiance against the segregationist *social* order, the imposed *spatial* order it evolved, and both orders' enforcement. The fiery revolt in the poems adheres to a vision that is at once apocalyptic and utopian, for it desires to "burn and destroy White Power" to make room for a more just order.[66] Here, Kgositsile captures the same spirit as another defiant diasporan, Aimé Césaire, whose *Notebook of a Return to the Native Land* lauds "[t]he only thing in the world worth beginning: / The End of the world of course."[67]

There are certainly multiple ways to end the world as we know it, and *some* of the work—the conceptual work—can be at least initiated and conveyed on the page. Indeed, the poem seems to exacerbate the dichotomy between action and language that this and other poems actually labor to overcome. For, like the fire it invokes, Kgositsile's poetry here commits itself to the destruction of the existing racial and spatial orders by engaging the imaginative order of his audience. This he undertakes through recourse to imaginative geography, notably by tailoring his map of the world, much like the speaker of Césaire's *Notebook* in this chapter's epigraph, in accordance with "the geometry of my spilled blood."[68] The poet's political vision reveals itself not only by underscoring how spaces of black dispossession contain their own seeds of resistance—thus giving weight to bell hooks's theory of social margins as the locus of radical possibility[69]—but also by *linking* the two social margins, Sharpeville and Watts. Kgositsile creates this association in part through the strategic placement of words on the page, a key formal option the poet expertly exploits here and elsewhere.[70] Indeed, consider the way Kgositsile arranges Sharpeville and Watts in relation to one another. In "When Brown Is Black," the line "*from* Sharpeville *to* Watts" establishes a continuum,[71] and in "Brother Malcolm's Echo," the parallel alignment of each proper noun and present participle—

WATTS happening
SHARPEVILLE burning

—visually conveys their political parallels. Through repeated coupling and spatial manipulation of the poetic line, Kgositsile intervenes in the ways Sharpeville and Watts are understood—which is to say, how they are typically construed as wholly unrelated places and events. He continues this spatial linking across numerous poems in *My Name Is Afrika*, including the temporally focused poem "Time," which charts how "This moment / like a tyrant strides / across Meadowlands or / Harlem streets."[72] "Time" allies the conditions of the noted district where former residents of a razed Sophiatown (the Harlem of South Africa) were forcibly removed and New York's most famous, culturally vibrant black locale, even while playing off of the rural and urban connotations of the names that suggest a continuum.

The earlier discussion of ghettoization focuses on the way both South African and American states enact power through the racialization and administration of space itself. But state power is exercised not only in how its subjects are spatially organized, but also how they conceive of their organization. The racial state, in other words, has a vested interest in the ways its subjects imagine their positions, socially as well as geographically. David Theo Goldberg argues that racial states "must be seen as not a static thing but as a *political* force fashioning and fashioned by *economic*, *legal*, and *cultural* forces (forces of production, of sociolegality, and of cultural reproduction)."[73] To this overview, we must add epistemic forces and, indeed, imaginative geographies. Fostering strong transnational ties among its black citizens was emphatically not the objective of either national government. Founded upon colonial stratifications and structured according to more contemporary dominant racial and spatial logics, the South African and American states have devised and manipulated imaginative maps to serve their interests and those of the privileged classes they empower. The uniqueness or exceptionality that each state has proclaimed—along with their respective rigid, nationally bounded categories—must thus be understood as part of a larger effort to reproduce dominant imaginative geographies according to discreet national (and intranational) units that ultimately channel the power of the sovereign racial state. Both states pursued these ends and means to an extraordinary degree. The implementation of bannings, censorship, surveillance, and incarceration of dissidents at the hands of the Security Police in South Africa and, in the United States, the FBI's violence against radical black organizations seeking international ties and support in the 1970s, among other illustrations, demonstrate both states' commitments to (a) delimit information in general and (b) scale down their subjects' sense of possibility to the boundaries of the nation. They were, in any case, invested in disaggregating the South African and American contexts while activists were establishing transnational ties to combat racial injustice. Some state efforts failed, while others succeeded with deadly precision, but, to differing degrees, each state labored to advance its own kind of narrow imaginative geography by imposing a strictly national(ist) vision.

In this light, Kgositsile's poetics of space intervene precisely in this imaginative order. Kgositsile presents an alternative geography wherein these places—the social struggles they represent and the communities of resistance that create them—are connected and instances of black self-assertion are internationalized, each part of the same global struggle. Put differently, he frames Sharpeville and Watts (and Meadowlands and Harlem) not as disconnected places that coincidentally marked Kgositsile's consciousness, but rather as part of the same extended transnational geography of racial struggle—a geography Kgositsile's work asserts, reveals, and discursively produces. Like Hughes's "Question and Answer" a few years earlier, his bridging of black South African and American struggles critically resists national compartmentalization. Resolved to bridging noncontiguous spaces, the Pan-Africanist's spatial poetics militate against an imaginative order of isolationism and contravene the singularizing logic of the racial state that profits from the spatial *and* imaginative ghettoization of its black subjects. To briefly return to Kgositsile's apocalyptic theme, this alternative geography labors to destroy conceptual arrangements of the world that encode black insurgency as mere individuated, occasional incidents and, thereby, foster political, cultural, and cognitive separation. In so doing, this poetry mounts a double opposition to political *and* imaginative apartheid. It is, after all, this battle against the latter—imagined separation—that strengthens the campaign against the former—apartheid proper.

Alongside the destructive impulse, then, lies a constructive one that nurtures it, insofar as it offers an avenue for future transnational engagements. Kgositsile's poetics at least partially help define what aspects black peoples from multiple sites of struggle have, or could have, in common in lands of divide-and-conquer, fragmentation, and displacement. In this sense, the alteration of cognition, or *recognition*, becomes the prerequisite for the *recognition* of the proverbial common ground that Kgositsile, among others, espouses. But it must be said that Kgositsile's work here does not just render visible this sought-for common ground; to the extent that it offers its audience an alternative way of perceiving transnational relationality, it also helps produce (in the constructivist sense) the grounds of engagement and his ultimate goal, transnational solidarity. Laura Chrisman rightly cautions against the assumption that all transnationalisms are inherently progressive in nature (and that all nationalisms are regressive), but Kgositsile's poetry very self-consciously advances a progressive politics through geographic reorientation, guided by what Chrisman calls an inclusive anti-imperial collectivity.[74]

Dilemmas of Distance and Difference

Kgositsile's linking of South African and U.S. sites provokes a reevaluation of physical space and its conventional meaning. In effect, his poetry asks us to conceive of geography differently—here, governed far less by physical *contiguity* than by experiential *continuity*. His movements have certainly helped determine which spaces formed his literary points of reference, but the poet's work registers an alignment between his land of birth and land of exile that well exceeds his singular trajectory. Indeed, his poetry returns again and again to the social and political conditions of each country that, however uniquely assembled they may be, stress a continuum. The locations that Kgositsile cites are separated by thousands of miles, but they share a singular problem of racialized space that minimizes the meaning of distance as separation and difference.

The diminished relevance of distance comes most clearly to light in Kgositsile's four-part poem sequence entitled "Point of Departure: Fire Dance Fire Song."[75] The poem's first section, "The Elegance of Memory," is a moving elegiac meditation on the challenging but transcendent conditions of exile. The section opens with the following:

> Distances separates bodies not people. Ask
> Those who have known sadness or joy
> The bone of feeling is pried open
> By a song, the elegance
> Of color a familiar smell, this
> Flower or the approach of an evening . . .

> All this is NOW[76]

The full poem sequence brings time and space into powerful synthesis. Kgositsile's emphasis on "mov[ing] to the meeting place" in the second section highlights the poem's general urging to overcome distances, both temporal and spatial, that an exile and an exiled people continually face in the service of a revolutionary spirit.[77] Indeed, the poem's striking first line—"Distances separate bodies not people"—affirms the indissoluble nature of human relationships by differentiating between physical beings and the emotional bonds that connect them. The speaker elaborates upon this point three stanzas later by affirming that:

> The elegance of memory,
> Deeper than the grave
> Where she went before I could
> Know her sadness, is larger
> Than the distance between
> My country and I. Things more solid
> Than the rocks with which these sinister
> Thieves tried to break our back[78]

The speaker's reference to the "sinister / Thieves" signals the (colonial) theft at the heart of the exile's predicament, and the identified rocks suggest that, at bottom, that theft is geological and geographic—an expropriation of land that helps break bodies and spirits alike. The elegance of memory delicately sketched out in this poem lies in its power to prevent wholly succumbing to this theft: to overcome the material space and passage of time that wrenches apart those separated by exile. Recalling the emboldening advice his now-deceased grandmother, 'Madikeledi, imparted ("Dont ever take any nonsense from *them*, / You hear!"[79]), the speaker finds her spirit of self-possession still present even if she has passed on and he resides in a different country.

From this memory of his grandmother, the speaker turns his attention to a more "extended" family, as the final stanza of this section invokes the metaphorical "sister" and "brother," whom he directly counsels:

> There are memories between us
> Deeper than grief. There are
> Feelings between us much stronger
> Than the cold enemy machine that breaks
> The back. Sister, there are places between us
> Deeper than the ocean, no distances.[80]

The speaker acknowledges a physical gap while attempting to minimize its isolating impact. Kgositsile's poem denies the spiritual or psychic breach that distance represents, and it conveys this through a skilled use of line breaks and prepositions. In the first iteration of his oft-repeated, relational preposition "between" (a stanza preceding the one above), Kgositsile stresses division by ending the line with "between," cleaving the prepositional phrase in two, with the preposition on one line and its related nouns ("My country and I") on the following line. This prepositional severance expresses the speaker's social separation. However, by the last stanza of the poem (quoted directly above), he thrice deploys the prepositional phrase "between us," which he refuses to split with a line break, thus maintaining the phrase as a coherent unit. So while the poem raises the painful problems of distance and division, by its conclusion, "between" conveys the opposite sense: connection, as a bond that two people share.[81] Here, the basis of connection is memory itself, a force that elegantly eliminates physical distance-as-separation and instead permits people (if not bodies) to convene at a "meeting place" or to commune on a more profound, shared plane of existence—a "memoryscape" of sorts.[82]

The transnational dimensions of this poem become all the more evident in the prefatory note that opens the poem: "A wise old man told me in Alabama: 'Yeah, Ah believes in nonviolence alright. But de only way to stay nonviolen' in dis man's country is to keep a gun an' use it.' Four years earlier, another wise old man told me the same thing near Pietersburg in South Africa. He said his words of wisdom in Sepedi."[83] Here, the necessary defense of black life and property against the threat of white racial violence is a defining experience shared by people of color in America and South Africa, as the epigraph frames self-defense under particularly hostile racial conditions part of their somewhat literal common ground. Emphasizing collective experiential proximity that threads together Alabama and the area around Pietersburg (now Polokwane), Kgositsile repeats the spatial suturing found in earlier poems.

The poet-in-exile more explicitly reaffirms this association between America and South Africa—remarking, in 1978, that "America is so much like South Africa" and, in 1992, referring to the United States as "another South Africa."[84] But the geographically expressed forms of relation in his early poetry open up an approach akin to Leon de Kock's trope of the seam. De Kock offers the seam in his quest to define a distinctly South African literary tradition, whose unity "resides less in its being a self-aware and interreferential field than in its being yoked together by geography and circumstance and by alphabetical-numerical arrangement."[85] The absence of an all-encompassing, integrated literary tradition mirrors the fragmented state of identity formation in the country, which runs along the old historical lines of language, race, ethnicity, and culture. In literary and social context, alike, de Kock posits the seam as a complex site of convergence and difference. Historically, the conjuncture of different people has played host to both the upholding of absolute difference and the wholesale denial of difference, each violent forms of erasure. Yet, for de Kock, the trope of the seam therefore becomes "a place where neither oneness nor difference can be maintained without reference to the knowledge of its double."[86] For our purposes, the seam articulates a nonuniform unity. Indeed, it enables a way of thinking about similitude without suppressing cultural and experiential difference, and vice versa; it functions as "the site of joining together that also bears the marks of suture."[87] In admitting its own representational sutures, it also lays bare the considerable labor of suturing itself and the desire to suture that lies behind the act. On the face of it, then, the seam helps illuminate how Kgositsile's threading together of black South African and African American spaces charts their commonality without collapsing their distinct characteristics (including language). His poetic suturing, in other words, marks cultural particularity while nevertheless outlining shared ground.

Remapping the Cartographies of Struggle

Kgositsile was not alone in his attempt to symbolically suture together South Africa and the United States during this period. In fact, a growing tendency in the United States to associate the conditions and racial status quos of both countries took root in all forms of black expressive culture, not least of which was music. In early 1976, five years after the publication of *My Name Is Afrika*, Gil Scott-Heron and his long-time collaborator Brian Jackson released their album *From South Africa to South Carolina*.[88] Scott-Heron and Jackson met and began working together at the historically black school Lincoln University, where they formed the group called Black & Blues. Although geographically isolated in Oxford, Pennsylvania, Lincoln nevertheless featured a black international student body and became a meeting ground of sorts for African American and African students including Kwame Nkrumah, Nnamdi Azikiwe, and very briefly Kgositsile.[89] Scott-Heron's own transnational consciousness found expression in the lyrics of *From South Africa to South Carolina*, whose title alone highlights transatlantic relation.

The album opens with the hit song, "Johannesburg," a tune that Aldon Nielsen reminds us riffs off of a commercial jingle for Thunderbird malt liquor ("What's the word? Thunderbird") that Gil Scott-Heron revamped from a ditty for profitable private consumption into a liberation anthem that calls upon the collective power of the people.[90] Emphasizing the centrality of communication in politically fraught times, the song opens with a plea for more (and clearer) news about South Africa: "What's the word? / Tell me, brother, have you heard / from Johannesburg?" The speaker's questions are motivated by a general uncertainty about developing political resistance to apartheid:

> They tell me that our brothers over there
> are defyin' the Man.
> We don't know for sure because the news we get
> is unreliable, man.

The song underscores how receiving news of opposition to the apartheid state—from popular local defiance to organized work stoppages ("They tell me that our brothers over there / refuse to work in the mines")—in the form of rumor only sows seeds of uncertainty that impede coordinated international support, an outcome not entirely accidental. While introducing a performance of "Johannesburg" in the 1982 documentary *Black Wax*, Scott-Heron notes that "[t]here are folks who are struggling in Namibia and Southwest Africa, and constant reports that would encourage people who are supporters of the southern Africans are suppressed to make us feel as though nothing is going on." Such misinformation—not just within South Africa but also in the West where the prevailing conservative Reagan and Thatcher governments regularly twisted the terms of political struggle, often by what June Jordan later identified as "American censorship"[91]—risked compromising transnational solidarity and depriving progressive communities in the United States of models of struggle worth replicating. Under these terms, acquiring and disseminating proper information are profoundly political acts. Because "sometimes distance brings / misunderstanding," the song aims to forestall the physical gap from becoming a gap in popular support. More than this, "Johannesburg" sounds a call for remedying the unreliability of information (by safeguarding against its distortion and then amplifying it), for keeping South Africa a part of people's everyday conversations, and for continuing the struggle against the apartheid regime by politically maneuvering in the United States.

The song also issues an explicit call for unification, as Scott-Heron's injunction—"We ought to come together"—during the song's extended keyboard solo makes clear. Formally speaking, "Johannesburg" orchestrates the practice of coming together, not through simple unison but by call-and-response. In the studio version of the song, a chorus uniformly answers Scott-Heron's recurring question "What's the word?" with the name of the apartheid-riven city. A live version of the song recorded in 1982 at Washington D.C.'s Wax Museum (added to the 1998 reissue of the album) brings the practical and pedagogical dimensions of "Johannesburg" into even sharper relief. Scott-Heron first cajoles his audience into serving as the chorus who answers his query "What's the word?" but, after their weak initial response in the song, Scott-Heron humorously interrupts the show to rib the crowd for its lack of organization. He begins the song anew to more successful coordination. While mocking the crowd that casually promises to answer his interrogatory call but fails to follow through—he jokes that only ten members of the audience did their part at the right moment—Scott-Heron urges his audience toward greater readiness, on multiple registers. "Che Guevera has told us, 'You got to be ready. You can't tell when it's gonna come,'" he teases them. Scott-Heron makes an instructive tie between the musical elements of timing and coordination, on the one hand, and the precepts of revolutionary struggle, on the other. In political as in musical endeavors, it would seem, discipline is paramount, timing is everything, and practice makes perfect. The song's pedagogical exigencies, then, involve training the audience to inquire about antiapartheid resistance with concerted effort—to know the word on Johannesburg, and if they do not, to demand it—so they can pass along the crucial information.

The song, however, insists upon a more immediate relationship to South Africa than black transnational advocacy. Folded in between repetitions of the chief question ("What's the word?") at the song's end, "Johannesburg" closes with a remarkable string of geographic similes. Scott-Heron declares that

> L.A.'s like Johannesburg
> New York's like Johannesburg
> Freedom ain't nothin' but a word
> It ain't nothin' but a word

Marking the absence of an achieved freedom on American soil, he goes on to liken the apartheid city to Detroit and, in other versions of the song, Philadelphia and D.C. In the fadeaway, Scott-Heron answers the precise question his claim begs (in what way are these American cities like Johannesburg?): ventriloquizing the policing discourse of law and order, he intones, "So 'let me see your ID,' 'let me see your ID.'"

In a later song, Scott-Heron redeploys the racialized rhetoric of surveillance and suspicion that has particularly plagued black men in South African and American urban areas. "Let me see your ID" became the name of the song produced for the 1985 all-star collaborative album *Sun City: Artists United against Apartheid* that, like "Johannesburg," would bring the antiapartheid movement into the stream of American popular culture. Leading Grandmaster Melle Mel (of Grandmaster Flash and the Furious Five), Miles Davis, Duke Bootee, and

The Fat Boys, among others, Gil Scott-Heron fleshes out the meaning of this pernicious command in his life:

> I had never met anyone from southern Africa until I had started going to school. I was going to Lincoln University down in Pennsylvania. There were South African refugee students there . . . and we started to compare experiences. And they were telling me that, in South Africa, you gotta carry this little black book that tells everybody whether you're supposed to be in a given area or not. Damn, [Scott-Heron realizes] there's a parallel to my life, 'cause I have to do that when I go to Philly.

Leaving no room for ambiguity, the refrain "Let me see your ID" immediately follows. Scott-Heron's spoken words establish the patrolling of black bodies as a transnational phenomenon that daily overdetermines lives in both America and South Africa. The authoritarian command requiring black people to justify their presence recalls precisely the spatial regimentation and management that Kgositsile traced between Sharpeville and Watts. Here again, we are reminded of the prohibitions on claiming space, belonging to it, or freely moving across it as common (experiential) ground that black South Africans and African Americans share intimately. Beyond this, Scott-Heron's words not only point to the ways that Lincoln University served as the site of Scott-Heron's burgeoning political insight,[92] but they also underscore the central role a South African presence in the United States played in shaping African American consciousness.

Gil Scott-Heron's attention to the analogous experiences of black American and South African citizens appears to acknowledge the differences between their two countries and the similarities that nevertheless link them over and above those differences. For example, his rendering of U.S. cities as "like" South African ones avoids making them interchangeable equivalents but stresses their similar features nonetheless. He brings the same nuanced attention to relation with the cover illustration of the *From South Africa to South Carolina* album (see Figure 4). The cover's tight thematic relationship to the album's music is more than a happy coincidence; it was driven by Scott-Heron's own instructions to the graphic designer, Iceman. In the liner notes to the 1998 reissue, Scott-Heron explicitly references his "special appreciation of album covers." He adds that "I wanted the covers for the work that we produced to say more about what might be in the grooves" and, therefore, "began to describe concepts to artists for both our covers and inside pages."

Comprised of both the front and back of the album when laid out, the cover design features a guerilla-gorilla figure in traditional militia garb—green

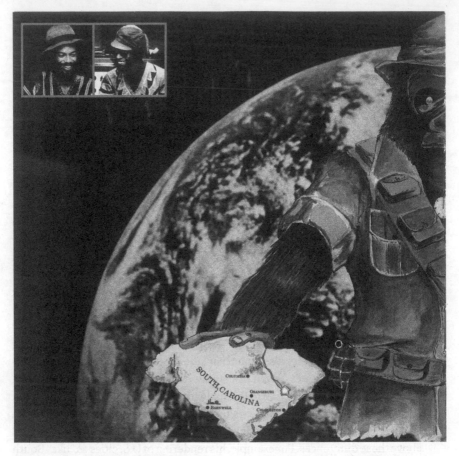

Figure 4. Cover of Gil Scott-Heron's and Brian Jackson's album *From South Africa to South Carolina*, © 1975 (back and front views).

uniform and accompanying bandoliers—an evident spoof on the stereotypical western conceptions of the revolutionary soldier. But the rebelliousness of this figure stems as much from his bold, defiant gesture as it does from his apparel. Standing in front of a rising earth that conveys the planetary nature of the political struggle, the guerilla-gorilla holds in each of his hands cartographic cutouts: one, a map of the state of South Carolina (a synecdoche for the United States); the other, a map of South Africa (and its territorial holding, Namibia). Gripping the two landmasses, the guerilla-gorilla compels viewers to reckon with the relationship between them. Their roughly triangular shapes stress

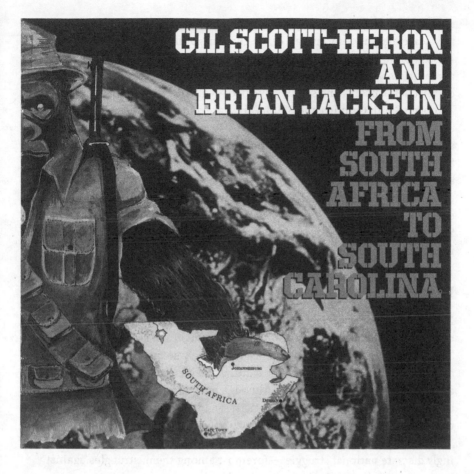

analogous social geographies, and the semiconsonant names of indicated cities (Orange*burg*-Johannes*burg* and Charles*ton*-Cape *Town*) bespeak twin histories of imposed European nomenclature upon non-European spaces.[93] But in 1976, one fundamental feature connecting both racial geographies was a continued need for liberation; as Scott-Heron sings in "Johannesburg," "we all need to be strugglin' / if we're gonna be free." The global scale upon which struggles for justice must be waged in order to bear fruit consequently comes into view.

Much like in Kgositsile's poetry and Langston Hughes's "Question and Answer," the very act of holding these two cartographic spaces in relation to one another—once again, stressing their experiential and social continuity over their physical contiguity—forms part of the guerilla-gorilla's revolutionary action. Repositioning these geopolitical spaces to redefine their relationship militates against a conventional view that takes these cartographies to occupy wholly distinct hemispheres and seditiously opposes a (nationally) separatist logic. Although South Carolina and South Africa are quite evidently not the same, they appear to be much closer spatially and conceptually than previously understood. In his introduction to "Alien," another song in the documentary *Black Wax*, Scott-Heron offers this telling reflection about people of color: "[I]t seems as though, oftentimes, there are attempts to split us up, divide-and-conquer, keep us at odds with one another, so that we never define the things that we have in common. But we have more things in common than we do that separate us." Scott-Heron's cultural engagement, at least in part, involves rearranging common-sense assumptions about commonality and separation.

The Problem of National Space and Belonging

If the illustrated cover of *From South Africa to South Carolina* remaps how we conceive the world to be arranged, it offers a powerful visual key for interpreting "Johannesburg" and other geographically attentive songs on the album. It is an equally apt visual analogy for the cultural and imaginative reconfiguration at the heart of Kgositsile's poetry. Although emanating from specific generic traditions, the poet's, the musician/lyricist's, and the cover artist's texts all act to *re*cognize the imaginative geographies of their audiences. And, laboring to "define the things that we have in common," they affirm links between seemingly discrete national struggles—foremost among them, struggles against state-sponsored campaigns of cultural and imaginative ghettoization.

Kgositsile's transnationalizing vision, in particular, is explicitly geared to an abiding suspicion of the function and effects of nation-states and their boundaries. For a South African exile in the African diaspora, matters of nation-states and their borders are inevitably vexed. Prior to apartheid, the boundaries of the South African state were forged by a constellation of actors—from imperial mining magnates to breakaway republics, European charter companies to colonial administrators—all of whom sought to confiscate inhabited land for their various, sometimes conflicting, purposes. During apartheid, the national boundaries that had been solidified in 1910 served to shield the sovereign white minority state from considerable external pressure, enclose its captive population, expel dissidents, prevent their return, and deny outsiders access to the country. These national boundaries and the practices that upheld them became the defining lines of South African exilic existence; they distinguished, cleaved, and distanced South Africans from one another to uphold a system designed to serve a white minority.

Once in the diaspora, the bard with a deeply spatial sensibility would come to find that the problem of space was not the province of South Africa alone but manifested itself in the United States, among other places, as well. First, he encountered the manipulation of sociogeographic space to maintain and innovate upon segregationist strategies like the American ghetto. Second, as a consequence of continuing mechanisms of exclusion, it became apparent that the concerns of exile were notably similar to the concerns of diasporic communities formed through involuntary migrations—as in the case of many black Americans who considered themselves *in* but not *of* America long before the Black Power era but especially during this period. The figure of the diasporan as alien and exile saturates black cultural expression in the West, not least of all in music: "How can we sing a song of joy in a strange land?" questions the Rastafarian anthem, while the Negro spiritual laments the fact of being "a long way from home." South African Peter Abrahams explicitly cited this black American song in a letter to Richard Wright, but his strong identification with the spiritual stressed its applicability to his own life in exile. If Abrahams saw this alienation as a personal bond between Wright and himself, it seems that, for Kgositsile, it could potentially serve as the basis of a wider, more explicitly political community. The conditions of the exile and the diasporan converge at the geographic and existential state of the alienated outcast. The problem they share stems from well-entrenched geographies of exclusion,[94] and the vexed possibilities of freedom within landscapes that are fractured to isolate, restrict mobility, and impose an imaginative separation of (black) inhabitants. The problem of space, it bears emphasis, is both internal to the nation-state (the ghettoization of black bodies from white-concentrated government and civil society) and external (the relationship between different black communities in noncontiguous spaces). But Kgositsile's poetics point to the promise of convocation that lies in transnational resistance to this shared problem of space and (un)belonging.

Kgositsile has continued to revisit the problem of space across the decades, and geography has persisted as a theme and poetics in the period after apartheid's formal demise.[95] "Crossing Borders without Leaving," an essay penned by Kgositsile about his 1990 return to South Africa after his three decades abroad, chronicles his unsettling experience of walking through the downtown of his once-familiar Johannesburg. Fully disoriented by the twenty-nine years of urban change in a once familiar cityscape, he finds himself once more a stranger in his own land: "No memorial points of reference. Therefore, return? Return to what? . . . This place is foreign. I might as well have been wandering . . . through any other part of this planet that I am not native to."[96] Having failed to return him to his point of departure, Kgositsile's extensive journey heightens a keenly felt lack of belonging. Several days later, while visiting the Alex Arts Centre in the township of Alexandra, he climbs the staircase to the music room only to find an array of photos of familiar African American jazz figures lining the wall: Duke Ellington, Count Basie, Miles Davis, Thelonious Monk, Charles Mingus, John Coltrane, Charlie Parker, Dizzy Gillespie, among others. Upon this discovery, his relationship to his "home" shifts: Kgositsile observes that his "whole being glows and [his] soul melts."[97] At the same time, he hears young jazz musicians in adjoining rooms "working out their history, *defining their space* . . . with their instruments."[98] Not long after, he encounters young South Africans reciting his own poetry, sounding as though Kgositsile himself had recorded it. "Perhaps *that* was my Homecoming!" he exclaims.[99]

Kgositsile's homecoming offers a particularly complex model of home, for here, the warmth and comfort of home manifests itself not in contrast to that which lies beyond it, but, rather paradoxically, in recognition of the more familiar outside of one's home. The returnee's home is finally rendered home through the presence of that which originated from abroad, instead of the unfurling of what is "authentically" national or intimately but distantly familiar. Kgositsile is welcomed by virtue of cultural work—from black American jazz music to his own poetry written abroad—having fluidly moved across rigid political boundaries, having circulated "in" from beyond the South African territory. The former exile is able to cross borders without once again leaving because black cultural production refuses to abide by national boundaries and has already done the crossing.

The homecoming scenario approximates a transnational version of philosopher Henri Lefebvre's curiously "interpenetrating" social spaces; according to Lefebvre, "[s]*ocial spaces interpenetrate one another and/or superimpose themselves upon one another*. They are not *things*, which have mutually limiting boundaries and which collide because of their contours or as a result of inertia."[100] Here, the traces of African American artists in the South African township and the reading of Kgositsile's poetry produced during his time abroad infuse the space of the Alex Arts Centre to create a potent coexistence of South African and American cultural forms and practices. Situated in the resulting generative mélange, the poet occupies a cultural seam of sorts between the two.

Kgositsile's rendering of African American culture in South Africa prompts us to more critically revisit de Kock's model of the seam for thinking about South African pluralism. The homecoming scene highlights the transnational flow of people and cultural production that preceded and accompanied Kgositsile's return. The extensive geographic range of this flow raises and complicates any strictly national focus of the seam, for it well exceeds South Africa's territorial footprint that it privileges. In "South Africa in the Global Imaginary," de Kock briefly notes the permeability between the inside and outside of the country; he also raises the "*representational* dimensions of cross-border contact," but his inquiry hews quite closely to the material boundaries of the nation-state.[101] It does so for the very good reason of trying to give some collective definition to the identities and art of peoples who were roped together by imperial designs. But what happens when long-standing flows of African American and so many other cultures circulate—via thousands of returning exiles, to note just one example—and firmly take root in South Africa but are still considered external to it? How to account for deeply formative cultural elements that originate from outside the country but, once having embedded themselves, remain unrecognized as part of the national fabric? Both Kgositsile's journey and oeuvre demonstrate that, whatever seams constitute the terms of life on the southern tip of Africa, some are undoubtedly transnational in nature. The seam cannot, therefore, be restricted to traditionally South Africa's intranational relationships alone; Kgositsile reminds us that, conceptually, it must acknowledge the more transnational engagements that have shaped South African cultural, political, and intellectual life. For those engagements press us to consider precisely the elements from "elsewhere" that also constitute seams—cultural forms like jazz and poetry or more material streams of migrant labor from southern and central Africa. Even as the country claims the mantle of democracy in the post-apartheid era, these too frequently fall out of formulas of South African-ness. But they nevertheless require us to reconceptualize definitions of "the national."

Kgositsile's writing effectively troubles any simple distinction between what is and is not national in character. The transnational flows that he represents (in both senses of the word) contravene any adherence to prevailing narrow state nationalism. Like his poetry, his essay accepts little in the way of national boundaries—neither their impermeability, their legitimacy, nor their value. It remains consistent with his long-held antipathy for nation-state boundaries that he would bring to bear against the nationalist fervor of post-1994 South Africa. In a 2008 interview, the poet casts a scrutinizing eye upon his fellow citizens' uncritical embrace of the concept of the nation and their mistaking national liberation for the achievement of freedom. Ever the ardent anti-imperialist, Kgositsile challenges a post-apartheid—or what Loren Kruger has called a "post-*anti*apartheid"[102]—reification of the country's arbitrary physical and imaginative boundaries predicated upon Europe's late-1800s designs for colonial states. He asks rhetorically, "Why were we willing after liberation to get rid of those Bantustan boundaries but we are not willing to get rid of the colonial boundaries which are the bigger Bantustans [created by the cynical scramble for Africa]?"[103] Those imperial geographies, he argues, form the basis of the unreflective nationalism that erupted into xenophobic violence in 2008 and spilled the blood of so-called "foreigners."[104]

Kgositsile, then, points to the collective amnesia about the early, more imperial global movements centuries ago that continue to set the course of national formations across Africa. He likewise reminds us of the violence that those forgettings underwrite. But there is no reason to limit the discussion to South Africa, alone. His own trajectory reminds us, after all, that the United States is constituted by a multitude of transnational influences and cultural seams—however un- or underacknowledged they may be—including, of course, those emanating from southern Africa. As Eugene Redmond and Margo Natalie Crawford have argued, the influence of African artists and intellectuals on African American cultural production at the very least complicates any simplistic notion of what "African American" means. Kgositsile's participation in the Black Arts Movement reveals a denser, more complex narrative of cultural formation. Crawford notes that his participation suggests "that the story of the black diasporic relations during the Black Arts Movement is only beginning to unfold."[105] As that heretofore infrequently told story continues to unfold, his poetics prod us to consider a variety of key but still-unresolved questions: How can we properly account for movement and forms of relation that will not adhere to the logic of national boundaries? How do we allow for extranational dimensions of culture that are in fact not extranational at all, but rather deeply intrinsic to it? If the cartographer's boundaries facilitate a certain type of identity, what others do they inhibit or foreclose, and to whose detriment? Moreover—we might hear Kgositsile challenging us—what identities or solidarities might such conventional geographies discourage us from imagining? And why submit to their limitations, in any case?

CHAPTER 4

Cultivating Correspondences; or, Other Gestures of Belonging

"As she fell asleep, [Elizabeth] placed one soft hand over her land. It was a gesture of belonging."

—Bessie Head, *A Question of Power*

"I look forward to a correspondence with you."

—Letter from Bessie Head to Alice Walker (December 22, 1974)

"I view my own activity as a writer as a kind of participation in the thought of the whole world. No other occupation provides for such an international outlook as writing. I have my national, my African side but I am also very much an international kind of person."

—Bessie Head, "Writing Out of Southern Africa"

The preceding chapters have taken up different ways black writers engage themselves transnationally in order to negotiate the alienation endemic to their racial geographies. Some writers stayed to confront the terms of their countries while setting their literary compasses to coordinates beyond their national boundaries. But many writers left their home countries, often electing exile and traveling with some frequency. Wright and Abrahams charted their flights out of their countries and powerfully represented the lands they left behind, while Kgositsile left denouncing the laws of his land and graphed new cartographies of black transnational belonging that helped bolster a freer arrangement of the world to come. Bessie Head, too, joined the growing ranks of South African exiles, but exile assumes a multitude of forms. Head left South Africa on an exit permit after having been denied a passport and entered neighboring present-day Botswana, where she would reside and write almost her entire oeuvre in the subsequent twenty-two years until her death in 1986. Crossing the border with only an exit visa rendered her a stateless refugee acutely aware of how national boundaries matter. Until she received Botswana citizenship in 1979, Head was unable to access the mobility she initially desired and, instead, assumed a largely sedentary life that set her apart from many, more mobile, metropolitan-bound, and predominantly male literary counterparts abroad.[1]

Head's statelessness and relative immobility fundamentally shaped the kinds of engagements that she pursued, the commitments she championed, and the relationships she developed—all of which powerfully played out in her writing. Head's literary corpus, however, includes more than her frequently studied published essays, short stories, and books to also encompass the vast stores of letters that Head penned throughout her life. Among the extensive correspondence she wrote in exile are four sets of letters to and from African American women writers—Nikki Giovanni, Alice Walker, Toni Morrison, and Michelle Cliff[2]—that spanned the mid-1970s to the mid-1980s. The subject of this chapter, these epistolary exchanges are noteworthy for the detailed ways that these authors discuss each others' literary works and social worlds, their intensity of expression, and for our purposes, the kind of transnationalism they put into practice.

As I outline in this chapter, Head's exchanges with Giovanni, Walker, Morrison, and Cliff reveal what we might call a locally grounded transnationalism that is both reflected in the correspondence and generated by it. I understand grounded transnationalism to signify in at least two principal ways. First, like much of her nonfiction, Head's letters directly address her state of political and geographic containment, but at the same time, the activity of letter writing aims to moderate its isolating effects. Head's correspondence with these writers accordingly registers, defines, and seeks to negotiate her grounded condition. But the content of the trafficked letters, including their accompanying books, essays, and magazines, raises a second, much more literal register of "ground": the exchanges between Head and some of her correspondents reveal a pattern of representations focusing on earth itself, the geography of the garden. More than reflecting the horticultural preoccupations of their authors alone, their repeatedly referenced mixed-use gardens lay bare a kind of cultural labor, particularly as they cut across the Atlantic and model a new way of thinking about transnational relation. Throughout *Grounds of Engagement*, I have been arguing that artists' quests for more just social and political arrangements take variously spatialized forms of expression. Whereas Kgositsile's and Gil Scott-Heron's answers to containing racial geographies spurred their efforts to remap the space between South Africa and the United States—in effect, demarcating a noncontiguous black community by suturing these countries' municipal and national geographies—Head's and her correspondents' responses conversely operate on a far more minute scale. Almost paradoxically, the small plots of earth recurring in their writing represent not the firm entrenchment of exclusive localism or isolationism but, to the contrary, the writers' imagining of community according to much more expansive horizons. As representational sites wherein authors work out alternative forms of belonging, these figurative gardens fashioned by women who have reason to question the terms of national belonging register an investment in forms of relation that contravene nationalist logic. A product and means of these writers' transnational reimaginings, their gardens emerge as the tropological ground of engagement between the authors.

The authors' engagements rest on two distinct forms of correspondence here: a literal, epistolary correspondence, on the one hand, and a thematic and formal correspondence in their writing, on the other. I posit a relationship between these two forms of correspondence but do so without asserting a hard causal link between the two, whereby the letters between the writers produce, in any direct sense, similarities in their styles, structures, and underlying philosophies. Rather, I argue that their circulating texts occasion self-reflective meditations upon the possibilities their social and literary correspondences open up. The writers explicitly discuss the terms of their cross-cultural connections—their similarities and differences—and as the authors' letters and microgeographic tropes of the garden circulate, they make visible certain shared interests and alternative modes of relation. But in doing so, they simultaneously expose the challenges of and impediments to extended long-distance community.

The figure of the garden, then, marks both the convergences and divergences among the writers. Indeed, for all the positive attributes of transnational traffic, we would do well not to exaggerate its power or uncritically cast this process as an unmitigated triumph of the human spirit over all adversity. Above all, it must be stressed, the epistolary cultivation of community I highlight here remains an attempt directed by desire[3]—neither inherent fait accompli nor foregone conclusion and, thus, always in process, never complete. As all forms of cultivation go, it is prospective, contingent, frequently tentative, temporary, and subject to various promoting or inhibiting factors. The sought-after community is always in formation, and the cultural ground that takes shape through the authors' efforts to engage across time and space remains almost necessarily under constant revision. This is not to suggest, however, that the protean cultural ground has no lasting impact. On the contrary, the letters and the published texts the authors sent one another constitute a profound record of the productive outcomes of these efforts. As with the relationship between Wright and Abrahams, these transatlantic exchanges left a lasting imprint upon the interlocutors' writings and literary culture beyond the actual engagement. But the pursuit of transnational community, an often temporary form of relation, does not always pan out in ways originally sought, or even the ways its students might hope for or expect.

The story of epistolary cultivation, in other words, is also the story of what does not take—the story of transnational engagements halted or never fully begun. It includes the relationships between Head, Walker, and Cliff most evidently framed by the figure of the garden, but it likewise involves relationships that do not yield the same intended generative outcomes. The connections Head sought with Giovanni and Morrison did not come to fruition in ways the South African author had wished, for several reasons, only some of which seem apparent. To extend the horticultural metaphor further, attempted engagements do not fully bloom or bear fruit either because they are cut short or do not take root. The acknowledgment of relationships that do not firmly take hold amid those that prove themselves more satisfying or desirable among its participants renders a much more comprehensive picture of the field of black transnational engagement. Such an accounting extends our knowledge into how and why direct transnational engagements are established and persist, or do not. We should be exceedingly wary of simple criteria for what counts as successful or failed—or, better yet, avoid such designations altogether—but assessing people's disappointments, disjunctions, or missed connections must also constitute a part of the story of black transnational engagement.

In order to develop this argument, I begin by considering Bessie Head's exilic life and her quest for belonging that motivated the grounded transnationalism she expressed. I then investigate one of its most exemplary practices: her letter writing, with particular attention to the set of letters between Head and her four African American correspondents. Some of their epistolary exchanges and writing published around the same period feature repeated references to gardens, whose political and imaginative implications are considered at length. I conclude by framing the practice of letter writing as a form of cultivation that re-centers our attention on the labor that transnational engagement requires, even as it yields a whole spectrum of outcomes.

Grounded Transnationalism

In "Geographies of Pain: Captive Bodies and Violent Acts in Myriam Warner-Vieyra, Gayl Jones, and Bessie Head," Françoise Lionnet offers a compelling rubric for cross-cultural literary comparison. Her analysis isolates a thematic commonality—black female characters' murderous confrontation with oppressive patriarchal structures—that resonates across writing by black women from different locales across the African diaspora: Gayl Jones from the United States, Myriam Warner-Vieyra from Guadeloupe/Senegal, and Bessie Head herself. Arguing against essentialist constructions of a "shared 'Africanness'" as the basis for common themes across texts, Lionnet instead locates cross-cultural correspondences in a "performative intertextuality," itself the result of "the ideological and cultural matrix that generates the work."[4] Her approach offers a historically produced and contingent commonality, a "common ground," so to speak, which rests on analogous conditions of gender-based oppression in racialized societies that inspire literary imaginings of violent justice in numerous texts.

"Geographies of Pain," then, outlines a productive framework for thinking about transnationally resonant literary tropes across wide swaths of geopolitical space without being beholden to the logics of national borders or literatures. It enables us to read cross-culturally via parallel comparison—an assessment of correspondences or thematic parallels across established literary categories and a powerful approach, indeed, for identifying counter-hegemonic literary traditions. At the same time, it is worth inquiring into the nature of the "cultural matrix" that facilitates Lionnet's charting of a "geography of pain." What are its terms? How did it emerge, and through what processes? Who and what produces it, and under what conditions? How and for how long is it maintained? These questions provoke a longer view of cross-cultural relation, which Lionnet's approach seems to implicitly encourage.[5] They require, in other words, an approach that pushes past a synchronic snapshot of similarity, for a strictly present-focused analysis may lead us to lose sight of the histories of transaction and circulation—themselves bound up with histories of racial-sexual domination—that have helped produce that matrix. A synchronic snapshot, alone, risks obscuring the development of cultural infrastructure that yields the resonances often identified in parallel comparisons. From this perspective, transnational cultural matrices come into view as neither uniform, spontaneous, static, nor permanent but the consequence of various forms of engagement painstakingly cultivated across time and space instead.

The evidence of that engagement turns up in the transactions between the writers themselves, and no greater illustration of literary transaction may be found than in one of the writers Lionnet features in her essay: Bessie Head. Head's twenty-seven years in South Africa constituted a series of physical and social displacements, which fueled her acutely felt, oft-cited lack of belonging. She was born in 1932 at the Fort Napier Mental Institution in Pietermaritzburg, her white mother having been committed by her family following bouts with mental illness; she never learned the identity of her black or coloured father.[6] An Afrikaner family initially adopted Head but, upon discovering her mixed-race origins, quickly returned her. Although she was subsequently adopted by a coloured family who raised her, Head did not learn of her family roots until she attended an Anglican mission high school in Durban and was painfully separated from her adoptive family. As an adult, Head relocated to Cape Town in 1958 to write for *The Golden City Post*; briefly moved to Johannesburg to work at the paper's main branch; and, just as fleetingly, involved herself in politics by joining the Pan-Africanist Congress. Upon her return to Cape Town, she married fellow journalist Harold Head, but the strains of a difficult marriage coincided with the untenable terms of life under apartheid, and in 1964, she fled South Africa with her young son, Howard, in tow. Head ventured across the northern border and headed directly for Serowe, a rural, predominantly Bamangwato village in the eastern part of the British protectorate of Bechuanaland (renamed Botswana at independence), to begin teaching. A remote, semiarid village situated on the edge of the Kalahari Desert, Serowe represented quite a departure from the lush urbanity of Durban, Cape Town, and Johannesburg that Head knew well. Her teaching career ended shortly thereafter, but—save for brief periods in nearby Radisele, Palapye, and Francistown—Serowe inadvertently became her permanent, if uneasy, home.[7]

Head's move to Botswana partially assuaged her most intense unease, but it also ironically extended the alienation she endured in South Africa. The exit permit the apartheid government issued severely restricted her mobility, rights, and opportunities. For Head, Serowe was foreign territory in more ways than one: An Anglophone South African, she never fully learned Botswana's dominant Setswana language. Beyond her legal limbo of statelessness and linguistic outsider status, she found herself on the outskirts of various longstanding and newly forming local communities.[8] In a letter to a confidante, Patrick Cullinan, Head couched her sense of persistent alienation in decidedly spatial terms: "I've always had to live in someone else's house—the unwanted stranger. You just gravitate naturally to the outer bounds of any environment."[9] Far from shutting her down, Head's continuous experience of marginality precipitated a transnational worldview, for she regularly peered beyond those outer edges of her environment in search of community free of the estrangements she had confronted with painful regularity. As Rob Nixon has noted, "the sheer force and variety of the dispossessions suffered by this *deracine* provoked her to pursue, and with great vigor, alternative forms of belonging."[10] Her quest for new community, then, gave rise to a transnationalism crucially defined by both her place (her residence in Serowe) and her practice (her literary engagements).

It is too often assumed that, in Serowe, Head was wholly removed from the world, destined to live out her days in a cultural desert. Perhaps no one did more to maintain this impression than Head herself, and by all accounts, she led a lonely existence, made all the more solitary by two serious psychological breakdowns during the 1970s.[11] But Serowe was more a rural crossroads of local and global vectors than a desolate island cut off by political lines, sands, or seas. The largest village in southern Africa, with over 30,000 inhabitants by 1964, it stood as the seat of the Bamangwato kingdom ruled by the Khamas, Botswana's most powerful chiefs across the twentieth century.[12] While the majority of Serowe's residents were Batswana, the village played host to numerous transnational guests, as it was located along a corridor trafficked by South African exiles and refugees who either settled in the area or were channeled out elsewhere.[13] Moreover, the village drew volunteers, development experts, and political activists from Europe, North America, and other parts of Africa interested in supporting southern African independence. In short, even in the seemingly remotest of locations, Head may have been painfully removed from her known world but was hardly cut off from the world at large.

The geographic and social terms of Head's location greatly informed her writing. The semiarid, rural village became a setting-template of sorts across Head's early fiction, most evidently for *When Rain Clouds Gather*'s Golema Mmidi, *Maru*'s Dilipe, and *A Question of Power*'s Motabeng. Her villages' social landscapes facilitate her trademark staging of outsider characters' entry into an alien world, while the harsh, quiet bareness of their natural landscapes symbolically lends itself to her characters' searching reassessment of their psychic and spiritual conditions. Head's devoted attention to local life and landscape also took the form of an elaborately researched nonfiction study, eponymously entitled *Serowe: Village of the Rain Wind*—followed by a historical novel about her adopted village, *A Bewitched Crossroad: An African Saga*. At every turn, however, Head's depicted villages are situated within a wider world, rendered visible by the continued presence of outsiders and allusions to historical developments well beyond Botswana's boundaries. Her texts, then, express a transnationalism that was inextricably threaded through her surrounding local environment. Rob Nixon has cast Head's writing in terms of a "rural transnationalism" born of her own relocation to the spare Botswana countryside populated by different walks of life. Head's work regularly registers "the ceaseless border crossings of imperialists, missionaries, refugees, migrant workers, prostitutes, school children, teachers, and armies that score Southern Africa as a region."[14] Nixon's emphasis on regional migration reframes colonies and countries across southern Africa—seemingly silo-ed by their politico-economic relationships to their respective imperial metropoles—as part of a more laterally connected, cross-colonial landscape.

Head's literary life would also extend beyond the regional scale to an even wider arena of engagement. Locally grounded but simultaneously enmeshed in a literary milieu that exceeded southern Africa, Head approximated what Dilip Menon has elsewhere termed "local cosmopolitanism."[15] Menon's concept outlines a relation to the wider world beholden neither to a culture of travel nor to exclusively colonial coordinates but guided, instead, by pragmatic worldly imaginings. He contends that elected affinities have too often been obscured by conventional constructions of nations as discrete formations; colonies as exclusively routed through intellectual traditions of their colonizers; and transnationalism as characterized by unrestrained fluidity. Lamenting that scholars "too easily let both the cartographic exercises of colonialism as well as the national worship of borders shrink the space of our conceptions of geography,"[16] Menon insists on recovering a "*locally rooted cosmopolitanism* that declares affiliation with other worlds and places," both western and non-western, and establishes a nexus of relations on terms not prescribed by the routes of European imperialism.[17] He offers, as example, A. Balakrishna Pillai, a sedentary early-twentieth-century Indian scholar who absorbed and threaded together literary traditions from across the globe in the journal he edited, *Kesari*, from his home state of Kerala.

The simultaneously local and translocal approach that Menon ascribes to Pillai bears out similarly in Head's own literary practices. Unable to travel until her later years in Botswana (1977 to 1984),[18] Head could only journey imaginatively via her literary channels to the rest of the world. From her remote location, Head read widely and voraciously, internalizing the writing of others and unapologetically reworking a variety of texts and traditions—making Head, as Desiree Lewis observes, an intellectual *bricoleur*.[19] It is in this sense that Head characterized, in her essay "Writing Out of Southern Africa," her "own activity as a writer as a kind of participation in the thought of the whole world. No other occupation provides for such an international outlook as writing. I have my national, my African side but I am also very much an international kind of person."[20] Hardly polar opposites in her writing, the local and transnational weave through her work, as much in the varied cast of characters that populate her narratives as in the broad, explicitly humanist energies that emanate out of her quiet corner of the world. A glimpse at some titles in her own library—composed of books sent by friends, admirers, and publishers—conveys the expansiveness of Head's literary horizons: Volume VIII of *The Complete Works of Swami Vivekananda*, Boris Pasternak's *Doctor Zhivago*, D. H. Lawrence's *Sons & Lovers*, Bertolt Brecht's *Mother Courage and Her Children*, Sol Plaatje's *Mhudi*, Michelle Cliff's *Claiming an Identity They Taught Me to Despise*, and Claudia Tate's volume of interviews *Black Women Writers at Work*. An avid reader of scholarship, Head also consulted studies, including John Mbiti's *African Religions and Philosophy*, Ronald Blythe's *Akenfield: Portrait of an English Village*, and *Papers of John Mackenzie*, edited by A. J. Dachs.[21]

Head's numerous readerly and writerly relationships remind us that transnationalism is not only a perspective or worldview, but a practice cultivated within and in response to the predeterminations of geographic remove. It is born out of the transmission of ideas, visions, commitments, and strategies, but that transmission is conducted in the physical world of circulating people and texts. Head developed a set of practices, characterizable as a grounded transnationalism, that emerged out of her relatively immobile state but continued into the years when she could travel somewhat more freely. Of the numerous engagements that register Head's transnationalism as a materially based practice, none are more illustrative or significant than her extensive correspondence with interlocutors abroad. The letters cast to and from her "quiet backwater"[22] throughout Head's most sedentary years represents the exiled author's concerted effort to join in and shape a discourse that exceeded her newfound local and national boundaries—thereby fashioning a grounded transnationalism simultaneously tied to and loosed from her immediate social and natural surroundings. To borrow from Édouard Glissant, Head's letters enabled her to exercise a poetics of relation resolved upon being both "there and elsewhere, rooted and free."[23]

Letters across the Atlantic

Alongside fiction, the epistle—with all its philosophical connotations—was very much Bessie Head's art form, as the sheer volume, range, and density of her letters attest. Her papers, archived in Serowe's Khama III Memorial Museum, reveal Head's extensive correspondence with a vast array of friends, agents, publishers, scholars, writers, and admirers. The subject of justly growing scholarship in recent years, her letters are the partial consequence of the author's need to conduct her literary business remotely; but beyond the communication with metropolitan publishing circles, Head's more intimate letters express her personal concerns, guiding philosophies on life and literature, and interpreta-tions of texts she voraciously consumed. In her give-and-take with others, Head honed her literary and social sensibilities while engaging their views about craft, specific texts, and world events at large. Numerous scholars have noted that Head "self-consciously practiced the letter as a literary form," and like the genre of autobiography, those literary letters also became a means of meticulous self-fashioning, a way of forging a highly wrought persona to present to her cor-respondents.[24] The fact that she began keeping carbon copies of the missives she wrote further suggests that Head understood her epistles to be part and parcel of a wider literary culture. Taken as a whole, her correspondence reveals Head's diligent efforts to connect, be heard, and extend her interpretive influence.

Precisely because it involves more than one person, correspondence has a constructive social function beyond the act of writing the letter. Examining a collective of Christian Zulu letter writers based around the Ekukhanyeni mis-sion station in late-1800s Natal, Vukile Khumalo argues that the network of exchange "was not just a line of communication, it was an environment in which these letter-writers lived, acted, and shared their thoughts." Over time, this network evolved into what Khumalo calls a sphere, "an imaginary environment where the letter-writers felt free to converse among themselves about issues that affected their lives."[25] Couching Head's correspondence as an equivalent to conversation would be to miss their particularly literary designs:[26] whereas the Ekukhanyeni epistolary network was driven by social and political expediency, Head's personally tailored exchanges—although frequently addressing past or present political matters—devoted themselves to the self-conscious exchange of thought and production of culture.

Whatever the distinctions between the two types of networks, Khumalo's framing of letters helps us better appreciate Head's and her correspondents' exchanges as a creation of an alternate social sphere. Head's epistolary rela-tionships evolved their own terms of sociality, each with unique social codes and performances.[27] The transnational epistolary sphere coexisted with her and her correspondents' respective local social spheres, and the inevitable interplay between the two underscores the negotiation of space and place across the Atlantic world through letter writing. In Khumalo's words, epistolary exchange represents an effort to "conquer space through ink" as a means of "establish[ing] connections that d[o] not rely on physical, face-to-face proximity."[28] In Head's case, that establishment of connections is all the more significant because of the initial impediments to her mobility. The epistle thereby offers some measure of reckoning with the problem of geographic distance; it contravenes the physical gap, while nevertheless remaining the inherent product and sign of separation.[29]

Sometimes painfully so: its limited solution to the problem of separation sometimes also meant the authors faced its discouraging constraints, including its lack of immediacy. The aims of letter writing to develop an interpersonal or intercultural imaginary environment, thus, sometimes lie in tension with the frustrations that distance and mediation can engender.

Head's exchanges with four African American women writers—Nikki Giovanni, Toni Morrison, Alice Walker, and Michelle Cliff—from 1973 to 1985 aspired precisely to create this kind of alternative social sphere. Head corresponded with each writer separately amid a wider pool of correspondences that she maintained, but as a discrete set, their exchanges are marked by what Anthony O'Brien has called the "pleasures of recognition, the writing of a likeness,"[30] often given to mutual proclamations of awe, respect, and affection. And given the prevalent themes in each authors' works, their letters unsurprisingly touched upon social and political concerns, past and present. With one exception, the transatlantic traffic that ensued became a means of assessing ongoing American and African struggles for liberation, discussing the relationship between black citizens in South Africa and the United States, and contemplating the possibilities for an ethical future. But, as the exchanges continued, some interpersonal tension and disappointment arose in ways that highlight the physical distance the writers' letters moved across.

A variety of factors led to Head's epistolary exchanges with her African American counterparts, but those exchanges point to the authors' corresponding aesthetic interests, particularly in the ways they explored questions of power in their work, ways that departed from the dominant paradigms of their day. They penned books and letters during and after multiple forms of nationalism swept across the African continent, North America, and Europe in attempts to secure black self-determination. An accompanying resistance to the aesthetic orthodoxies that the white literary establishment hailed as the essentials of "high art" likewise defined the period. Head and the black women she corresponded with played a part in this resistance, not least through their choices to make black women and their communities the centerpiece of much of their literary work. But they also questioned, revised, and maneuvered around what Madhu Dubey has called the prevailing nationalist aesthetic. Exploring the multiple dimensions of black women's lives in a patriarchal white supremacist society, their writing "dialogizes the ideological discourse of black nationalism," often subverting or confronting some of its terms, even while accepting others.[31] Their work in the wake of the 1960s and '70s celebrates the value of community, but, prompted by the exclusions of black nationalism, objections over its (hetero)sexist and reproductivist framings, and worries that it could author post-colonial modes of domination, it casts a suspicious gaze upon the most prevalent constructions of the nation, white or black, as the exclusive carrier of identity or locus of allegiance.

To varying degrees and with different motivations in mind, the authors shared their misgivings about the most dominant expressions of black nationalism as the primary means of mobilizing against racial oppression. From her remote locale in southern Africa, Head surveyed the rise of African nationalism that fueled decolonization with equal parts interest and trepidation. She quickly developed a Fanonian antipathy to nationalism as both incomplete decolonization and a new name for dominion over the disempowered poor.[32] Head's concerns partially dovetailed with her African American correspondents' complex negotiations of black nationalism in a U.S. context, where black nationalism sought to defend and establish forms of sovereignty for a racial minority. The writing of Walker, Morrison, Cliff, and Giovanni all envisioned community in one form or another, but these visions did not easily accept doctrinaire forms of the nation and very frequently challenged the gendered contours of conventional nationalist logic articulated in their work. They sought alternatives to the withering negations of racist, patriarchal, and colonial structures that inhered in ways that the nation and nationalism were deployed around them. Walker and Cliff fashioned art to usher the passage from the psychic and social fracturing to new forms of wholeness and belonging, as Morrison explored the deep historical registers of intracommunity bonds and their ruptures in her writing. And while Giovanni exhibited the least resistance to black nationalism, she nevertheless reported to Head her disagreement with its more masculinist iterations.[33]

Parting company with their black male counterparts' tendencies to stage grandiose clashes with the white racial state, civil society, or its representative figures in their writing, these black women writers frequently redirected their readers' attention to the personal, the everyday, and the ordinary as repositories of variegated black life and, therefore, critical sites of cultural politics.[34] They did so by endowing their female characters and their relationships with functions and dimensions that far outstripped the narrow roles generally scripted for them by male and white female predecessors and contemporaries. Indeed, the work of the five authors helped make room for women's stories in black literary traditions—American and South African—that overwhelmingly privileged writing by, about, and sometimes for men, black nationalist or not.

In response to this masculinist tradition, Morrison, Walker, Cliff, and Giovanni (among others) dedicated themselves to a related cultural project that exceeded their independent artistic ventures: cultivating a greater collective presence of black women in the literary world. Across their careers, they engaged in black feminist institution building in their formal relation-ships with publishing houses and journals as well as in their informal support of black women's writing.[35] As fellow writers, editors, and literary advocates in the United States who knew and interacted with one another, they aimed to pro-mote and sustain black women's writing as sign and shaper of struggle through autonomous self-expression. The promotion of black women's cultural expres-sion well exceeded the American territory, particularly at a moment when black American attention was turned toward the African continent. In this light, Head proved to be of particular interest. Head herself was already versed in African American culture prior to this set of exchanges. In South Africa and Botswana, Head had long followed news about the American freedom struggle along with much of the black American literature and music that made its way to southern Africa. Before leaving South Africa, Head briefly corresponded with Langston Hughes to procure, unsuccessfully, financial and professional assistance.[36] Even upon arriving in Serowe, she befriended an African American activist, Jane Kerina, who assisted refugees and whose political views, argumentative style, and independent spirit had a profound impression on Head.[37] So when black American women writers began corresponding with the South African exile, Head fit well within their efforts to forge black feminist solidarities across the United States and far beyond it, especially as the global antiapartheid movement gathered steam across the 1970s and '80s. Black feminist, transnational, and antiapartheid commitments necessitated creating bonds with black women art-ists across the African diaspora, and the four African American writers shared an interest in Head's work and in amplifying its radical humanist messages.

The resulting transnational contacts and relationships involve other ideolog-ical convergences and differences as well. The authors' relationship to feminism, for example, reveals a range of multifaceted views. Walker developed womanism in the 1970s as an alternative to a U.S. feminist movement led by white American women with concerns that infrequently reflected the lives of black women; she would, however, serve as an editor at the mainstream feminist magazine, *Ms.*[38] By contrast, Head refused to align herself with the feminist movement, despite the fact that her texts denounced sexual dominance and showcased women in the process of liberating themselves. Fearful of any movement's exclusionist practices and of being conceptually boxed in, she eschewed being celebrated as a feminist icon, even if that was precisely what drew Walker, Cliff, and oth-ers to her.[39] Furthermore, Head did not share some of her counterparts' open-ness to or acceptance of fluid or queer sexualities; her writing, published and unpublished, suggests she subscribed to a very rigid, heterosexual code and was subject to flashes of homophobia. However, Head's befriending of openly lesbian or woman-centered African American writers with far more progressive views on sexuality may help us revisit and revise standard assumptions—in ways that cannot be fully explored here—about the meaning and extent of Head's sexual conservatism.[40] Whatever their personal and political orientations, Head's interlocutors aimed to open up dominant literary culture to black women's voices that had too often been restricted to the margins, and Head's work remained of particular interest.

The transatlantic relationships conducted through these correspondences proved quite consequential in the realm of African American literary production, which continues to bear the marks of Head's imprint. The story of this correspondence is, in many ways, the story of black American writers' growing conscientization and outspokenness about apartheid South Africa and, for related reasons, the story of Head's gradually growing prominence on the American literary scene—an account which remains strikingly unaccounted for and underappreciated. For example, Giovanni discussed Head's work with numerous African American writers, including Margaret Walker, who likewise admired Head and met her (in Iowa and Jackson, Mississippi) years later during Head's brief stay in the United States.[41] Morrison, who briefly corresponded with Head while an editor at Random House, has since credited Head (among others) with inspiring her particular way of representing black life in her fiction—namely, as the center of her narrative world, free of recourse to a legitimizing white presence or gaze.[42]

Walker and Cliff have even more overtly acknowledged Head's significance. Walker ushered Head's short stories—including "Witchcraft" and "The Collector of Treasures"—into print in the United States during her tenure as editor at *Ms.* magazine, and, years later, she nominated Head as an "unsung writer" to receive a Mother Jones diploma in the January 1986 issue of *Mother Jones*.[43] Walker variously incorporated Head in her work: A section of her second collection of poetry, *Revolutionary Petunias*, opens with an excerpt from Head's second novel, *Maru*—which she also acknowledges as a touchstone in an early 1973 interview.[44] In *Good Night, Willie Lee, I'll See You in the Morning*, she dedicates the poem "Having Eaten Two Pillows" to Head, whose own language forms the basis of Walker's lines.[45] Walker also dedicates her second book of short stories, *You Can't Keep a Good Woman Down*, to Head, among a large list of luminaries. Perhaps most literarily of all, the character "Bessie Head" briefly appears in Walker's wide-ranging 1989 novel, *The Temple of My Familiar*.[46] Walker even had hopes of publishing her correspondence with Head, along with Head's letters to and from another American confidante, Betty Fradkin.[47] As for Cliff, she would read Head's work alongside her own at public readings,[48] and she acknowledged Head's impress on her life and art by dedicating her first novel, *Abeng*, to Head (and Jean Toomer). Small wonder, then, that Hershini Bhana Young credits Head with a "pivotal role in the creation of a diasporic community of black women writers."[49]

The precise nature of this community remains a matter of some interpretation. O'Brien situates Head's exchanges with Giovanni, Morrison, Walker, and Cliff between two radical letter writing traditions that, when combined, outline a radical nonmetropolitan black feminist network: First, a European feminist tradition, whose privately circulating missives have a "disruptive effect on ideologies of the public-private dichotomy and on masculinist genres, their opening up of strategies of autonomy and opposition." Second, O'Brien aligns this epistolary traffic with earlier sets of African and diasporic authors, whose letters crisscrossed the Black Atlantic world.[50] While O'Brien hails the radical outlines of these transatlantic exchanges, Desiree Lewis's assessment suggests a more tempered approach. Lewis underscores the shared interests and alignments between Head and her counterparts across the Atlantic, while at the same time noting Head's resistance to wholesale identification with them or their political commitments.[51] Identification and affirmed kinship at times quite intensely resonate across these letters, but with Head, they do so temporarily and, as such, invite some caution against too cavalierly reading this community as a settled matter. The sequence of letters between these writers, rather, attests to an intimate epistolary sphere in tentative formation, ever aiming to "conquer space through ink."

• • •

Of the four sets of epistolary exchanges with African American women writers, Head initiated half of them. In 1976, she contacted Toni Morrison in her capacity as editor at Random House in an effort to place two separate manuscripts: a volume of short stories entitled *The Collector of Treasures* and her nonfiction study of her newly adopted home, *Serowe: Village of the Rain Wind*. Having previously received a copy of *Sula* from Nikki Giovanni,[52] Head was already familiar with Morrison as a writer, but their brief correspondence focuses rather formally on the publishing business at hand. Head's passing reference to *Sula* prompts Morrison to offer a discussion about the novel at a later point.[53] That discussion does not materialize; their correspondence ceases shortly after Morrison notifies the South African exile that the traditionally organized departments of Random House had rejected both of Head's genre-bending manuscripts. Morrison signals regret about the outcome and eagerly solicits any future novel, but Head—either hurt by the rejection, desperate to find a suitable publisher, or both—simply asks her to forward her manuscripts elsewhere.[54]

Prior to this, Head reached out to Nikki Giovanni in the earliest set of letters— beginning in 1973 and ending abruptly in 1975—that resulted from the writers' rare face-to-face encounter. While Giovanni had been on a State Department– sponsored reading tour across the African continent, Head was invited to the Botswana capital, Gaborone, to meet her. The two writers were already aware of one another prior to this meeting: Giovanni had learned of Head from the latter's estranged husband, Harold Head, who had migrated to the United States and met Giovanni in John Oliver Killens's Writer's Workshop at Fisk University before settling in Canada.[55] Also before meeting Head in 1973, Giovanni had blurbed the American edition of Head's 1971 novel, *Maru*, wherein she asserted a deep affective bond between them and affirmed literature's capacity to foster sisterhood across a geographic breach: "Bessie Head always reminds me of a classmate I should have had—but didn't. A friend I should have shared secrets with—but couldn't. . . . None of these were possible because I was on one continent and she was on another. But through *When Rain Clouds Gather* and now *Maru* I can share some of her longings and some of her pains. And perhaps she feels my hand reaching—and shares some of my joys."[56] The blurb's intimated friendship had deeply moved Head years before their meeting, and their few days in Gaborone together brought their affinity for one another into material form.

Keen to maintain the tight connection, Head immediately began writing Giovanni upon her return to Serowe. Her initial letters conveyed her effusive enthusiasm, at times reaching up to eight single-spaced pages typed on legal-sized paper in order to expansively address matters personal, political, and spiritual. Some letters include Head's commentary on Giovanni's books (including *Black Feeling, Black Talk, Black Judgement* along with *Gemini, Re: Creation*, and *My House*) furnished by her newfound friend; they offer eloquent disquisitions on Giovanni's writing style and perspective, interspersed with Head's own views on art and politics. Head frequently pondered their friendship: "You said to me: 'We share the same views.' It's not only that. We share the same approach to writing—that it is a piece of music, and a lot of your love poems are very beautiful music."[57] Head also discusses Du Bois's *The Souls of Black Folk*, Eldridge Cleaver's *Soul on Ice*, and James Baldwin's and Giovanni's jointly authored *A Dialogue*. Head's vast reading frees her to weigh in on black freedom struggles in South Africa and the United States, often delineating their similarities and differences. In one letter emphasizing her familiarity with violent state suppression in South Africa, Head notes a "wide gap between my experience and your own, which isn't so terrible." She quickly follows up with a qualification:

> But where our experience draws close together is in [Giovanni's] lines like this: "Black people come from an oral tradition. We sat by the fire and told tales . . . We had a beginning and an end for we didn't know what tomorrow would bring. *We were prepared to deal with the unknown.* . . . Our laws were people-directed. . . ." (. . . [Y]ou will see from my research, the truth of your own words as told to me by the old men of Serowe. That means that a huge chunk of the African way of life went over to America! I'll also send you the story of how people are abruptly shot dead in South Africa, so you can compare.)[58]

In the same letter, Head also signals her philosophical objections to black nationalist politics: "[O]ne day black people might not be there as black people and objects of injustice but they would have suffered a sea change 'into something rich and strange'; so the most eternal gesture would be love and not black power, for instance. . . . I also hate a camp—I can't identify with a cause."[59]

For her part, Giovanni affirms Head as "one of the best writers writing in English"[60] and facilitates a connection between Head and Margaret Walker, author of *Jubilee* and professor at Jackson State University. At one point, Giovanni signals the possibility that a visiting position might be opened there for Head, who indicates a general interest in leaving Botswana. (Margaret Walker would later meet Head in 1977, when Head was a fellow at the University of Iowa's International Writing Program and invited her to Jackson State University for a short visit in December that same year.) Giovanni also briefly reports her impressions of the world as she continued her travels. In contrast to Head's extensive missives, Giovanni's initially typed responses become shorter handwritten notes, and their progressive brevity and comparative infrequency draw increasingly sharp complaints from Head. At one point, she writes Giovanni that she had become "anxious that I was losing track somewhere, that letters were going into a void and I wasn't sure of how to communicate anymore."[61] Head's frustration culminates months later in a furious message terminating their correspondence. Many of her initially effusive epistolary relationships came to notoriously tempestuous ends,[62] but Head's decision here is marked by a refusal to accept what Head took to be a lack of reciprocity and a deep disparity in the authors' investment in their relationship. As Desiree Lewis observes, Head's "ardent declarations of intimacy were largely an expression of her desire, while her sense of persecution painfully registered the extent to which the misunderstanding, miscommunication and everyday social problems of a real world frustrated this desire."[63]

The letters to and from Giovanni are the most elaborate and effusive of her four engagements with African American women writers, but Head's correspondence with Giovanni and Morrison conclude on considerably different notes than they began. Head's epistolary engagements with Alice Walker and Michelle Cliff took place over longer periods, each lasting approximately four years, and both Walker's and Cliff's letters share a certain reverential tone for their South African correspondent, a tone often reflected back by Head herself. As the evidence of Head's influence in their work suggests, their high esteem of Head rendered her an elder-contemporary of sorts, despite Head's relatively young age. Just as noteworthy for our purposes is the fact that the figure of the garden repeatedly surfaces across both sets of correspondence. Plots of planted earth figure as much in their letters as they do in their contemporaneously published fiction and poetry. Indeed, Head, Walker, and Cliff—avid gardeners in their own right—turned to horticulture as either passionate hobby or sustenance, but they also adapted it to serve their writerly needs as a trope of self-expression in their writing. As such, their various gardens ultimately help delineate a new, quite literally grounded form of transnational relation.

In 1974, declaring herself "an admirer of your work," Alice Walker wrote Head to solicit some short stories to publish in *Ms.* magazine, whose editorial board Walker had recently joined.[64] Walker avidly followed Head's writing, becoming arguably her "most conspicuous advocate in the U.S."[65] She had been drawn to *When Rain Clouds Gather*, Head's first novel, which she had lent to Giovanni,[66] and was especially enamored of *Maru*. Head, who was seeking a publisher for her two manuscripts, had a variety of short stories on offer. The initial professional contact catalyzed a set of more intimate exchanges between the authors, peppered with an array of adulations: Walker referred to Head as "My darling sister" and the affectionate abbreviation "Bess," while Head on occasion addressed her correspondent as "My dearest 'Other Half'" and signed herself "your relative."[67] Their correspondence took place as Walker moved from Mississippi to New York City to take her job at *Ms.* but also faced the painful close of her marriage to Mel Leventhal, which she discussed with Head. The bulk of the letters between them represent an interchange of words and worldviews, personal, political, and literary in nature. Sometimes accompanying Walker's missives were sample issues of *Ms.* magazine, but more important to Head were copies of Walker's own writing: a short story collection (*In Love & Trouble*), poetry volumes (*Once* and *Revolutionary Petunias*), novels (*The Third Life of Grange Copeland* and *Meridian*), and several uncollected pieces. As she did with other authors she befriended, Head penned detailed reflections on theme, craft, and artistic vision that she mailed back to Walker.

The letters proved to be the most literarily and philosophically expressive of the set Head wrote to the black American women writers, and Walker recognized these as gifts. "Your letters," Walker marveled, "are the most beautiful and thick-with-thought letters I think I've ever received."[68] Among these was Head's copious commentary on Walker's 1970 novel, *The Third Life of Grange Copeland*, that opens out into a more broadly literary and political discourse. Its capaciousness merits extensive quoting:

> First of all, let me admit humbly that I have not achieved anything near such a vast social statement. [*The Third Life of Grange Copeland*] is a magnificent book and I can well understand the hostilities it would arouse because black people would not like to see themselves like that—basically paranoid. I think they'd rather see themselves pretty as they appear in the pages of *Ebony* magazine and its adverts, looking not too much different from white people, in their pursuit of fantastic clothes, beer and cigarettes.
>
> I make a deep identification with the book because really, it is like a big chunk of Southern Africa, with the same patterns of life, the same paranoia which is like an inward turning whip that devours black people. I woke up a little during the 1960's, firstly because African liberation vibrated through the continent and a little of it reached South Africa, where I was then. . . . [I]n my very early life, the pattern of the Copeland's [*sic*] life was one I lived through. As I recorded in *A Question of Power*, my real mother (who was white) was thrown into a loony bin by her own family for sleeping with a black man. . . . Life doesn't offer you miracles! I think I feared that *death world*. For about seven years I managed to move around on my own, carefully shuttling my way between libraries and work. The suicide attempt and a terrible feeling of loneliness made me marry a man with that same death pattern, like Brownfield Copeland. . . . [Y]ou are so accurate in pointing out that liberation isn't only an equality with the white man, if such a thing is needed . . ., but that black people get to grips with themselves and find out what their value as human beings may be. Unfortunately, it is an acknowledgement of all you acknowledged in *Grange Copeland* and then a "where do we go from here?" How do we create ourselves anew and not necessarily have, as our highest aim—dinner at Tiffany's. Tiffany's might only be for Harry Belafonte and Sidney Poitier and that might be a death too and not what the people really want. I think the white man thinks we want that, that's why he hogged all those places so jealously to himself. Yet people want the big, wide flexible universe to dream in. . . .

So I deeply appreciate THE THIRD LIFE OF GRANGE COPELAND.

The rest that I wanted to add is just bits that weild [*sic*] the book into a beautiful whole; the delicate touches of Southern landscape and scenery, the fruit, the cotton, the flowers, the smell of hay and rain. . . .

. . .

P.S. . . . A note I also wanted to make is that long ago in libraries in S. Africa I had some acquaintance with American writing and used to choose American writers above British for their vigour. But your stuff is an evolution and a powerful one on Steinbeck & Co., like it knows where its [*sic*] going. As for Baldwin, he is a prophet, to me. He, his mind, has a way of devastating America. He really sits on the judgement throne, in spite of his personal complexities. Maybe I identify so strongly with black writers because I am black.[69]

Ranging from an ideological critique of black aspiration to an assessment of American literature, Head's missive is as intriguing for what it reveals about what she does (and does not) know about life in America as what it pronounces in the way of political and social analysis. Head mirrors back to Walker her concerns about the ways in which oppressed peoples respond to their oppression, a concern that fuels Head's well-known misgivings about black nationalist projects. At the same time, however, Head's attention to psychology, the dubious affectations of equality, and the revaluation of black life all interestingly align with Steve Biko's contemporaneous expressions of Black Consciousness.[70] Head's challenge to treating equality (understood as a benchmark set by the white world) as liberation, in particular, demonstrates her overlapping views with black nationalism. Such shared ideological ground with nationalist projects, despite Head's trenchant critiques of their implementation and the terms of community they imply, has received scant critical attention but lends further credence to Dubey's thesis on black women writers' complicated negotiation of the nationalist aesthetic.

Head's emphasis on the liberation of the individual's mind and spirit tightly converges with Walker's own social and artistic perspective, as they discover in their correspondence. What so conspicuously characterizes their respective early work is the struggle against the deformation of the soul in a dehumanizing world shot through with racism, sexism, and a thirst for dominance. Head's awe for Walker's *The Third Life of Grange Copeland* is a case in point. Walker's first novel turns on the transformation of Grange Copeland, whose growing self-possession stands in contrast to his son Brownfield's succumbing to the corrosive racism and violence endemic to the postbellum "plantation world" of Georgia sharecropping.[71] To underscore this point, in the 1988 afterword to her book, Walker stringently maintains the "necessity of keeping inviolate the one interior space," the soul.[72] The conditions of her characters' "interior space" lie embedded in the 1920s rural landscape of racial dispossession, a geography of pain if there ever were one. Her novel's profound spatial sensibility conveys how land and architecture are not just signs of abstract social power, but also its brutal, material instruments. Without ownership of land or crops, Brownfield faces a relentless hypermobility akin to that of Richard Wright's family in *Black Boy*. Subject to predatory white landowners' whims, Brownfield and family are tossed from one gray, dilapidated shack to another, encased by an alienating architecture of race.

Head's praise for the "delicate touches of Southern landscape and scenery" in *The Third Life of Grange Copeland* signals her discerning interpretation, for it is here that Walker locates her characters' redemptive, resilient spirit. That spirit finds expression in floral and vegetable gardens—projects that nourish body and spirit—that thread through Walker's novel. Brownfield's boundedness to the depleted land, implied by his name, finds its foil in the regenerative practices of Mem, who nurses a bed or box of flowers at each decrepit cabin (save the last one)—tenuously but conscientiously staking her small claim through adornment and growth. When boldly plotting her escape from sharecropping by renting a house in town (before Brownfield's vindictive reversal), Mem glows at its indoor plumbing, electricity, and "garden space for flowers and greens."[73] Her steadfast gardening, Melvin Dixon reminds us, "offers refuge and exercise of her will over the family's frequent moves," whites' exploitation, and Brownfield's abuse.[74] Even Grange's vegetable garden located in front of his newly acquired farmhouse signals an abundance and self-sufficiency rooted in ownership, a rarity for surrounding black families.[75] Thadious Davis observes that, across Walker's writing, "it is the natural configurations of landscape itself, represented by gardens and growth, that signify what is enabling in the lives of oppressed people."[76] In *The Third Life of Grange Copeland*, those natural configurations are designed for (if not always achieving) the most copious yield.

Head's attentiveness to Walker's "Southern landscape and scenery, the fruit, the cotton, the flowers, the smell of hay and rain" additionally underscores the authors' shared interest in the relation between power and geography—particularly, the garden, a staple trope across Head's writing—that made her all the more receptive to Walker's (and later Cliff's) landscapes. Head's abiding interest in gardening and horticulture was spurred early by gardens at her childhood home and residential high school, St. Monica's in Durban. After arriving in Botswana, Head briefly worked in the experimental Bamangwato Development Association farm in Radisele, which propelled her to pursue a short course of study on tropical agriculture, and once back in Serowe, Head drew on these experiences as an instructor for a gardening group, composed primarily of Serowe women. The group was one of multiple skill-specific units to form the Boiteko ("self-help") rural community development project spearheaded by South African expatriate and prior founder of the Swaneng Hill School and cooperative Brigades Project, Patrick van Rensburg. Apart from these communal efforts, Head was allocated a personal garden next to her home, where she steadfastly tended her vegetables, flowers, and gooseberry bushes, and prepared seedlings for the Boiteko garden.[77]

Gardening and writing became the principal preoccupations that structured Head's life, and these two chief passions very much worked in tandem, sometimes in conjunction. Like literature, gardening crucially helped restore Head back to good health and stability after periods of great distress, particularly after her second mental breakdown in 1971.[78] A source of sociability, personal pleasure, and survival (economic and psychological), Head's gardens also became fertile ground for her creative writing. The Radisele project became the template for the experimental farm in *When Rain Clouds Gather*, for example, while the Boiteko garden served as her model for the cooperative plot in *A Question of Power*.[79] Head also notably harnessed the language of agriculture— "cooperative," "communal," "development," "cultivation," "transplantation"—for her own literary-philosophical efforts to conjure her characters' conditions and aspirations. While the trope of the garden may generally be given to all kinds of metaphors for nurturing, growth, and plentitude, Head represents land and agriculture as labor-intensive and trying, where the yield is transformational but hard-fought. Across her oeuvre, they routinely mark other forms of work, social and metaphysical.

Agricultural enterprise organizes many of her social worlds in Head's texts. In *When Rain Clouds Gather*, for instance, arid conditions force the people of Golema Mmidi ("to grow crops") to "make the land the central part of their existence," and while the novel revolves around predominantly male figures, Head highlights the lives of female "tillers of the earth."[80] Outsiders—including South African freedom fighter-in-exile, Makhaya Maseko, and British agriculturalist, Gilbert Balfour—work their way into the social fabric of their adopted home through the experimental farm, whose success requires modifying local customs and natural resources alike. The novel thus establishes a "symbiotic relationship between nurturing the environment and being sustained by it";[81] likewise, the people originally from and beyond Golema Mmidi simultaneously alter and are altered by the social landscape. Rather than a hubristic venture to make the desert bloom, revamped agricultural practices are geared toward rendering people of Golema Mmidi self-sustaining and less vulnerable to both natural and political ravaging. Producing a self-sufficient harvest in an only seemingly barren landscape is imbued with a more democratic and participatory politics of ensuring people's independence from former colonial masters and post-colonial profiteers. In *A Question of Power*, Head's third novel, the village's collective garden is where transplants—horticultural and human—can take root and "a great experimental centre where everything new [is] tried out," but it also serves as the epicenter of communal engagement, a site where "people of totally foreign backgrounds are made to work together and understand each other's humanity."[82] The garden in Head's work, however, is no Edenic sign of paradise and social harmony; prejudice and abuse certainly figure into the social order.[83] Nor does her figured landscape represent an "alienated ground of contest" as it often did in the writing of Head's South African literary peers, James Graham has noted; and Maureen Fielding reminds us that the reclamation of land in Head's work takes place in far more subtle ways than does the revolutionary struggle that surrounded the former protectorate, Botswana.[84] Indeed, Head's gardens are grounds of engagement where troubled social relations are manifest and worked out.[85]

As characters work out their social relations by way of working the land, agricultural plots form staging grounds for their metaphysical development. It is one of the hallmarks of Head's writing to link the inner, psychic, or spiritual conditions of her characters with their surrounding natural worlds, whose descriptions are charged with metaphor and meaning. For instance, the garden not only provides Makhaya an entry into a new social network free of apartheid's ills; with its labor and time for reflection, both the garden and its workers nudge along his gradual psychic restoration from the exile's "inner torture" and memory of a South African hell. Head biographers and critics have, indeed, noted the healing properties of the author's tangible and literary gardens, in which practices of mutual interdependence yield possibilities for moral growth.[86] Such properties are most associated with *A Question of Power*, wherein the name of the novel's village, Motabeng ("place of sand"), simultaneously connotes nonarable land and a terrain of psychic instability that correspond to Elizabeth's more spiritual turmoil. The village's cooperative garden, however, provides a sanctuary from Elizabeth's raging soul-drama, thus becoming a locus of reconnection, restoration, and reorientation. Linda-Susan Beard considers the garden an integral "part of Elizabeth's metaphysical education [that] works towards 'the total de-mystifying of all illusions.'"[87] This metaphysical education is what finally enables Elizabeth to touch the land with calm in "a gesture of belonging."[88] Whatever victories Head offers are the outcome of laborious struggles, the arduous cultivation of soil, soul, and society—a point that she communicated regularly to Walker, among others, in her letters.

Walker's own missives to Head are not as extensive or detailed as her correspondent's, but they reflect an unmistakable reverence and intimacy. Walker even encloses some hand-drawn illustrations expressing her high regard for their friendship. In one letter that alludes to her stronger sense of well-being after a challenging period, Walker notes her emerging strength:

> I am regaining my peace of mind. This is due largely to summer being the season for my gardening. I have planted lots of flowers and vegetables and I am supremely happy when I am tending my tomatoes, say, or watering the marigolds. We are now planning (at Ms.) a two page spread of apartheid laws in the Magazine. I feel sick reading them, and as I read them, I think of you, your beautiful soul and spirit, your beautiful and holy work/life. It sends me into a rage (I think of other people too, of course, living under those "laws" but it is you, because we have "met" that my heart hurts for).[89]

Walker's missive offers a glimpse into the ways that publications guided by the vision of their editors engaged in the transnational advocacy against the apartheid regime during this period. The specific knowledge of South African politics that this advocacy requires lies in contrast to the abstracted, mythical constructions of the African continent that Walker has repeatedly invoked in her writing.[90] More important for our purposes is how Walker's letter affirms an affective correspondence between the cultivated environment and the soul's "interior space." Establishing a direct line between the practice of gardening and emotional health, Walker's characterization of her Brooklyn plot gels with Head's own understanding of the garden as a site of restoration and psychic growth. Walker then extends the vitality of her garden to her friend by drawing three cheerful flowers named "Howard," "Alice," and "Bessie" at the bottom of her letter (see Figure 5).

Other letters from Walker convey her desire not to lose the bond with Head, when her southern African correspondent expresses impatience at not receiving a letter or when she appreciatively accuses Walker of "pinching from my philosophies" in her own published writing.[91] Indeed, she evinces a respectful deference to Head. She takes Head's mixed response to the newly released *Meridian* in stride and engages in a back-and-forth about the novel. At other moments, frankly illustrating how letters emphasize distance, Walker shares her frustrations with the epistolary form, as well, wishing "that we could talk in a normal way . . . Letters leave out so much."[92] In fact, Walker was quite eager to meet Head in person and, in 1977, raised the possibility of a trip to southern

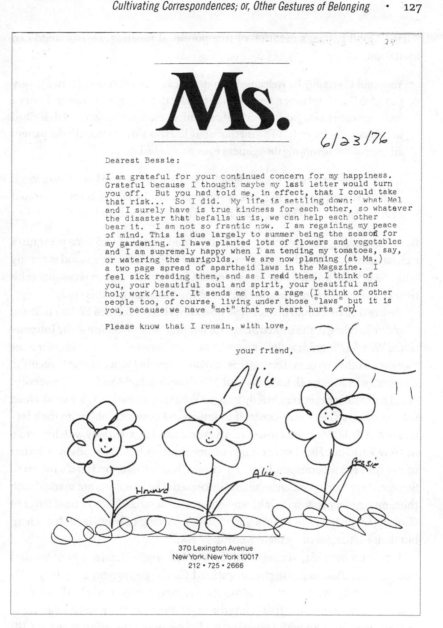

Ms.

6/23/76

Dearest Bessie:

I am grateful for your continued concern for my happiness. Grateful because I thought maybe my last letter would turn you off. But you had told me, in effect, that I could take that risk... So I did. My life is settling down: what Mel and I surely have is true kindness for each other, so whatever the disaster that befalls us is, we can help each other bear it. I am not so frantic now. I am regaining my peace of mind. This is due largely to summer being the season for my gardening. I have planted lots of flowers and vegetables and I am supremely happy when I am tending my tomatoes, say, or watering the marigolds. We are now planning (at Ms.) a two page spread of apartheid laws in the Magazine. I feel sick reading them, and as I read them, I think of you, your beautiful soul and spirit, your beautiful and holy work/life. It sends me into a rage (I think of other people too, of course, living under those "laws" but it is you, because we have "met" that my heart hurts for).

Please know that I remain, with love,

your friend,

Alice

Howard   Alice   Bessie

370 Lexington Avenue
New York, New York 10017
212 • 725 • 2666

Figure 5. Letter from Alice Walker to Bessie Head, with hand-drawn flower garden, June 23, 1976 (Bessie Head Papers, Khama III Memorial Museum, KMM 76 BHP 24).

Africa. Upon Walker's mention of this potential meeting, Head extends an invitation:

> You would certainly be welcome to come this side in February. Serowe is very peaceful and mundane and my only life too. Nothing exciting happens. I work a lot in a garden in my yard. At night I type a bit or read. It was Serowe I described in *A Question of Power*: "... The rhythm of its life was slow paced, like the patient stirring of cattle turning thoughtless eyes on a new day ..."

> Let me know for sure if you would really like to come here and I can draw a rough map of where I live. It's miles in the bush and off the beaten track, so I would have to give you long and detailed instructions on how to find me.[93]

Besides stressing her two chief activities, Head's note of welcome presents a rich snapshot of place that conjures a mood. Head follows this mood mapping with the offer of a visual map to help orient her interlocutor in ways that echo the exchange between Rive and Hughes at the beginning of this study.

Before this visit could materialize, however, Head informed Walker that she would be heading to the United States for her four-month tenure at the International Writers Program at the University of Iowa, where Head would encounter numerous other writers. During this stay, she traveled to lecture at Concordia University in Montreal, Canada, and Mississippi's Jackson State University. Head and Walker met very briefly in New York City in early 1978, just as Head was concluding her American visit to return to Botswana, although their letters reveal little about their meeting. Walker invited Head to stay with her while in New York, but Head spent much of her time with Betty Fradkin, another of her American correspondents. After one final letter upon Head's return to Serowe, their correspondence quizzically ceased. The letter was not marked with the tempestuousness or definitiveness that characterized Head's final letter to Giovanni. The terms of Head's and Walker's parting of ways seem less clear, but their exchanges nevertheless abruptly end.[94]

In September 1981, Michelle Cliff forwarded Bessie Head a copy of her first book, a collection of prose poems entitled *Claiming an Identity They Taught Me to Despise*, along with a note of admiration. She had procured Head's address from African American activist and educator Gloria Joseph, who had met Head in Gaborone in 1980 while advising on Botswana's education system. Cliff shared with Head a copy of her new work, she explains, because Head's books "have given me so much insight and knowledge" and reports having read aloud Head's story "The Collector of Treasures" at her own public reading the previous year.[95] If Head's work resonated with Cliff, it is likely due to the fact that Cliff's own book addressed very similar themes. A series of fragmented meditations, *Claiming an Identity They Taught Me to Despise* charts the lives of women across a world riven by imperialism, patriarchy, racism, and classism. Together, the prose poems attest to a struggle not only for survival and autonomy, but for a sense of wholeness as well. Cliff has elsewhere remarked that the identity being claimed in the volume's title is "Jamaican and black" and the identity of "a whole person."[96] While marking moments of painful fragmentation (collective and individual), the volume is driven by a searching quality that aims for a new state of being—an approach that, indeed, resonates with Head's own writing.

As both writers have indicated, Cliff's and Head's similarly searching approaches were prompted by their own early struggles with identity.[97] Cliff's attention to Head's writing, then, also points to related patterns in their social circumstances. The Jamaican-born Cliff was not compelled into exile, but she did share with Head the unique estrangements of expatriation away from the land of her birth. Emigrating to the United States quite young and attending graduate school in England before returning to reside in the United States, Cliff has not fit the classic designation "African American" in the ways that the multigenerational, U.S.-born Walker, Morrison, and Giovanni have. Nor has she easily conformed to the category of blackness. As a light-skinned Creole woman, whose visual presence in Jamaica and the United States brought her social privileges, Cliff may have connected to Head, whose painful predicaments as a biracial woman within her country's hierarchical schema she frequently explored in her first several novels. Such fraught predicaments—from their mismatch with crude identity categories and others' simplistic assumptions of racial belonging—seem to have made both of them suspicious of the politics of authenticity while equally committed to demands of racial justice. Moreover, refusing to embrace their imposed racial identities and privileges they bestowed, each sought to actively claim the African heritage both of their worlds taught them to despise.[98]

Taking place over an extended period with some stretches of silence, Head's correspondence with Cliff was not as extensive as that with Giovanni or Walker, but it exuded a similar mutual respect, warmth, and connection. Her prompt reply to Cliff's initial contact was full of praise for her first book, explaining that she read it "with great pleasure. It reminds me strongly of the writing of Lorraine Hansberry. There is the same quiet, pretty pacing of thought and feeling, a precision of language that makes meaning utterly and absolutely clear and the same talent for the small poignant statement that lives in the memory forever."[99] Head elaborates on Cliff's praiseworthy style, noting that the latter's "very clarity of language and meaning suggests a control over the experience, an intellectual control that leaves one with a sense of peace, not alarm. . . . I think that this is the basic magnificence of your own book, that your life depends on coming face to face with your own self."[100] Head closes by affirming the power of literature to surpass the challenges of exile and of living in the deeply troubled and turbulent southern tip of Africa: "That has been my major problem, a feeling that I should have gone somewhere. All this being so, it gives me a little happiness that you liked some things I wrote. Gloria [Joseph] is like that too, as though the world of writing can triumph over a terrible environment like southern Africa."[101]

Claiming an Identity They Taught Me to Despise in many ways marks Cliff's own grappling with her environment and is especially attuned to the political dimensions of land and place discernible in Head's letter. In the prose poem "Obsolete Geography," for example, the speaker explores the Jamaican landscape shaped by the violence of colonial rule and its aftermath that often play out through intimate family relations. Recalling quizzical childhood memories, the speaker ultimately discovers a host of undercurrents beneath the surface of a once-familiar Jamaican social geography:

> Behind the warmth and light are dark and damp/behind the wet sugar, cane fields/behind the rain and river water, periods of drought/underneath the earth are the dead/underneath the wood fire are ashes to be emptied/underneath the distance is separation/underneath the slaughter is hunger/behind the mysterious births is my own/behind the fertility are the verdicts of insanity/behind the women at the river are earlier women/underlying my grandmother's authority with land and scripture is obedience to a drunken husband/underneath a tree named with my mother's name is a rotted cord.[102]

Zeroing in on histories of colonialism, patriarchy, colorism, and economic exploitation, much of Cliff's writing works to unearth power in its sedimented, less evident forms.

The agricultural plot serves this purpose in "The Garden," a nine-part meditation on gender, land, and race. Cliff's variously invoked gardens are vexed sites, indeed, where unwelcome forces and underlying violence repeatedly mar efforts to cultivate a plentiful garden. At one point, this comes in the form of a man who destroys meticulously arranged rows of crops while offering the speaker his assistance; at other points, it manifests as the speaker guiltily wages "hand-to-hand combat" to kill pests or as frost requiring her to practice a "strange destruction."[103] Cliff's gardens additionally foreclose any naturalizing assumptions about women as innately nurturing beings, fecund (Mother) Earths, or explorable sites of pleasure. The garden, in fact, develops into the setting for a deep familial struggle: the speaker strives to "assure that everything lives"[104] against her mother's accusations of being "unloving and unnurturing." Gardening represents a "pitched battle" against the "powerful weeds" that function as a metaphor for her "mother's and sister's demands." This "contaminated" space becomes threatening enough for the speaker to imagine "a snake or animal lurking somewhere."[105]

This personal drama broadens out onto a more systemic consideration of women's (re)productivity in another section, where the speaker weighs society's brutality toward childless women against the deaths that mothers (Mary Wollstonecraft, Charlotte Brontë, Mariah Upshur, and the Virgin Mary) have historically had to bear—most sacrificially, their own. Part 7's "history of women and gardens" catalogues specific women's relationships to agricultural, horticultural, and botanical labor of different sorts: a formerly enslaved woman photographed by Dorothea Lange; Emily Dickinson "tending exotica"; the four Nebraska homesteading Chrisman sisters; Fannie Lou Hamer in a cotton field; Maria Sibylla Merian's sketching of the botanical bounty in colonial Surinam; peasant workers in European art; Jamaican market women; as well as her grandmother and herself.[106] Cliff's list conjures a tradition of women resolutely working (physically or artistically) the planted earth. But it also intimates their knotty entanglements—some far less fortuitous than others—with colonial formations and coercion, as all the women's determined gardening takes place on terrains of domination, usurpation, and displacement. Cliff's literary gardens, then, are deeply fraught, if not dystopic, loci characterized by loneliness and destructive forces, historical and natural, that frustrate human designs.[107]

Head briefly acknowledged Cliff's deeply conflicted associations with cultivated land in a later short note acknowledging receipt of the book; alluding to the prose poem, she signed off by wishing Cliff "no snakes in your garden."[108] In 1983, Cliff wrote informing Head that she had dedicated *Abeng* to her (and in memory of Jean Toomer) "[b]ecause of who you are & what you & your work has meant to me," adding that it "gave me great pleasure to do it." Beyond this announcement, she mentions her burgeoning mixed spring garden in Montague, Massachusetts, which admits of far fewer struggles and wrenching relationships than her literary gardens explore. Somewhat akin to Walker's Brooklyn garden, Cliff's horticultural plot represents prized refuge: "I am also occupied with my garden," she reports, "So far I have peas coming & lots of asparagus, herbs, cabbages, broccoli, spinach, strawberries—and daisies, floxgloves, poppies, pansies, and johnny jump-ups. I still feel safe here—perhaps that is not so good, since I tend to be a bit reclusive."[109] As a site of relative solace and safety, Cliff's personal cultivated space is a remarkable counterpoint to the charged historical and natural encroachments represented in "The Garden." It, furthermore, offers a point of connection with her reclusive counterpart in Botswana. Head's response to Cliff's letter explains how honored she is by Cliff's dedication of *Abeng*: "This is the first time something like this has happened. . . . [Y]our letter is like a mile stone in my life, some landmark and proof of human affection for my existence. I am inclined to love life and people and a terror had built up in me that I only saw horror and hate all around me." From one avid gardener to another, Head adds a note of thanks "for news of your garden and all the wonderful things growing in it."[110]

Cliff's *Abeng* takes up the legacies of Jamaica's colonial history primarily through the family narrative and adventures of protagonist Clare Savage, a young Creole girl. Her quest for autonomy—attainable, in her mind, upon menstruation—is set against her own color and class privileges, rendered all the more visible by a darker and poorer majority that includes her friend Zoe. Although Clare does not (yet) resolve these tensions, the narrative gestures toward her growing consciousness. In a follow-up letter almost one year later, Head offers her characteristic insightful commentary on *Abeng*, stressing along the way the similarities between herself and the novel's protagonist, Clare, as well as Cliff. "I found that no book had been more aptly dedicated," Head enthuses. "Clare is a kind of mirror of my own youth. What surprises me are the many similar details." Further highlighting the novel's style, Head notes their common authorial approaches: "It is tight and cool. Messages about slavery, poverty, and exploitation come across very clearly. I have something else I share with Clare—there is something tough and masculine in me that will suddenly make me do bold, unexpected courageous things." Extending this point, Head emphasizes Clare's "blending of toughness and delicate femininity," which, for Head, recalls Frank Sinatra's phrase of a "tomboy in lace." Imagining a strong physical resemblance between Head, Cliff's protagonist, and—she presumes—Cliff, she speculates that Cliff might be mistaken for Head by British reviewers were she to be published in England.[111]

Cliff's reply to Head's missive reaffirms their deep correspondence in multiple ways. She raises the social relatedness of the United States and South Africa, noting their "differences lie in the 'quality' of oppression only it seems. The essential hatred permeates both countries." More personally, Cliff also claims the same "tomboy-in-lace" qualities that Head identified with in the character of Clare.[112] As if to hammer this point home, in the final letter between them, in 1985, Cliff wittily addresses Head and signs herself off as "Tough Guy, Twin Soul, Two."[113] Their letters end here, however, perhaps the consequence of Head's declining health that would lead to her early death in April 1986.

The Politics of the Cultivated Earth

The political dimensions of gardens come into sharp relief in the American and African post-colonial contexts of each author, shaped as they are by racialized processes of land expropriation, displacement, and labor exploitation. V. Y. Mudimbe argues that the etymology of "colonialism"—whose Latin root, *colĕre*, means "to cultivate or design"—reflects, beyond land expropriation proper, a western will "to organize and transform non-European areas into fundamentally European constructs."[114] The histories of southern Africa and the Americas attest not only to geographic and ecological dominion, but also to the violent social and epistemic reordering behind the hubristic enterprise of "cultivating" raw materials and people. The magnitude of the western hemispheric plantation system, a patchwork of vast land tracts dedicated to the mass production of crops for private profit, offers ample illustration. So too does Europe's incursion into southern Africa that began as the agricultural settlement Cape Town—an initially modest, fragile refreshment station built around a vegetable garden to supply passing sailors extending Dutch maritime trade interests throughout the Indian Ocean basin.[115] (These examples also point to how colonies were turned into remote gardens of sorts for the European metropole, furnishing it with crops, resources, and exotica.) That these initial agricultural exploits grew into imposing colonial formations claiming sovereignty over enormous territory and its inhabitants and subsequently developed into powerful modern countries underscores the connection between gardening and racial statecraft.

If the plantation and the colonial garden are animated by exploitative political economies, so too are the seemingly isolated farm and idyllic pasture wholly imbricated in national narratives and economies guided by early and later forms of global capital.[116] In South Africa and the United States—as in other areas of the world where the worked land buttresses racially defined forms of livelihood, ownership, prosperity, citizenship, rights, knowledge, sanctuary, and freedom—even the small vegetable patch or elegant floral designs are overlayed across a political terrain. In *My Garden (Book)*, for example, Jamaica Kincaid reminds us that everything from the institutionalization of Linnaeus's binomial nomenclature to the emergence of the botanical garden is shot through with the turbulent reordering of empire.[117] As if to showcase Mudimbe's claims, Kincaid scrutinizes the history of horticulture (her own prized hobby) to lay bare the extensive reach of European linguistic and material seizures, acts of dispossession, and imperial practices that efface indigenous political, cultural, and knowledge systems across the globe.

For all their implication in histories of imperial domination, gardens have nevertheless long served the needs of the dispossessed. Writers and scholars alike have recognized the ways that oppressed peoples put the productive plot of earth to use for their own artistic and psychological necessities.[118] Well beyond physical sustenance, subjugated populations have, indeed, used horticultural turf to lay claim to land—if not by outright ownership (often denied them), then by ordering, working, and rendering it productive by their own hands. As miniature terrains on which to anchor one's identity and being (individual or collective) and to exercise some relative amount of control, gardens have been means by which the subjugated could restore their psyches and exercise their subjectivities. Although focused on gardens in literal war zones, Kenneth Helphand's notion of defiant gardens underscores the ways in which gardens have historically served as "sites of assertion and affirmation" in contexts of "extreme or difficult environmental, social, political, economic, or cultural circumstances."[119] As the personal and published gardens of Head, Walker, and Cliff attest, gardens mark a refusal to abide by the dehumanizing physical and social environment, if only by modifying a minor portion of the terrain. As their varied gardens equally bear out, gardens have also long been women's spaces. This is not only because gardens have classically figured as metaphors for women's beauty, hidden pleasures, or fertility, or because ornate gardens in patriarchal societies have been safe, sanctioned spaces of entertainment for women of leisure. Women have also been associated with the garden because, in many parts of the world, they have worked both expansive fields and small private plots for sustenance. They have, likewise, often produced gardens as sites of creativity beyond the care or control of men.

The latter point returns us to Alice Walker, whose own theorization of the garden brings an intersectional approach to highlight a largely unrecognized tradition of black American women's expressivity. In her 1974 essay "In Search of Our Mothers' Gardens," Walker laments the stymied conventional artistic production by black women who had been denied formal creative outlets under America's regime of racism and patriarchal servitude. "What did it mean for a black woman to be an artist in our grandmothers' time?" she ponders, and her answer lies in the oft-unseen "millions of black women" whose creative force reshaped their surroundings.[120] Instead of seeking black women's expressive culture on the exceptional page, stage, or gallery, Walker locates it quite literally in the everyday of her mother's front yard. Over and above the underpaid field work and unpaid domestic labor, Walker's mother planted "ambitious gardens" to adorn "whatever shabby house we were forced to live in."[121] Her mother's artful labor, she explains, colorfully altered the dismal physical and social structures Walker's sharecropping family was compelled to inhabit:

> Whatever [Walker's mother] planted grew as if by magic, and her fame as a grower of flowers spread over three counties. Because of her creativity with her flowers, even my memories of poverty are seen through a screen of blooms— sunflowers, petunias, roses, dahlias, forsythia, spirea, delphiniums, verbena . . . and on and on.
>
> . . . [W]hatever rocky soil she landed on, she turned into a garden. A garden so brilliant with colors, so original in its design, so magnificent with life and creativity, that to this day people drive by our house . . . and ask to stand or walk among my mother's art.[122]

Walker's analytical return to her mother's garden as a metaphor for black women's cultural production offers several key points worth enumerating here. First, her mother's garden introduces beauty across an otherwise barren, hostile social landscape in ways that show us how, as Cheryl Wall has argued, for Walker, the "garden is the initial signifier of the beautiful."[123] Walker's essay recenters black women's aesthetic virtuosity and pleasure as critical elements of black American life, not subordinate to political matters but, rather, part and parcel of them. Second, Walker's skillful gardener exerts a quiet but evident agency in a sphere riddled with social and spatial inequalities. For Walker's sharecropping family repeatedly displaced across the segregated southern terrain, the small cultivated garden offers a necessary salve. "People plant gardens to control wilderness, to establish boundaries of human endeavor against the onslaught of nature, and to harness beauty as a exercise of taste and will," Melvin Dixon observed in his pioneering spatial analysis of African American literature, *Ride Out the Wilderness*. But Walker's mother's perennial gardening (irrespective of address) also helped to "beautify each subsequent residence and to stave off feelings of uprootedness and dislocation. The garden stabilized the family's sense of home, identity, and beauty, in the midst of disrupting change."[124] Walker's redefined garden is thus saturated with the stabilizing, restorative, and empowering function of aesthetic pleasure in a hostile world. Where black freedom is partially hemmed in by white physical, political, and economic structures, the garden evinces a counteractive, reorienting will. It becomes the artful island of self-possession in a desolate landscape of dispossession, and that, in Walker's eyes, is the crucial work of creative self-expression. Third, if the garden marks the site of artistry and self-possession, it also serves as a metaphorical placeholder for other commonly practiced art forms that black women have mastered over the centuries, including storytelling and quilt making. Identifying these everyday acts of cultural production enables Walker to recuperate a long lineage of otherwise unrecognized black women artisans, who painstakingly but often indiscernibly passed down their talents to younger generations. Through the garden, then, Walker gathers and claims a diachronic community of black female cultural progenitors.

The personal gardens of Walker, Cliff, and Head certainly speak to the restorative comforts, empowerment, and artistry of gardens as miniature zones of relative autonomy.[125] The gardens featured in their published writing, however, point to a considerable divergence in their associations and goals. Angeletta Gourdine has noted, for instance, the differences between Walker's garden and Cliff's: "While Alice Walker can 'search her mother's gardens' and excavate a tradition that sustains her and allows her to sow seeds connecting her to the past and projecting her into the future of womanists, Cliff's gardening 'is a pitched battle against' her mother and her sister and is 'thus contaminated.'"[126] Their figured gardens address different social, political, and interpersonal struggles, and they do so in distinct manners: some represent the struggles and, others, the respite from struggle. But if their gardens variously scrutinize questions about space, social power, and identity, they nevertheless gesture toward the issue of community. Whatever configuration or disintegration it conveys, the garden as a trope in their writing marks a search for community and an exploration of its terms, especially in light of the broader social and political questions.

The type of community that the figure of the garden can correspond to is arguably precisely what would interest these writers. Head's, Walker's, and Cliff's gardens offer a very different scale of belonging than that of the nation, whose model of community took precedence in the Cold War contests across the latter half of the twentieth century. The nation became the form through which political legitimacy and sovereignty could be secured, and the nationalisms of the racial state, its black nationalist opposition, and the emerging post-colonial state all served to solidify it. Whereas nationalism requires an allegiance to the nation—often coterminus with a vast territory—that trumps any other alliances, identities, and forms of belonging, the garden evokes a fundamentally different register of relation, at once subnational and extranational. In one sense, the modest geographic scale of the garden gestures toward a ratcheted-down scale of belonging and outlines an intimately known world where the constituents are identifiable and claimed. This microgeography indexes a carefully cultivated community created through acts of affiliation and friendship—premised on what Leela Gandhi calls "elected affinities"[127]—whose desires, allegiances, and imaginings are not bound up with the abstracted nation but with the more grounded, intimately scaled lateral relationships. This smaller scale redirects us toward the microcosmic ordinary and everyday that retains, for example, the black female autonomy and close connection Walker pinpoints in her essay but which are quickly obscured by the construct of the expansive nation.

By the same token, the figure of the intimate garden serves as the basis for a geographically extended form of relation. Gandhi's concept of "affective communities" reminds us, after all, that intimacies can stretch far and wide and cut across political and cultural boundaries. While Walker employs it to reveal a collectivity of black women artists, the garden need not necessarily be restricted to a diachronic community; it also serves as a medium for marking a synchronic transnational community. Numerous scholars, from Rob Nixon to Sonali Perera, have located that wider synchronic community in the figure of Bessie Head's rural village.[128] In her analysis of Head's represented rural village, Eleni Coundouriotis casts Head as a participant in a discourse that she calls, after Ronald Blythe, an "internationalism of the planted earth."[129] Blythe—author of *Akenfield: Portrait of an English Village*, which served as a model for Head's own eponymous study of Serowe—imagined a confraternity among rural agrarian villages (be they in England, Vietnam, or France) by virtue of their symmetrical relationships to the "planted earth."[130] That shared orientation, in turn, forms the basis of an identification with a much wider circle of humanity. She observes that, for Blythe, "agricultural life enhances a basic commonality among humankind. The boundedness of the village is important to Blythe in the end . . . because it renews our sense of the 'elemental' life we have in common as a world community. The local gives way to the universal and presents an opportunity for a kind of cosmopolitanism that is anchored in our relationship with the earth and that transcends national boundaries, thereby sensitizing us to our common humanity."[131] Coundouriotis traces a transnational imaginary likewise running through Head's figured Botswana village, a literary construction that enables her to open out onto a larger community. Coundouriotis argues that Blythe's and Head's related conceptions of the village bypass the nation as an organizing ground to claim instead a more transnational community. In effect, they practice what cultural geographers have called "jumping scale."[132]

By this logic, the authors' analogous orientations toward miniature plots of planted earth—in Serowe (Head), Brooklyn (Walker), or Montague (Cliff)—position them in evident relation. Although much smaller in size than a village, their gardens also jump the national scale to outline a transnational community. However, they do so by more than symmetrical relationships to gardens alone, as one of the crucial differences between Head's and Blythe's approaches makes apparent. Blythe's "internationalism of the planted earth" assumes a deep symmetry among coexisting but discrete agrarian villages around the globe. The "inter" of his internationalism signals a parallel, not transactional, positioning; it rests on latent relation that could, but need not, develop into dynamic interaction. Far more than parallels, the gardens of Head, Walker, and Cliff become tropological grounds of active transnational engagement. What initially appears to be the very archetype of singular rootedness is, in practice, extensively rhizomatic.[133] If the authors' fecund plots of earth render visible key symmetries across transnational geographies, it is their epistolary exchanges and textual transactions that actualize their salience. The sharing of these gardens—their circulation and recognition—renders them meaningful and a basis for bonding. And as they move across the ocean to be shared, these figured gardens outline a grounded transnationalism.

The Labor of Cultivation

The relevance—and aim—of grounded transnationalism is abundantly evident in Alice Walker's seemingly whimsical drawing, which quite literally illustrates how circulating gardens function as grounds of engagement (see Figure 5). According to the text of her letter, Walker regains her peace of mind by tending to her plot of planted earth, now flourishing in "the season for my gardening." Walker's personal plot is her restorative terrain, consistent with the ways her gardens appear across her fiction and nonfiction. Her visually depicted garden below the typed text is bountiful in a different way: three cheery flowers ("Howard," "Alice," and "Bessie") appear to be nurtured as much by their companionship as by the bright sun. Their sharing of the same earth expresses an emotional closeness and a metaphorical common ground that also bespeaks Walker's desire to overcome the geographic distance between them. Invoking and projecting her desired community, she discursively produces the shared ground of communion upon which she and her friends may grow. In this way, Walker's drawn arrangement represents her own declarative gesture of transnational belonging.

This drawing is also self-reflexive, for the assembled flowers are the yield of Walker's and others' figurative gardening: a black transnational feminist community cultivated through the process of letter writing. The communal ground that Walker's illustration envisions is, indeed, the principal aim of the authors' epistolary writing. Much like the physical gardening they relished, Head, Walker, and Cliff tended to the conditions of their friendship through their exchange of letters and accompanying books. Literal and metaphorical gardeners, Head,

Walker, and Cliff sought the creation of a common ground—one all the more meaningful because it could extend far, across local geographies. This was particularly important to Head because the length, frequency, and depth of her letters convey her commitment to fashioning a wide intellectual circle while based in rural Botswana. With another correspondent, Paddy Kitchen, who also shared Head's interest in gardening, Head occasionally exchanged actual seeds through the mail.[134] With her U.S.-based counterparts, however, Head was interested in seeds of a different sort: the letters, books, and ideas with which to cultivate a community of literary sustenance and support. Indeed, at its best, the writers' epistolary gardening produced for each of them a sphere of companionship—outside a predominantly white, male, and metropolitan culture industry[135]—where they could independently reflect upon their art and the prospects of liberation.

Cultivation, of course, is a practice, and it requires proper skills and knowledge applied with deliberation and adeptness. It also rests upon the proper circumstances and conditions, only some of which are in the control of the cultivator. The cultivation of community relies on these same factors, and some attempts fall fallow while others flourish. It is perhaps more apt to say they flourish for a period, a season, or until the circumstances and conditions change. The letters between Bessie Head and her African American women correspondents—most notably, Walker and Cliff—point to some engagements that took root and, to extend the analogy further, attest to some remarkable intellectual cross-fertilization. These were variously temporary engagements while other attempts at cultivation did not take (as in her exchange with Morrison), but neither were inconsequential. Indeed, for one thing, these engagements bespeak Head's rather consequential literary influence within the field of African American letters. In addition, the epistolary exchanges center our attention on the attempt—the effort itself driven by the urge to belong—rather than an accomplished or settled state of being, all of which Head seemed to understand quite well. At the conclusion of *A Question of Power*, as Elizabeth begins to recover from her excruciating encounters with the harrowing "intangible forms"[136] that plagued her, she "place[s] one soft hand over her land." We learn that "[i]t was a gesture of belonging."[137] Many readers, relieved by Elizabeth's relative peace after her descent into hell, understandably place the emphasis on the prepositional gerund. But Head's phrasing requires equal, if not more, attention to the preceding noun, "gesture." "Belonging" pinpoints the end-goal and the driving desire, but a "*gesture* of belonging" alerts us to the effort, the attempt itself (independent of the outcome), which the novel raises to a new level of significance bestowed in this scene with respect and quiet dignity.

Above all, recognizing the attempt brings into focus the labor at the heart of black transnational engagement. Beyond the physical gardens Head, Walker, and Cliff fastidiously tended, the authors' writing across the Atlantic Ocean exposes neither inertia nor spontaneous generation but deliberative labor, instead. In her poem entitled "Women's Work," Cliff yokes together numerous scenes of laboring women across space and time in a way that commemorates the oft-ignored struggles and lives of women ("We are still learning to recognize what we see").[138] In her study of African American women's literature by the same name, Courtney Thorsson identifies organizing, cooking, dancing, mapping, and inscribing as forms of black women's cultural work that helps produce both self and community.[139] The letters of Head, Walker, and Cliff prompt me to add gardening to this capacious list of women's work and to draw out its transnational dimensions. Gardening is by turn demanding, painstaking, tedious, exhausting, therapeutic, rejuvenating, gratifying, or anxiety-producing. The same must be said for epistolary exchanges. At one point or another, these women writers, Head especially, worked to make connections and to maintain them for some time. Even when attempts to connect across wide swathes of space do not bear the fruit originally intended, such efforts entail extensive labor that too frequently remains under-recognized or, worse, illegible under our analytical lenses. A fuller assessment of efforts to develop relationships across vast distances, whatever and however they yield, permits us to see the needs and desires that the labor represents—all of which inevitably shape the contours of black transnationalism. Chapter 5 explores what that labor—the labor of authors' engagements taken up in this and preceding chapters—helps to generate in the period of the 1980s as the global antiapartheid movement gathered momentum.

CHAPTER 5

Constructive Engagements

The global antiapartheid movement began as the Nationalist Party–led apartheid regime started implementing its policies in the late 1940s. With commitments of different agencies, committees, and organizations amassing across the decades, this movement developed into a formidable planetary front with prongs in countries across the African continent, Asia, Europe, and the Americas. In the United States, black radical organizations responded even earlier to developments in South Africa and began marshaling black and white leftist support for the increasingly resistant victims of the regime at the southern tip of Africa. In fact, organized African American political efforts supporting black South Africans' early protests against white rule ramped up in the mid-1940s as the Council on African Affairs led a pre-apartheid solidarity movement.[1]

Black Americans' preoccupation with South Africa dates back to the late-nineteenth-century black missionary movement,[2] but two chief mid–twentieth-century political developments extended this interest more popularly within the black community. The first involved the fluid nature of postcolonial Africa. The rapid succession of independence movements that swept across the African continent brought black Americans into greater awareness of contemporaneous African affairs, and the 1950s and '60s decolonization of Ghana, Kenya, Côte d'Ivoire, and the Congo drew particular attention from African Americans still bearing the brunt of racist violence and systematic discrimination. But the subsequent political quagmires facing emergent postcolonial African states from the late 1960s on—coups, civil wars, autocratic leaderships, and the related rise of neocolonialism in the Cold War era—largely cooled popular African American enthusiasm for politics on the continent. They also produced a narrowing effect: according to historian James Meriwether, a more exclusive focus on the struggles of still-colonized Africa—particularly, South Africa—helped black America "circumvent the knotty dilemmas" posed by postindependence crises.[3] Mainstream black America began to more restrictively follow and identify with the struggle in South Africa.

The second development is the apartheid regime's violent crackdown on dissidence in the country, which drew swift and growing condemnation worldwide. Following the lethal force of police in Sharpeville in 1960, the state's infamous 1976 assault upon protesting schoolchildren and young activists in Soweto (and other townships) was a pivotal point in how the international community understood apartheid. The brutal excesses of the regime shocked the world, and they particularly jarred the African American community. With Bull Conner's Birmingham and "Bloody Sunday" in Selma seared into memory, black Americans recognized racialized state violence as a phenomenon not limited to the United States. Thus, in addition to sharing everyday experiences of social, residential, and educational segregation, African Americans began identifying with their South African counterparts based on violence, trauma, and mourning precipitated by the white racist state. The apartheid regime's cynical promises of reform throughout the 1980s were belied by the repressive actions of police and security forces employed in the face of mounting popular resistance after the Soweto Uprising. Widely broadcast across the globe throughout this period, the state's violent strategies to maintain order on its own terms further turned the tide of public opinion and generated support for solidarity movements outside South Africa.

By the early 1980s, antiapartheid efforts in the United States had made crucial inroads as a result of a broad coalition movement primarily led by African American activists and organizations. Its chief battlegrounds were the university campus, the church, the union hall, the arena of popular culture, and the corridors of power in Washington, D.C.—all of which focused on the imperative to divest American resources from the apartheid state and cut off its economic blood supply. The Congressional Black Congress made reshaping American foreign policy a central priority immediately after its inception in the late 1960s, and it encouraged the formation of TransAfrica, the oldest lobby for Africa and the Caribbean, led by Randall Robinson to craft a multipronged interventionist strategy.[4] The American struggle to end apartheid in South Africa was both the manifestation of black advancement in national government and the spatial and temporal extension of domestic civil rights battles that defined America at midcentury. For Robinson, the difference between black people bearing the brunt of racism across the globe were largely nominal: "I could see no real distinction between my American experience and the painful lot of Haitians, South Africans, Mozambicans, Angolans, Zairians and Afro-Brazilians."[5]

U.S. domestic efforts to exert pressure on the South African government came to a head as Ronald Reagan took office in 1981 and assumed an amicable Cold War–driven policy toward the apartheid state. Seeing South Africa as a stable, resource-rich ally in its global fight against communism, the Reagan administration positioned itself "on the side of the whites" in South Africa in the hopes that a new black majority favoring the Eastern Bloc would not be installed.[6] Reagan supported a so-called reformist approach rather than forcing the regime to relinquish power; denounced the ANC and other antiapartheid organizations as terrorists; and adopted the conservative policy dubbed "constructive engagement" by Chester Crocker, the assistant secretary of state for African Affairs, that flatly rejected the application of economic sanctions.[7] With the administration actively discouraging a democratic South African state, the antiapartheid movement within the United States battled the White House's approach and forged an extensive popular front comprised of grassroots efforts. These mobilized college students, activists, local civic and religious leaders, popular cultural figures, and politicians to end the country's notorious foreign policy.

Grounds of Engagement has shown that extensive human and material movement transnationalized the imaginations and work of black writers on either side of the Atlantic and, consequently, reshaped the literary landscapes of their respective countries. Channeled through the medium of geographic representation as a means of expressing and comparing their experiences, these writings reframed how black South Africans and Americans conceived of themselves and their relation to one another. In this chapter, I extend this argument by demonstrating how the multiple reimaginings are both the cause and consequence of "constructive engagements," although emphatically not the kinds of diplomatic and economic relations the Reagan administration favored. The constructive engagements under consideration here encompass a variety of claims of kinship, assertions of transnational similitude, interpersonal relationships, and expressions of solidarity in black South African and African American literature that addressed the prospects of liberation. By "constructive," I do not necessarily mean to sound the uncritically celebratory bell that exalts the human transcendence of national difference, distance, and separation. Nor do I aim to imply that the engagements were inherently or unmitigatedly positive;

certainly, some examples taken up earlier involved more complicated relation-ships. Rather, I mean to emphasize two related aspects of the decades-long relationship between black South Africa and black America: that relationship's constructedness and the solidification of that relationship's self-evidentness or seeming inevitability.

My attention to constructive engagements, then, is essentially an inquiry into the development of a common sense, understood here as a collective way of thinking about collectivity.[8] Although that development was hardly restricted to literary expression alone, I take up literature as emblematic of larger cultural and discursive practices to chart how a general sense of black transnational similar-ity became so common. I suggest that a substantial part of this forming common sense derives from the extensive cultural transactions between South Africa and the United States. Part of my objective has been to position these cross-cultural transactions in an antidiffusionist frame that demonstrates a mutual redefini-tion of imaginaries and literary production on both sides of the Atlantic. We have already seen the ways that Peter Abrahams helped coax Richard Wright through the exigencies of exile even as he benefited from Wright's mentorship. Through his poetics, Keorapetse Kgositsile sought to reconceptualize the ways that African Americans understood their relationship to South Africa. And Bessie Head's influence upon Alice Walker, Michelle Cliff, and Toni Morrison clearly manifests itself in their letters and in the books they published. The personal and textual engagements explored in earlier chapters, however, were not isolated, one-off connections but, instead, produced further repercussions that rippled out into the wider literary sphere. They led to new transnational connections and inspired a fresh wave of literary work, also often geographic in sensibility. This chapter traces out some of the "afterlives" of earlier trans-national engagements to consider how those prior engagements' generative effects play out across the 1980s. It does so by tracking a handful of familiar authors from prior chapters, folded in with several new figures and relation-ships all positioned here within the wider sweep of the 1980s cultural terrain. I show that the consequences of earlier interactions open out onto subsequent engagements in ways that require us to continue reevaluating the presumptive flows of cultural influence and what we mean by the term "constructive."

South Africans in Black America

In addition to the political developments taking place on the African conti-nent, two key cultural factors contributed to the sensitizing and conscientizing of African Americans about the racial regime in southern Africa, namely, the presence of South Africans and the availability of South African texts in the United States. The physical presence of South African writers as exiles, immigrants, or sojourners in America played a crucial role in shaping black Americans' understanding of the apartheid state and its relationship to the United States. South Africans' visibility in America—as participants in antiapartheid campaigns testifying to the brutal enforcement of South Africa's racial hierarchy—not only helped escalate the American divestment movement, but also altered the focus and texture of African American writing that registered the horrors, challenges, and resilience of South Africans under apartheid. Perhaps most visible among writers was Dennis Brutus, who led the successful campaign to ban South Africa from the Olympic Games from 1964 to 1992. His political activism, cultural activism (such as his cofounding of the African Literature Association in 1975), and his poetry proper—including *Letters to Martha*, *Poems from Algiers*, and *A Simple Lust*, volumes that chronicled his incarceration on Robben Island and his subsequent life in exile—catapulted him and the cause to end white minority rule into wider visibility on American shores, where he relocated.[9]

Some South African writers found visiting or longer-term appointments at American universities as the basis for some economic stability. Institutions of higher education became the locales for the practice of their art, their pedagogy, and their politics—sometimes uneasily so, given both conservative and progressive tendencies in the professoriate. Dennis Brutus (at Northwestern University and the University of Pittsburgh), Es'kia Mphahlele (Universities of Denver and Pennsylvania), Keorapetse Kgositsile (Columbia University, University of Denver, North Carolina A&T State University), Mazisi Kunene (UCLA), A. C. Jordan (UCLA and the University of Wisconsin at Madison), among others, all taught African literature and creative writing courses and reached thousands of students and faculty interested in antiapartheid activism. Unsurprisingly, then, the college campus became one of the initial battlegrounds for the American antiapartheid movement.

In the spring of 1987, Richard Rive also briefly joined the American academy as a visiting professor.[10] Although less explicitly activist, at home or abroad, than many of his compatriots in exile, Rive likely assumed his temporary appointment in the Department of English and American Literature at Harvard University as a kind of cultural ambassadorship in opposition to the South African state. It was not his first trip to the States: in 1965, Rive left Cape Town for New York City to pursue his master's degree at Columbia University's Teachers College, where he studied African American literature under Professor Robert Bone with an aim to examining the significance of Harlem Renaissance writers on the protest generation of South African writers that followed decades later.[11] During his academic year there, he took advantage of his proximity to Langston Hughes to borrow books from and interview his mentor for his own research. Upon completion in 1966, Rive returned to Cape Town but visited the United States several times thereafter. By his final American sojourn in the mid-1980s, Rive was a reputed scholar of Olive Schreiner, on whom he wrote his doctoral dissertation at Oxford, and an accomplished South African fiction writer; he had published two volumes of short stories (*African Songs* in 1963 and *Advance, Retreat* two decades later), a novel (*Emergency*) in 1964 and, in 1981, released his autobiography entitled *Writing Black*.

Decades after his initial epistolary exchanges with Langston Hughes, Rive remained preoccupied with the significance of place as a defining feature of his thinking and writing. Just before his visiting appointment, Rive completed *"Buckingham Palace," District Six*, his second novel, which is set in his birthplace, Cape Town's primarily coloured district that was redesignated a "white area" and slated for clearance in 1966. Falling prey to the Group Areas Act of 1950 that authorized forced removals and demolition to assure that demarcated geographic zones corresponded with racial identity, the district was cleared in less than two decades. Having not been repopulated, the open area in the heart of the city exposed more evidence of apartheid's violent enactment. In his early hand-drawn map to Hughes just prior to the neighborhood's designation as a white area, Rive identified District Six as his own birthplace with a heavy "X"—a disturbingly appropriate mark, given the area's eventual fate.[12] But Rive, who had moved out in his younger years, would revisit District Six artistically with such regularity that he proved "unable to write beyond the razing of his birthplace."[13] Repeatedly commemorating the life and loss of District Six, Rive would help render it the Western Cape's archetypal symbol (an analogue of Johannesburg's Sophiatown) of the apartheid regime's destruction of community through the grievous refashioning of South Africa's physical and social landscapes.

"Buckingham Palace," District Six dramatizes the growing affective bonds between the residents occupying a stretch of modest houses on Caledon Street, wryly nicknamed "Buckingham Palace," and their neighborhood's eventual dissolution as officials cast the majority of its residents from the City Bowl, where the District lay, out onto the inhospitable Cape Flats. The novel's protagonist, Zoot, closes the narrative with a powerful lament: "We knew that District Six was dirty and rotten. Their [white society's] newspapers told us so often enough. But what they didn't say was that it was also warm and friendly. That it contained humans. That it was never a place—that it was a people."[14] Zoot's characterization underscores the view that human relations are the primary constituents of

a given social space. Absent the members of community, whatever the condition of its buildings and infrastructure, District Six is no more. And yet if places are primarily the people who compose them, the memory of one permanently holds the memory of the other. As Zoot notes upon the departure of Mary, the local madam, "Buckingham Palace will be razed next week, but Mary will still be here. And even when District Six is gone, there will still be Marys here."[15] District Six achieved a doubled status upon its material destruction. On the one hand, the District represented the pinnacle of coloured community that would become, as Grant Farred notes, "*the* memory of social cohesion" formed by common circumstance and attachment to a specific locale in the Capetonian landscape; on the other hand, its decimation dealt an irreparable loss that was at once culturally damaging and culturally formative.[16] With the figured community scattered about, it could no longer be reconstituted in any pragmatic or meaningful sense. Written in retrospective lamentation, Rive's novel is shot through with the irreplaceability of District Six, and it does much to advance the absolute singularity of place.

Rive assigned *"Buckingham Palace," District Six* as one of several books in his undergraduate survey of South African literature at Harvard University. The class notes of one of his students, Jim Kornish, reveal Rive's primary emphasis on place as a defining feature of South African writing, especially in the protest tradition.[17] Students learned, for example, that "for something to happen it must be defined in terms of place" and "sometimes the name of the place takes over the book."[18] Rive asserted that this was particularly the case in literature that took up District Six as setting or subject—in his class, represented by Alex La Guma's *A Walk in the Night* and Rive's own novel. Given the ill-fated setting of the texts, the loss of place featured as an equally salient part of discussion, for dislocation stressed the tragic rupture of community and the disoriented state of characters. This focus quite logically led to the next theme of exile as expressed in the poetry of Arthur Nortje.[19] As if to drive home the centrality of place, Rive made sure students encountered it as an essay question for their final exam: "Discuss the authors' use of place and movement in *A Walk in the Night* and *Buckingham Palace, District Six*, and show how they are appropriate or otherwise in each novel."[20]

On several occasions, Rive also brought South African and African American writing into conversation. In a course section on Soweto School poets, Rive assigned Sipho Sepamla's "This Land" (from his 1977 collection, *The Soweto I Love*), which he introduced to the class alongside Langston Hughes's 1932 poem, "Our Land."[21] With an eye to the geographic, Rive's pairing says as much about his own preoccupations as it does the two poets he compares. Whereas

Hughes's verse deploys a bleak, dismal American landscape to lament African Americans' oppressive political and economic environment, Sepamla's Black Consciousness–era poem penned decades later defiantly asserts black South Africans' deep, multigenerational possession of the land in spite of whites' usurpation of it. The two poems' juxtaposition points to crucial variances in how black subjects—as alienated demographic minorities, in Hughes's poem, or subjugated but deeply rooted majorities, in Sepamla's poem—conceive of their surrounding social space at different points across the twentieth century. Rive's interpretation of these two poems went unrecorded, but his pairing of them underscores the thematics of geography he not only put into practice in his own literary production, but also identified in other writers' output.

Rive likewise expressed his ongoing preoccupation with the geographic in his autobiography, *Writing Black*, in which all but four of the twenty-five chapter titles bear the names of specific places to which Rive traveled, such as "Greece," "London and Paris," "Soweto," "Rio and Miami to Texas," and "England Again." A travelogue infused with philosophical reflections, social commentary, and memories of literary friends, *Writing Black* charts Rive's journeys and places that marked his perspective. His attraction to "Western European sophistication and unsophistication," he avers, stems from the impress of his urban upbringing. He distinguishes himself from the "propounders of négritude" and primitivism (which he associates with Hughes's early poetry) who emphasize the drums and dramas of largely rural life, and in so doing, Rive so closely associates himself with his cityscape that it becomes his identity: "I am Johannesburg, Durban and Cape Town. I am Langa, Chatsworth and Bonteheuwel. . . . I am urban South Africa."[22]

If the novel, course notes, and autobiography—in addition to the maps and reflections Rive sent Hughes decades earlier—all point to Rive's acutely geographic imagination, they appear to emphasize the perpetual inimitability of place, the deep singularity of a specific locale. Places, in each instance, possess an unreproducibility that makes them equal only to themselves. And yet, Rive's writing presents a doubled aspect of place. On the one hand, places are stamped with absolute uniqueness, formed as they are by an induplicatable constellation of physical geographies, people, histories, and very particularly arranged social relations. On the other hand, recognizable experiences and characteristics of place across space instantly invite conceptual linkage and assimilation into what is already familiar. Place is at once irreproducible and almost infinitely comparable. The extensive comparability of place surfaces multiple times in Rive's autobiography, and it is most pronounced in his ruminations on visits to the United States, where black social spaces ignite his comparative imagination.

Rive's 1979 tour of the American South, for instance, inspired him to reflect on what seemed familiar:

> I could sense little observable difference between the Midfield ghetto in Alabama and the Guguletu Location in South Africa. Both wear an air of neglect and resignation and one can feel in both areas the vibrations of the cauldron simmering below the surface, which could at any point explode into another Watts or Soweto. Black Midfield has no noticeboards to remind one of attitudes that enforce segregation. Black Guguletu has many such noticeboards. And that is the essential difference. The one place is created by attitudes, the other by laws catering to such attitudes; the one shows the unofficial, amorphous signs of discrimination, the other the official observable signs of discrimination. Both produce the same effects.[23]

"Little observable difference." While allowing for each locale's unique properties, including the physical markers that denote state legislated segregation over less evidence of entrenched custom (and prior or even continuing statutes), Rive nevertheless affirms an important discernible symmetry between South African and American social landscapes. He establishes this by way of two kinds of linkages: the geographic pairing of Midfield and Guguletu and, in a way that recalls poems by Hughes and Kgositsile, of Watts and Soweto. And Rive simultaneously gestures toward an ominous temporal linkage between the two pairs. Pointing to the substratum of festering discontent beneath the apparently languishing first pair, he foresees a repeat of the explosive second pair.

Rive would draw the connections between South Africa and the United States even tighter in a passage that highlights the way cross-cultural literature can effect a powerful sense of transnational relation. In his autobiography, he relates an encounter with African American writer Julia Fields, whom he met in 1963 while socializing with Langston Hughes in London. Fields, also a schoolteacher, revealed to Rive that, "while White racists were cruising in cars around her segregated school shooting into the classrooms," she would read aloud to her students "The Bench," Rive's short story that Hughes had published in his 1960 anthology, *An African Treasury*: "The story, she explained, was so immediate to their experiences that they listened because they also knew those segregated benches marked 'Whites Only.'"[24] Rive's (or Fields's) choice of the word "immediate," here, suggests an absence of distance or mediation between the situation in Rive's story and the Alabama students' experience of segregated social space. And yet, literature creates—that is, mediates—precisely this sense of proximity between the two experiences and fosters their recognition. If also an example of Rive's reputed self-congratulatory posture,[25] the detail illustrates how representations of racial geographies lend themselves to cross-cultural identification, how—facilitated by transnationally circulating texts (thanks to Hughes's editorial enterprise)—they are put to self-reflexive use. The initial exchanges between Rive and Hughes with which this study began spun off years later into a new generation of spatially attuned transnational engagements for Fields and her young students, who identified with Rive's story.

As Rive's example of "The Bench" makes clear, the physical presence of South African writers on American soil was only part of what facilitated African Americans' identification with black South Africans. Another major part of the cross-cultural equation was South Africans' textual presence via publications circulating within the United States. Midcentury black South African writing—including the 1950s appearance of Peter Abrahams's work and the 1960s anthology of Langston Hughes—drew some attention, especially within black communities. But by the 1980s, that South African textual presence was taken to exponentially greater heights by an intensified American distribution of writing by and about South Africans. As the antiapartheid movement gained popular momentum across North America, the American publishing industry responded to and, in turn, contributed to a spike in the public's interest in apartheid South Africa, which also manifested itself in television journalism, popular music, drama, film, and visual art.[26] The more widely available publications often aimed to inform a larger public about the South African battle against white minority rule, as in the proliferation of handbooks, readers, and pamphlets.[27] In addition to nonfictional or journalistic exposés and biographies on South African events and figures, South African dissident literature helped familiarize Americans with the terms, factual or fictional, of South African lives and predicaments.

The heterogeneity of the publishing industry during this period is worth noting, for a cursory look reveals a variety of stakeholders in the publication of transnational texts. The proclivities of major corporate presses amplified their listings in ways that shaped the popular American consciousness. For example, western authors dominated most of the nonfiction about South Africa, often crowding out analyses by South Africans. In terms of South African literary work, as major presses like Penguin, Viking, and Harcourt Brace skewed toward white dissident writing, they made the writing of white authors such as Alan Paton, Nadine Gordimer, J. M. Coetzee, André Brink, Athol Fugard, and Breyten Breytenbach more commonly available, reviewed, and known across the 1980s United States. In the 1980s, Heinemann remained the primary publisher of earlier black (South) African writing, but in the United States, it lacked the popularity of major presses. Still, it made available the writing of Dennis Brutus, Alex La Guma, and Bessie Head, among others, to knowing U.S. readers. Other small, more politically conscious presses further brought black South African voices into American circulation. Published by Thunder's Mouth Press, for instance, Sterling Plumpp's important 1982 edited volume, *Somehow We Survive: An Anthology of South African Writing*, presented a diverse cast of black South African writers, including Brutus, Head, Kgositsile, Barbara Masekela, Mongane Serote, Essop Patel, and Arthur Nortje. Ellen Kuzwayo's *Call Me Woman* was published in 1985 by Spinster Ink, the small New York–based lesbian feminist press. And, in 1986, George Braziller released exiled South African actor and playwright Duma Ndlovu's edited collection of predominantly black-authored South African plays entitled *Woza Afrika!* Academic and specialist volumes featured a panoply of South African writers that likewise brought black contributions to American viewers. A 1987 special issue of *TriQuarterly*, entitled *From South Africa*—edited by David Bunn and Jane Taylor, along with assistance from Reginald Gibbons and, again, Sterling Plumpp—brought work by black artists, writers, and intellectuals into greater view. Other multiracial anthologies followed, including *Sometimes When It Rains: Writings by South African Women*, edited by Ann Oosthuizen, and one marketed toward a young adult audience entitled *Somehow Tenderness Survives: Stories of Southern Africa*, which featured ten coming-of-age stories by Peter Abrahams, Zoë Wicomb, and Gcina Mhlope, among others. With a title that gives more explicit articulation to the implied impetus behind these publications, *Art against Apartheid*, a 1986 IKON special double issue edited by Susan Sherman and Gale Jackson, collated poems, essays, testimonies, interviews, visual art (photography, sketches, painting, sculpture), and song lyrics that supported the antiapartheid struggle, its vision of the future, or its relationship to other ongoing freedom struggles. The collection devotes a section to work by southern Africans followed by a section comprised of artists from outside the region. These volumes and others facilitated a growing black South African textual presence in the United States that also began shaping the American imaginary.

This is not to suggest that major publishing houses exclusively published white writers. The 1985 *Penguin Book of Southern African Stories*, edited by Stephen Gray, offered a diverse, boundary-crossing collection of short stories, followed two years later by André Brink and J. M. Coetzee's more generically varied edited volume, *A Land Apart*. Although the anthologies privilege a white literary tradition, they deliberately cut against a racial exclusion the South African state practiced. Furthermore, in 1985, W. W. Norton published to considerable acclaim *Poppie Nongena*, a novel (in translation) by Afrikaans author Elsa Joubert based upon interviews with a Xhosa woman. The American edition of

Winnie Mandela's *Part of My Soul Went with Him*, also published by Norton in 1985, also made a considerable impact.

As this last example indicates, black South African writing made its way to American bookshelves predominantly as memoir and autobiography during this period. This trend was driven by a hunger for personal, firsthand accounts of life under apartheid and heroic efforts to defy or escape it; as a whole, in the broad public imaginary, such a trend effectively relegated black writers to producers of reportage and sociology, as opposed to inventive creative writers.[28] The autobiographical fever inaugurated a wave of republications, including Bloke Modisane's 1963 *Blame Me on History*, which appeared for the first time in the United States in 1986 from Simon & Schuster. But perhaps no autobiography made more of a splash than Mark Mathabane's 1986 virtual instant classic, *Kaffir Boy*, the narrative of a driven young man's escape from apartheid South Africa to the United States through the sport of tennis.

Drawing upon prior autobiographies, *Kaffir Boy* had its own transnational literary dimensions. While the American edition features a *Washington Post* blurb that likens Mathabane's autobiography to Claude Brown's 1965 *Manchild in the Promised Land*, much of its formal techniques and energy derive from its semi-eponym, Richard Wright's *Black Boy*, and Peter Abrahams's autobiography, *Tell Freedom*. *Kaffir Boy*'s tone bears a stronger resemblance to Abrahams's tale, which likewise stresses family bonds. It shares the literary craft of neither *Black Boy* nor *Tell Freedom*, but like both of its antecedent texts, its narrative momentum is propelled by a teleological structure that plots out the dehumanizing injustices he faces, his refusal to accept them, and his ultimate flight out to a putatively freer place. Ironically, Mathabane finds his freedom in the American landscape Wright fled. But Mathabane's passages describing his childhood hunger most keenly recall Wright's own dramatic bouts with deep physical craving.[29] Hunger also drives Mathabane toward his passion for sport, although it barely outstrips another basic interest common to all three authors, reading and listening to stories.[30] Like Abrahams and Wright before him, he also uses anaphoric structure to present revelrous passages about his youth while recounting lessons he gained from his mother's stories:

> I learned that virtues are things to be always striven after . . .
> I learned that sagacity and quick wits are necessary in avoiding dangerous situations . . .
> I learned that good deeds advance one positively in life . . .
> I learned that good always invariably triumphs over evil . . .
> I learned to prefer peace to war, cleverness to stupidity, love to hate, . . . creation to annihilation.[31]

And like his predecessors, the conscious recognition that he is a "black boy" in a white world engenders a pained revelation of limitation: "As a black boy, the odds were heavily stacked against my establishing a normal, stable family when I came of age."[32] Mathabane's work self-consciously hearkens back to and adapts the constructions of its popular African American and South African precursors.

South Africa(ns) in African American Literature

In addition to South Africans' presence and gains in the antiapartheid movement across the United States, the wider availability of South African writing and cultural production throughout the 1980s assured the emergence of South Africa as a resonant theme in black American writers' works. South African politics, authors, and their writing began shaping the texture of African American literary culture across numerous genres. Essays by writer-activists like June Jordan and Audre Lorde indexed and generated an increasing black American interest in South Africa, primarily through an alignment of the United States and the apartheid state often achieved by geographic reference. Jordan's 1985 collection of essays, *On Call*, opens by admonishing the American mass media's silencing of black American experts on urgent matters, including the South African struggle. Her focus on South Africa's suppression of dissident voices echoes Gil Scott-Heron's concerns in "Johannesburg"; she repeatedly intones "I am learning about American censorship."[33] In "South Africa: Bringing It All Back Home," one of the volume's five essays referencing the apartheid state, Jordan acknowledges the centrality of the South African context to her political conscience: "South Africa used to seem so far away. Then it came home to me. . . . That was Birmingham. That was Brooklyn. That was Reagan. That was the end of reason. South Africa was how I came to understand that I am not against war; I am against losing the war."[34] Her closing lines—"South Africa is not so very far away; I am only waiting for the call"—advocate a politics of proximity and preparedness.[35]

As with Jordan, the calculated comparisons that Audre Lorde advanced stemmed from her discerning similar patterns between the suppression of black dissent in South Africa and the series of deadly police actions across the 1980s within black urban American communities. According to Alexis de Veaux, Lorde's biographer:

> The wanton killings of black South Africans, the killings of black Americans, government neglect of the social needs of black communities, the precarious nature of black survival against the backdrop of struggles for power on the world

stage, were all emblematic of connecting political realities, and Lorde felt "the urgency to unearth the connection between these assaults."[36]

Persistent signs of devalued and imperiled black life in South Africa and the United States led Lorde to make this deeply felt connection explicit in her essay, "Apartheid U.S.A.," originally published in 1986 as part of a pamphlet by Kitchen Table: Women of Color Press. Warning that "connections have not been made" between iterations of institutionalized racism the world over— represented here in instances like the teargassing at a Tembisa funeral and arson in the black community of Baldwin Hills, California—Lorde aims to mobilize resistance at home and abroad.[37] Countering narratives of exceptional American progress, she likens the 1980s political and social status of African Americans to that of black South Africans during the 1950s, "the period of the postwar construction of the apparati of apartheid, reaction, and suppression,"[38] and warns against the impending rise of a de facto American apartheid state. She identifies a mutually shared black vulnerability resulting from the entrenched machinations of racial capitalism in both countries: "The fact that African-Americans can still move about freely, do not yet have to carry passbooks or battle an officially named policy of apartheid, should not delude us for one minute about the disturbing similarities of the Black situation in each one of these profit-oriented economies."[39]

Lorde's recognition of the class dimensions of American and South African racism underscores what Achille Mbembe has called, decades later, an often lethal "contradictory relation between the instrumentality of black life in the market sphere, on the one hand, and the constant depreciation of its value and its quality by the forces of commercialism and bigotry, on the other."[40] Lorde's emphasis on biopolitics extended to her "politicization of women's health," as Simone Alexander has also noted, and Lorde explicitly linked the defiant action against South African and American racism to her own battle against cancer.[41] In the title essay from A Burst of Light, Lorde writes that she daily visualizes "the battles going on inside my body" with her cancer cells "tak[ing] on the face and shape of my most implacable enemies." She imagines these cells as Bull Connor being "smothered" "by a mighty avalanche of young determined Black marchers" and South African president P. W. Botha being "squashed into the earth beneath an onslaught of the slow rhythmic advance of furious Blackness."[42] As Alexander argues, Lorde's visualization not only strengthens the association between South African and American racism, but it frames racism as a social disease and systemic disorder that requires resistance in order to preserve black life.[43]

If perceiving interconnecting manifestations of social ills in both countries initiated Lorde's outspokenness about South Africa in print, it was her inter- actions through local and South African political circles that fueled her com- mitment. Her interpersonal engagement was primarily catalyzed by Gloria I. Joseph, Lorde's eventual partner, who had toured southern Africa years earlier and met, among others, Bessie Head in Gaborone. Joseph brought Lorde into the orbit of antiapartheid politics to collectively found, along with several others, Sisterhood in Support of Sisters in South Africa (SISA) in late 1984. The group of six women, called the Founding Mothers, was comprised of Zala Chandler, Johnnetta Cole, Andrée McLaughlin, and Barbara Riley, along with Lorde and the group's chief torchbearer, Joseph. SISA was established with a joint mission to raise consciousness about apartheid and to raise funds in the United States for women's self-help projects in South Africa—namely, community childcare organizations, the Maggie Magaba Trust (a scholarship fund designed to assist students), and the Zamani Soweto Sisters (a women's sewing and quilting coop- erative that supported literacy and training programs).[44] By 1990, the advisory board consisted of 26 members, including Toni Cade Bambara, Michelle Cliff, Angela Davis, Alexis de Veaux, Adrienne Rich, Sonia Sanchez, and Betty Sha- bazz.[45] With Joseph and Lorde as its chief representatives, SISA recognized South African self-help projects as "form[s] of political resistance to apartheid," and it sought to encourage "personal bonds between North American women of the African diaspora and black South African women; and promot[e] the responsibility of African American women to share economic and political resources far more available to them in the West with women of the African diaspora."[46] In *A Burst of Light*, Lorde documented her meeting with the Zamani Soweto Sisters in Bonnieux, France, over several days in June 1986, marking the stories of each of the women she encountered there.[47]

Lorde lent her time, resources, and substantial public voice to her South Afri- can sisters by headlining fund-raising events and speaking engagements. Her political engagement helped solidify her relationship with Ellen Kuzwayo, the South African activist who helped direct the Soweto-based self-help groups and the author of the popular 1985 autobiography *Call Me Woman* (whose American edition included a preface by Nadine Gordimer and a foreword by Bessie Head). Lorde met Kuzwayo in person several times, including in England, Canada, and Germany, and the letters between them were replete with mutual admira- tion and praise for one another's efforts to support the self-help organizations. Moreover, in her capacity as a founding editor of Kitchen Table: Women of Color Press, Lorde sought out writer Miriam Tlali directly and via Kuzwayo to publish more of her fiction in the United States and increase Americans' exposure to more South African writing.[48] She procured much information on South Africa from Kuzwayo, Joseph, and other activists from both countries. This included her friend and fellow member of the SISA Advisory Board, Michelle Cliff, who occasionally passed along press clippings and notes regarding the antiapartheid struggle. While corresponding with Bessie Head, Cliff also relayed to Lorde part of an "incredible letter" from Head in response to *Abeng*'s publication and dedication. Sharing evidence of the South African exile's isolation, she quotes Head's own words: "I am not really regarded as a person of the country [Botswana] or a writer of the country so people only vaguely see me pass and do not know what I am doing here."[49] Cliff fastidiously shared Head's voice with others, just as she would when reading aloud Head's short stories at her own literary readings. Lorde's efforts to share South African struggles and to connect them to black American ones found expression in her poetry, as well. Many of Lorde's poems that touch upon South Africa—including "The Evening News" in *Chosen Poems Old and New*; "Sisters in Arms," "Diaspora," "On My Way out I Passed over You and the Verrazano Bridge," "Holographs," and "Call" in *Our Dead behind Us*; and "Party Time" in *The Marvelous Arithmetic of Distance*[50]—articulate her concern for black women in "both profit-oriented economies" and affirm their profound transnational relationships, both intimate and political.

Lorde's poems, in fact, were part of the escalating evocation of South Africa across African American poetry that began decades earlier. As with other genres, the poetry of the 1980s exploded with references to South Africa and its connections to the American racial context, and as the antiapartheid movement intensified inside and outside South Africa, so too did its presence in black American writing. Numerous poems in this period celebrate and commemorate the spirit of the South African struggle and its warriors—for instance, Amina Baraka's "Soweto Song," Lucille Clifton's "winnie song" and "there," Sonia Sanchez's "An Anthem," June Jordan's "A Song for Soweto," Jayne Cortez's "Solomon Mahlangu: Freedom Fighter from Mamelodi," Toi Derricotte's "The Choice," and Elizabeth Alexander's "A Poem for Nelson Mandela."[51] Other poems, including Clifton's "there" and "this belief" and Brenda Marie Osbey's "Stones of Soweto," mournfully explore the pain and predicaments of life under apartheid, while Sanchez's "Letter to Ezekiel Mphahlele" and Tom Dent's "For Kgositsile" respond to the powerful presence and ideas of the South African writers in their company.[52]

Explicitly comparative poems—such as Jayne Cortez's "For the Brave Young Students in Soweto," Geoffrey Jacques's "Soweto Remembrance," and Bernice Johnson Reagon's "Chile Your Waters"—thread together multiple sites of racial and political justice.[53] In "living as a lesbian underground: a futuristic fantasy," Cheryl Clarke takes up this strategy, as well:

> Don't be no fool, now, cool.
> Imperialism by any other name
> is imperialism.
> Even Vietnam was finally over.
> It's all the same—
> *a*-rabs, gooks, wogs, queers—
> a nigger by any other name . . .
> Johannesburg is Jamesburg, New Jersey.
> Apartheid is the board of education
> in Canarsie.[54]

Similarly, Afaa Michael Weaver's poem, "South African Communion," explicitly registers how "the whole arrangement" of racial exclusion and exploitation produces the conditions for deep cross-cultural empathy. "It is not difficult to feel compassion / for the workers in South Africa," the speaker intones as he and his fellow black South Baltimore factory workers navigate a similar terrain of hostility and indifference:

> The faces we meet, the blank
> smiles, the beckoning fists, the yells are
> grandchildren of laws that did not allow blacks
> to set dusty foot on white pavement past nightfall
> . . .
> It is not difficult to understand greed here
> where freedom has been harvested, cut and laid aside
> to die, when a whole other similar paradise was carved
> from theft. The whole arrangement comes clear.[55]

Weaver's poem establishes corresponding experiences of social conditions as the basis for communion. Michael S. Harper brings transnational communion into even more immediate relation in his *Healing Song for the Inner Ear*, poems which register his rare visit to apartheid South Africa in 1977. "Arpeggios" features references to South African singer Miriam Makeba, and in "The Stutterer" and "The Militance of a Photograph in the Passbook of a Bantu under Detention," Harper renders his experience after his arrest in Soweto.[56]

Gwendolyn Brooks's verse also brought the South African struggle home. Brooks was aware of ongoing antiapartheid activism long before the 1980s, and her visits to Kenya and Tanzania in 1971 and Ghana in 1974 signaled her interest in developments in contemporary African politics and culture. Before her travels abroad, Brooks's friendship with Keorapetse Kgositsile during his American period of exile ensured that she was well acquainted with conditions in South Africa. It would prove a generative artistic relationship for both poets. Brooks's support translated into diligent mentoring of the younger Kgositsile, who learned much from the American poet's dedication to craft. In the exile's company, in turn, Brooks became appreciative of his unique aesthetic and more familiar with the liberation struggle in southern Africa; Brooks biographer George Kent notes that she admired "his personality and his poems," which "revealed absolute commitment to freedom, mastery of poetic techniques, and mastery of African, black American, and European cultures."[57] As Kgositsile's mentor and friend, Brooks penned a glowing introduction to his *My Name Is Afrika* that marked their artistic and ideological affiliation. Hailing Kgositsile as "one of the finest black poets of today," Brooks concludes with a poem, "To Keorapetse Kgositsile (Willie)," in which she praises her South African friend's artful lessons: "He teaches / strategy and the straight aim."[58] Brooks paid him further homage by incorporating the poem into a three-subject portrait entitled "Young Heroes," with the Kgositsile section leading off.[59] Their collaborative efforts also found expression in print, including in *A Capsule Course in Black Poetry Writing*, a four-part primer penned by Brooks, Kgositsile, Haki Madhubuti, and Dudley Randall.

This relationship bore additional fruit in Brooks's poetic output as manifested in her poems "Music for Martyrs," "The Near-Johannesburg Boy," and her long poem *Winnie*, all of which directly address South Africa.[60] In her 1986 "The Near-Johannesburg Boy," Brooks explores the mounting militancy and spirit of South African revolt—mobilized by the United Democratic Movement and the ANC's strategy to render the apartheid state ungovernable—that led to the decade's extended states of emergency in 1985 and '86.[61] The poem implicitly gestures to resemblances between the South African and American racial status quos, and it does so through geographic reference. It opens with a note explaining that the anonymous boy in question "does not live in Johannesburg. He is not allowed to live there. Perhaps he lives in Soweto"[62]—a note that stakes out the geographic dictates of daily life under white rule. The boy's positioning on the margins of the city of Johannesburg indicts the apartheid state's rigid geographies of exclusion; his nearness to (rather than presence in) Johannesburg indexes prohibition and denied access, just as the hyphen in the title denotes the boy's remove from the seat of power.

The poem's dynamism turns on the youth's journey "from woe to wonder," a journey pegged to two principal transitions: a key switch from a singular focus to a collective one and a shift from observation to growing action. The opening portion of the poem sets the scene:

> Those people
> do not like Black among the colors.
> They do not like our
> calling our country ours.
> They say our country is not ours.[63]

The poem's recurring "our" emphasizes a possession and belonging that contrasts with the law of the land. Indeed, the denial of black citizenship is intimately understood by the speaker, whose father is shot dead and mother bears her life with necessary fortitude. By the sixth stanza, the poem highlights how collective exclusion begets a general disaffection and movement. The gathering resistance takes a decidedly geographic expression, as the speaker and other black youths defiantly traverse the line of demarcation into the whites-only space they are forbidden to enter:

> Well, enough of the slump, enough of Old Story.
> Like a clean spear of fire
> I am moving. I am not still. I am ready
> to be ready.
> I shall flail
> in the Hot Time.

> Tonight I walk with
> a hundred playmates to where
> the hurt Black of our skin is forbidden.
> There, in the dark that is our dark, there,
> a-pulse across earth that is our earth, there,
> there exulting, there Exactly, there redeeming, there Roaring up[64]

The black youths' spatial transgression into forbidden territory (the repeated "there") represents the transgression of the social, political, and even existential order, for in occupying the territory ("earth that is our earth"), they assert their positive presence to one another as they try to repossess it and reverse their alienated state. The youths' scattered, nascent expressions of liberation ("exulting," "redeeming," and "Roaring up") is coterminous with reconfiguring the very terms of their relationships to one another, to white society, and to their newly reclaimed space. The poem closes projecting a fiery future:

> we shall forge with the Fist-and-the-Fury:
> we shall flail in the Hot Time:
> we shall
> we shall[65]

The youths' revolt against the racial-geographic order conjured in Brooks's poem echoes the tone and spirit of collectivity in Kgositsile's "When Brown Is Black" over two decades earlier. Indeed, it is hard to imagine that Brooks did not have in mind a specific former near-Johannesburg boy, now in exile, when she penned her poem. The invocation of the flail (both an agricultural instrument of harvest and a weapon of war) and of heat ("the Hot Time") approximates the productively destructive, fiery insurgency celebrated in Kgositsile's poetry, but here updated to capture the 1980s revolutionary action. In addition to signaling a struggle over rights and spatial mobility—Brooks noted in an interview with D. H. Melhem—"flail" introduces ambiguity by connoting what is "uncertain, disorganized, thrashing" and, as such, underscores the vulnerability of the gathering black collective.[66] The lack of punctuation at the poem's end extends that vein of ambiguity by conveying, in Brooks's view, an uncertainty and determination and, in Melhem's view, "continuing conflict."[67]

Ambiguity also expands the scope of the poem's spatial politics. Brooks's suggestion in the prefatory matter of the poem that "*Perhaps* [the boy] lives in Soweto"[68] opens up its referential field of applicability. The boy may not reside in Soweto, nor, for that matter, another of Johannesburg's townships such as Alexandra, nor even necessarily South Africa itself. If the boy's geographic nearness to Johannesburg expresses a political relationship to the dual seat of exclusive power and oppression—in other words, access to political power rendered in terms of spatial proximity—it applies to a variety of terrains. The poem, in fact, lucidly reflects Brooks's own spatial sensibility, born of her experiences in hypersegregated Chicago and fully displayed in her other work, from "kitchenette building" to *Maud Martha*.[69] Crafted by someone intimately familiar with racial lines of demarcation and proximity without access or welcome, the poem's referential openness invites readers to recognize other segregated cityscapes, not least the poet's own, especially in light of the fact that, by the 1980s, Chicago was popularly nicknamed "Joburg by the Lake."[70] Read cross-culturally, the "Perhaps" in the poem's headnote nudges open the boy's politico-geographic positioning to encompass, as well, that of, say, an African American youth on the south side of Chicago.[71] In this way, what is insurgently "a-pulse across earth that is our earth" telescopes between the black experience of a very local spatial-racial order and those of other similar orders much farther afield.

Constructive Engagements

African American poetry of the 1980s reflects an extensive effort to bring the relationships between South Africa and the United States into fuller view. Much like their predecessors in South African and African American letters over a decade earlier, from Langston Hughes to Bessie Head, the writers aimed to connect the terms of racialized life in South Africa and the United States. But unlike their predecessors, the writers of the 1980s as well as political activists had a new target toward which they could direct their attention: the Reagan administration's obstinate foreign policy of "constructive engagement" toward South Africa. While activists mobilized to pressure the American government to reverse course, black poets in the United States added their voices to inveigh against the government's cynical stance and its duplicitous (ab)use of language.[72] D. L. Crockett-Smith's "Constructive Engagement," for example, employs the very name of the Reagan administration's warm policy alignment with the apartheid state to ridicule the two racist governments' collusion. Mockingly likening it to the relationship between pairs of pissing dogs, cawing crows, destructive Japanese beetles, and stumbling winos, the poem balks at the supposition that the engagements between South African and American racial states could possibly be constructive, in any generative sense of the term.[73]

Michelle Cliff likewise plays with the terms of the U.S. government's policy in her own poem with the same title, but rather than underscore the two states' nefarious diplomatic and economic ties, Cliff redirects our attention to more affirmative connections between the states' more resistant subjects. Fueled by political commitments and bonds she forged with Bessie Head, among others, Cliff's participation in antiapartheid efforts included material support for community activists within South Africa, as in her membership on the board of SISA. It also emerged in her published work, including her long poem, "A Visit from Mr. Botha," which sardonically reimagines his 1984 visit to Europe as South Africa's head of state. In "Constructive Engagement," Cliff adamantly twists the name of the U.S. foreign policy (back) into a radical expression of affiliation and solidarity. The poetic persona opens by explicitly declaring her "constructive engagement/ with" the burdened subjects of the apartheid state:

> the sisters and brothers on the sun-blasted dried-out bantustans/ the gold-
> miners/ the white-baby minders/ the diamond miners/ the forced laborers/ the

Ford auto workers/ the house workers/ the urban dwellers/ the urban workers/ the coloreds/ the hungry ones/ the old ones/ the prisoners/ the ones whose children are dead/ the ones whose children are still alive/ the schoolchildren/ the law-breakers/ the ones who have no work/ the ones who have been reclassified/ the pass-carriers/ the ones whose passes have been voided/ the white-sewer tenders/ the ones who wear the Black Sash/ the lovers.[74]

A second stanza presents a cluster of "engaged" freedom fighters: "Mamphela Ramphele/ Albertina Sisulu/ Albert Luthuli/ Ruth First/ Winnie Mandela/ Helen Suzman/ Helen Joseph/ Steve Biko/ Nelson Mandela."[75] Both sets of invocations mark a respectful recognition of South Africans' courage and sacrifices notably absent from either government's abstracted and extractive policies. The persona's sympathetic engagements instead work to reinstate the more humane meaning of "constructive" by invoking elected affinities that cut against the cynical, Cold War alliances between the American and South African states.

In the third stanza, Cliff's attention turns toward a more individualized scene of loss and courage: a "Black girlchild" bravely testifies before an all-white court against a white man, who has run over and killed her 7-year-old friend. The narrative voice pauses to consider the girl's internal state:

Did anything stop in her when she saw her friend die? Does she dream about that afternoon? Is she afraid? Does she feel guilty for not saving him? Did she think she could save him? Does she understand what happened? Are there people who will protect her from this knowledge? Does she understand her own courage—for that *is* what it is—in standing up, school-dress, hair braided, in a white court before a white judge and a white jury and a white defendant and his white friends and white family who claim it was only an accident . . . and no amount of tricky questioning can shake her. . . . Can she realize that there are people who will hate her without ever meeting her? What will happen in her life?[76]

Rather than proffering an omniscient description of the scenario that foregrounds injustice but risks abstracting the young girl in turn, the series of more penetrating questions places her subjectivity and psychic well-being into sharp focus and, in so doing, models an investment not only in the young girl's present inner life, but in her future existence, as well. These probing questions demonstrate yet another form of constructive engagement, here more intimately scaled to refocus readers on the courageous subject.

Cliff closes the poem by imbuing the scenario with a critical indeterminacy of place. Her culminating defiant demand—"Tell me if you will whether this happened in New York or Pretoria, L.A. or Johannesburg. // Don't ever tell me that South Africa makes America better by comparison"[77]—troubles assumptions about the setting of the girl's court appearance. The indeterminacy of the scene's location disables the dominant contrastive logic of the day that employed the South African state's notoriety to dismiss charges of ongoing American racism (along the lines of "This isn't racism; apartheid South Africa, that's *real* racism"). Furthermore, as it showcases the indistinguishability of South African and American racial geographies and the charged predicaments they engender, Cliff's poem prompts readers to reconsider what difference the matter of location should have on our affective relation to the young girl. At bottom, the poem counters distancing strategies by evoking those who contest foreign or domestic state policies and those who bear them. Cliff models a far more compassionate form of relation than either racial state would enact: an antiracist engagement that is constructive in the sense of fostering individual and collective well-being through support for liberation efforts in both countries.

The elected affinities and sympathetic expressions at the heart of "Constructive Engagement" most evidently aim to build solidarity against both states' racial regimes. In addition to its direct political aims, the engagement that Cliff names and models is also constructive in an imaginatively and culturally foundational sense. The title poem also names the very process that the literature and authors taken up in this study participate in. In other words, it is a deft, self-reflexive description of what all of the texts explored here enact: a discursive practice that helps constitute the imaginative, social, and political terms of transnational engagement. In this light, "constructive engagements" refers to two related phenomena that deserve further elaboration: first, the emergence of a tradition of sorts wherein continuing associations and affiliations are based on multiple prior transnational engagements and, second, the accreted discursive effects of repeated comparisons between South African and American racial contexts.

First, the emergence of a thematic tradition. It is of particular importance that Rive's late writing and teaching, the poems of Brooks and Cliff, and Lorde's essays meditate on South African and African American relationships, for these surface in the wake of the earlier and contemporaneous transnational engagements explored in previous chapters. Given the critical tendency to trace how African American culture shaped South African culture, the drawn lines of literary influence from Langston Hughes and Richard Wright to South African writers like Richard Rive, Peter Abrahams, Keorapetse Kgositsile, and Mark Mathabane—or from James Baldwin to Nat Nakasa—may seem more obvious, legible, even predictable (without being unimportant). However, following the engagements registered in the last two chapters and this one, we can now also trace inverse patterns of literary impact: for example, drawing a line from some of Michelle Cliff's and Alice Walker's writing back to Bessie Head, Gwendolyn Brooks's work back to Kgositsile, Audre Lorde's efforts back to Ellen Kuzwayo (and indirectly, via Cliff and Gloria Joseph, to Head). We can also recognize Rive's literary presence in the 1960s primary school classroom via Hughes's *An African Treasury* anthology and his later physical and literary presence in the 1980s American university classroom, in addition to the surge in available South African publications in the United States. This is not to suggest that one writer was exclusively shaped by a single other one, who happens to neatly represent either the United States or South Africa. Influence is an unruly, diffuse, often ghostly property, and how it emanates or is absorbed is a complex process, indeed. I am not suggesting that a tradition was self-consciously crafted as such. But the subsequent generations of engagement—be they via interpersonal relationships or published work—nevertheless help illuminate a vein of South African–African American relational writing and reading that successively builds upon preceding interactions. The relationships explored in this study have rippled out in ways that have engendered further comparative or relational writings, other interpersonal relationships, or both. The cross-cultural engagements that took root across the 1980s, themselves the result of earlier exchanges or connections, represent a new set, which prefigure future engagements, as well—a new batch of texts that would explicitly meditate on South African and U.S. relationships. In this wider frame, these cross-cultural texts are both products and producers of a transnational(izing) consciousness, both evidence of its existence and propagators of its possibilities.

The essays, poems, autobiographies, and even class lectures considered here articulate a set of resonant black experiences by way of invoking similar geographic and material features of both countries. To different degrees, Rive, Jordan, Lorde, Brooks, Clarke, Weaver, and Cliff marshal a commonality or critical indeterminacy that brings the geographies of both racial states into tight relation. Consequently, invocations of place and sociogeographic space function as a shared lexicon that underwrites claims of comparability, similarity, relation, or affiliation of segregated life in South Africa and the United States. Not unlike Hughes's "Question and Answer," Kgositsile's poetics, Scott-Heron's lyrics, or Walker's drawing, these later texts stress an experiential proximity that belies the geographic distance between the two countries and, thereby, remap the ways readers might imagine themselves and their relation to their counterparts overseas.

The texts' black transnational imaginings set into relief the second type of constructive engagement at work: the effects, in a constructionist sense, of the texts' discursive interventions. I have been suggesting that, if decades of transatlantic traffic between black South Africans and black Americans result in a consciousness of relation at play on both sides of the Atlantic, that transnational(izing) consciousness has been textually mediated. The significance of the writings examined earlier is not merely that they mimetically reflect an emerging transnational consciousness; rather, these texts participate in a fundamentally productive enterprise that discursively creates and reinforces a conceptual ground for cross-cultural association. Whatever assertion or recognition of bonds between South Africans and African Americans featured in or effected by literature, these texts are predicated upon a *re*cognition made possible by the remapping of relation that the texts also engage in. Put differently, by advancing a specifically transnational "mode of apprehending the world,"[78] the texts help reconceptualize the known world and the means by which that world comes to be known. As creative responses to unacceptable problems of the past and present, they critically engage readers' current imaginations, yet do so with an eye to a freer future. The writers' and their works' remappings partake in a prospective project; to borrow Thongchai Winichakul's formulation, this kind of map is "a model *for*, rather than a model *of*, what it purport[s] to represent."[79]

Despite their prospective properties, these texts rest upon the sometimes obscured past of prior associations while giving the appearance, over time, of self-evident truth. Their repeated claims of continuity, assertions of similitude, and expressions of affiliation across the latter half of the twentieth century cumulatively affect how relation between black South Africans and Americans is imagined. The reinforcing invocation and reinvocation of a South African–African American relationship by writers from both countries (even if at times to reject it) effectively produces a bank of associations and a rationale from which subsequent writers would draw. The repeated, if varied, associations between both black communities have accrued in a way that their similarities have become generally given, naturalized, assumed, and indeed commonsensical. In this way, the body of texts from both countries, composed of many instances of constructive engagements, helped constitute the imaginative ground of transnational engagement. It supported the formation of cross-cultural networks and solidarities while, in true dialectical fashion, also being a consequence of them.

The constructedness raised by Cliff's poem, then, metonymically models the role literature plays in shaping and reshaping transnational cultural and political processes. The texts I have considered collectively aim to make black transnational connections meaningful, imaginatively viable, and generative of social and material change. To be sure, the kinds of transnational remappings the writers and their texts advanced raise a variety of legitimate concerns. As

Ifeoma Nwankwo and Brent Hayes Edwards have separately argued, efforts to stress cross-cultural symmetries with black counterparts elsewhere often elide significant differences, disjunctions, or nonalignments. The potential consequences of these elisions are skewed representation, mistranslation, or distortion under a homogenizing sign of *Blackness*.[80] It also risks obscuring disparities regarding who historically has had more power to represent. The ways in which black South Africans and black Americans characterized their relationship, for example, could not always be properly called neat mirror-image reciprocity. There is a difference between South African literature's explicit engagement with African American literature and authors, on one hand, and African American literature's taking up of South African geographies, figures, and events, on the other. In part, such asymmetries speak to the relative power disparities between black Americans and their South African counterparts. Legal or economic restrictions and differential access to media, markets, networks, and presses ultimately affect who and what gets heard. African Americans' hard-fought accessing or creation of cultural institutions in the absence of access has historically meant a relatively louder voice than their black South African counterparts in shaping national and transnational discourses, with the potent exception of several individual South Africans. In a disproportionately empowered world, the resulting terrain is, indeed, thorny—at times, appropriative; at other times, politically generative; but it is always peppered with the possibility of misunderstandings and missteps.

Without pretending that these differences do not matter, it remains important to recognize these South African–African American remappings as culturally constitutive processes. Whether or not we agree with the terms of comparison, claims of affinity, or their assumptions, these repeated remappings over time constitute a remaking. From an academic standpoint, these engagements may or may not appear reductive, but my point here does not rest on an evaluation of ideological soundness, historical accuracy, or strict sociological fact. From the vantage point of the cultural long view, they are constructive insofar as they have built up to a general way of thinking, shared cultural conception, or common sense that stakes out a strong relationship between two groups of people.

In this very strict sense, it might be said somewhat provocatively that there is no such thing as a cultural mis-mapping. The writers' repeatedly drawn transnational arrangements have solidified into a substantial map—one that may be reinscribed, reworked, and critiqued, but one that gained cultural and political force in the period of formal apartheid. Maps reflect the desires, ideologies, biases, and interests of their cartographers or commissioners.[81] So implies the persona of Césaire's classic *Notebook of a Return to the Native Land* when he reserves his right to a "special geography": "the world made for my own use, not tinted by the arbitrary colors of scholars, but with the geometry of my spilled blood."[82] At this point in my study, I would be hard pressed to deny scholars the right to use our own colors and scrutinize the represented worlds we encounter, and it remains important for scholars of transnationalism to tease out the significance of aporias, slippages, superimpositions, or erasures. But Césaire's persona importantly raises the politics of mapping. He reminds us that the elements and arrangements of a map legitimate specific experiences, privilege particular knowledges, and consolidate distinct bases of power. He also reminds us that hegemonic power works by representing its world and, by design or force of habit, erasing or distorting the worlds of others. The colors of scholars fail to reflect—perhaps, actively deny—the world order of violence and suffering that Césaire's persona knows, so he yearns for a geography that acknowledges it. When the dominant representation of the world does not correspond to one's knowledge or experience, it becomes necessary to create one that does.

Neither dominant maps nor their critical remappings are above critique, but Césaire's line better frames both within a context of political and representational power that govern their uses. To bring us back to the cross-cultural literature under discussion, elisions, silences, conflations, appropriations, reductions, mistranslations, and distortions are part and parcel of these black literary remappings, but they are deliberately so. That is to say, the black writers featured across this study, from Langston Hughes to Richard Rive to Bessie Head to Audre Lorde, were fully cognizant of the actual differences—demographic, linguistic, cultural, and historical—between individual places or geographies they brought together or even conflated in their work, and they sometimes registered these differences. They remapped quite consciously, not naively; their maps emphasized or established common bonds over and above the differences they understood precisely because doing so served a purpose: cutting against dominant, national arrangements that denied black freedom. The fact of this repeated remapping of black American and South African spaces and circumstances by numerous writers from both countries across decades should alert us to the power of the representational strategy as well as its driving motivations. Their constructive engagements must be understood as representational tools deployed to challenge the conventional ways we think about relation.

Furthermore, Césaire's critical attention to the chosen colors of scholars might inspire more self-reflection about the kinds of maps we draw or uphold—their values and their relation to power. After all, the kinds of geographies we legitimate may ignore or dismiss significant cultural orders taking shape, especially when we reproduce dominant arrangements uncritically. For the terms of the present inquiry, some scholars who resist tracing transnational trajectories and identities because they inaccurately capture the terms of black identity may be relying on a mythical stability or authenticity of national frames. A national map of blackness is no less a product of culturally constructive processes than is the map of black transnationalism. In other words, the same sorts of engagements and elisions of difference govern both national and transnational cartographies of black belonging. The difference, which is not negligible, is one of scale—the latter necessarily remaps more sets of experiences and relations—but not of kind.

"To Remake It"

This chapter has shown that interpersonal relationships between black South African and African American writers and the comparative texts they produced in the earlier decades of apartheid yielded a new constellation of engagements by the 1980s. I have traced out several examples that reveal how the latter set of relationships and writings variously built off of antecedent ones. Over the decades, the numerous writers' claims of comparability and similarity—frequently expressed in geographic terms—advanced in their writing accumulated into a common sense that tightly associated South African and African American contexts in the cultural imaginary. As I have demonstrated in prior chapters, writers and intellectuals established these associations well before apartheid's formal end in the 1990s. Our timeline begins in the 1940s, when Peter Abrahams and Richard Wright drew connections between their native lands, but they were drawn even earlier. What distinguished the 1980s from earlier decades was that black South African–African American connections were now de rigueur, as writers (and activists) continued to push for the recognition of this transnational relationship while the battle against apartheid raged on. This common sense was the outcome of constructive engagements from across the decades.

The operative terms "constructive" and "remapping" dwelt upon here cut against the general presumption that South Africans and African Americans are naturally or self-evidently linked. It is a presumption that even the writers sometimes aimed to promote, and its pervasiveness speaks to the success of their efforts along with that of other artists, intellectuals, and politicians. But this common sense, like all others, was socially produced, even as it passed itself off as natural.[83] Indeed, to chart a literary history of constructive engagements is to reveal a whole network of deliberate choices, willed transactions, strategic representations, carefully forged intellectual decisions—in short, the active building of a proverbial common ground. My aim has been to expose this history of constructedness precisely to interrupt naturalizing narratives that leave so much of the active black cultural production taken for granted or unrecognized, in both senses of the term. In the remainder of this chapter, I tease out several additional points about the constructedness of black South African and African American relationships that help give clearer definition to the transnational engagements expressed during and before the 1980s.

The first of these points is that expressions of cross-cultural similarity were not preestablished or inherently automatic. Some black South Africans and African Americans at times denied any substantive commonality between them; in other cases, they perceived their commonality to be temporary, partial, or tepid at best. This chapter and, indeed, much of this book have focused upon the efforts of black South African and African American writers to articulate, imagine, or reimagine their relationships to one another, but it bears repeating that this was not universally the case. As I have indicated at several moments, some writers were met with gaps they would or could not bridge, disjunctions they would or could not adjust. The list includes Nat Nakasa and some exchanges between Bessie Head and some of her interlocutors, as we have seen. It also, at times, encompasses even Richard Rive, whose autobiographical piece, "Taos in Harlem," alerts us to some points of cultural disjunction between him and his mentor, Langston Hughes. When Rive asks Hughes about "soul," Hughes suggests he would be unable to access it; in an earlier draft of this piece, Hughes responds, "Man, Richard, you Africans won't quite understand."[84] In the 1980s, the Xhosa imbongi David Manisi likewise encountered a divide, partly of his own making. His multiple performances in the United States were complicated not only by his own social positioning within South Africa and his oration in Xhosa, which required translation, but also by his framing of African and American relations. As Ashlee Neser notes, in his American performances, Manisi cast South Africa as the beggar to a wealthy United States, but his approach failed to create a connection precisely because the poet was unable to establish "a common cause and geography . . . as forceful reasons why parties owe duties to each other."[85] Instead, his poems explicitly introduced him as part of an African landscape wholly foreign to the American territory he was touring, a rhetorical move that set him apart from, rather than bonded him to, his audience.[86] As Neser's point makes clear, how the writer conceived of cross-cultural relation shaped his or her terms of engagement, and they did not always pan out as direct links.

The second point about constructive engagements follows from the first: they were not uniform or uniformly deployed, shaped as they were by different

worldviews and motivations. Aside from a general commitment to black liberation, many of the writers covered here did not share a singular ideological perspective. The kinds of engagements that Head sought to cultivate, for example,
varied considerably from those that Kgositsile aimed to establish. Moreover,
driven by different aims, authors necessarily put transnational engagements to
different uses. The most obvious impetus behind assertions of cross-cultural
commonality was to shore up solidarity to overthrow South Africa's apartheid
regime, imagined as part of a broader black transnational antiracist movement.
But it is also the case that these engagements helped black Americans and South
Africans confront their racial states independently. Engagements were not all
designed to build a unified transnational front; sometimes, more particularized
incentives were at play. Black Americans and South Africans, in other words,
invoked one another's contexts for domestic reasons as much as for transnational ones. Each context offered the other something in the way of symbolic
power, strategic analytical insight, example, leverage, or value in their localized
battles against racism. The invocation of one situation, accordingly, helped give
indirect expression to the other's predicaments or achievements. For South
Africans, the perceived relative successes of the U.S. Civil Rights movement
became the exemplary proof of the possibility of achieving the antiapartheid
struggle's goals. Black American political battles lent South Africans a certain
spirit of struggle against racism, if not always the strategies, to coexist with local
or continental narratives of anti-imperial struggle. African American writers
and intellectuals, moreover, helped South Africans frame their own frustration,
anger, and desire that fomented within a racial cauldron. For African Americans,
the valiant protests of South Africa's antiapartheid campaign (from acts of civil
disobedience to the 1956 Women's March to the turn toward armed resistance)
served as symbols to inspire resistance and shore up resolve across the United
States. South Africa also lent African Americans a critical lexicon with which to
name the persistent structural inequalities under continuing segregation. *Apartheid* became the appropriated term of analysis for black (and white) Americans'
political and economic conditions. It denounced the failures of the post–Civil
Rights-era dispensation, indicted the racist policies of a conservative American
state nefariously deploying a color-blind ideology, and indexed what ominously
loomed ahead if fragile black political gains kept suffering rollbacks. And as the
divestment movement made clear, the crisis in South Africa also encouraged
African American communities to mobilize themselves as a bloc capable of
shaping international politics by maneuvering its political weight domestically.

These different objectives shaped the kinds of comparisons that writers and
others developed. But, together, they underscore how one black population's

transnational comparison with the other performed critical ideological work in the service of more nationally specific political projects. In this way, engagements between black South Africans and Americans bear out the arguments of Michelle Stephens, Brent Hayes Edwards, and Laura Chrisman on the relationship between nationalism and transnationalism.[87] They show that transnational relationships and visions have often worked in tandem with—rather than in necessary opposition to—more nationally focused projects or forms of (black) nationalism, and vice versa. Nationally based struggles hardly prevented transnational linkages or solidarities; quite the contrary. As Lorde imagined it in "Apartheid U.S.A.," "[w]e examine these similarities so that we can devise mutually supportive strategies for action, at the same time as we remain acutely aware of our differences."[88]

Without wholly erasing the category of the nation or nation-state—which was frequently the source of black activists,' intellectuals,' and artists' frustrations and the target of their opposition—some iterations of black transnationalism aimed to mitigate its most pernicious powers. The transnational(izing) black South African and African American writers examined here imagined and sought forms of relation other than those furnished by their respective nation-states. Offering alternative sets of coordinates by which to orient oneself, their writing remapped geographies and relations in ways that resisted the primacy of the nation-state and the maps of belonging it underwrote. And it sought to undermine the ideological work that those state-based maps perform—namely, preserving the state as the ultimate arbiter of rights, privileges, and power, as well as maintaining a white supremacist order on which both South Africa and the United States have depended. By emphasizing variously figured common ground between black South Africans and African Americans, some writers generated maps to exceed the nation-state (extranational), others to function beneath it (subnational), but they typically produced maps to cut across its logic or its terms of community (transnational). Indeed, their figured grounds of engagement sought new terms of black belonging that would reposition black peoples as subjects within a collectivity of their own shaping.

The third point worth making is that black transnational engagement via remapping or other claims of commonality does not rest on the notion of a singular blackness. Rather than ratify race as a uniform or essential trait, it points to the ways that racial identity is itself mapped and remapped, actively redefined for political and ideological purposes. Katherine McKittrick has attended to "the classificatory where of race" in order to reveal the ways in which historical forces and social processes "make geography a racial-sexual terrain."[89] McKittrick argues that race and gender are constitutive of social space and that, in a white-dominated segregated society, "blackness is integral to the production of space."[90] If this is the case, when writers redraw the spatial and conceptual boundaries of black belonging, their resulting black geographies effectively redesign the contours of identities within the freshly configured spaces. In other words, if one black community's experience of racism spurs a search for corresponding black experiences in other locations across the globe, that comparative or relational enterprise inevitably rearticulates blackness as a historically contingent political identity. Blackness (or any other racial identity) reformulated through claims of similar geographies is—far from an expression of intrinsic racial essence—a placeholder for consonant experiences of racial hierarchies structured by white supremacy, which become the ground of comparison or relation. But that ground is not some essential biological trait, per se. Instances of South African and African American remapping help us appreciate more fully the ways, to use Kamari Clarke and Deborah Thomas's formulation, "people understand, perform, or subvert racial identities by mobilizing both knowledges gleaned from the particularities of their local circumstances and from the range of ideas and practices that circulate within their public spheres, showing that racial subjectivities are always 'coalitional, contingent, and performative.'"[91]

This is not to suggest that these remappings have not been couched in naturalizing language. Affirmations of blood ties and assertions of racial kinship have been staples of this transnational history, in fact. But that should not blind us to the performative dimension of those claims. Edward Said has distinguished between filiation, or direct genealogical descent, and its alternative when biological reproduction is impossible, a horizontal affiliation. He characterizes affiliation as a "compensatory order that, whether it is a party, an institution, a culture, a set of beliefs, or even a world-vision, provides men and women with a new form of relationship."[92] This distinction quickly blurs, however, when one becomes a metaphor for the other, in particular, when affiliative relationships of race mobilize the language of filiation, the metaphor of the family. The aim is clear: to establish a relationship as undeniable as blood ties and with as much of a built-in sense of obligation. The pronouncement of kinship is an assertion of a responsibility-bearing relation with an explicit or implicit injunction to act. In effect, claims of kinship are speech acts that perform ethically oriented discursive work, which is to say that claimants activate the salience of their claimed relation, along with whatever responsibilities that relation mandates. So, for example, when African Americans assert their brotherhood and sisterhood with black South Africans, or vice versa, it is done to raise and mobilize a set of obligations to, or on behalf of, one another.[93] In this framework, the claims of filiation are performed, but filial claims are no more authentic or less performed than affiliative ones, for literal and metaphorical families alike rely on such speech acts to establish rights, duties, or responsibilities.

The fourth and final point follows from all three preceding points: the common association between black South Africans and African Americans was not inevitable.[94] If connections between black peoples on either side of the Atlantic were neither predetermined, uniform, nor born of some innate connection, they were most certainly produced. It was the product of a wide range of imaginative, discursive, and cultural work over the course of many years. Among a panoply of activists, intellectuals, politicians, and other artists, the writers very deliberately labored to bring black South Africans and African Americans into relation, to build and reveal a common ground between them. Writers actualized the cross-cultural connection through their personal interactions and their art, which required deliberation, design, and execution. Indeed, the transaction, mapping, remapping, cultivation, and constructive engagement I have outlined across this study all highlight the extensive labor at the heart of black South African and African American writing, black cultural production, and black transnationalism, more generally. As I noted in the previous chapter, these terms implicitly stress the desire of writers who attempted to forge the connections they sought, but above all, they place considerable value on the forging itself, the arduous imaginative and material labor necessary for transnational engagement.

Seeing the labor of engagement enables us to draw out the often less visible work needed for other forms of black collectivity, as well. This is particularly the case with the concept of diaspora. My focus on black South African and African American literary relationships has dwelt on a type of transnationalism forged within the sociological sphere of the African diaspora but not in accordance with classical diasporic relations. Traditionally understood, diaspora names the set of lineal relations established as a result of large-scale and extended migration from one general area to a series of different discontiguous places. African diasporic relations are complex configurations of rupture and continuation, and they encompass communities far broader than families, per se; Saidiya Hartman has exposed the fraught fictions of kinship and the problematic family romance within this cultural relationship, too.[95] The cataclysmic terms of the transatlantic slave trade brutally ensured that direct genealogical lines could not be traced, that inheritance could be understood in general cultural terms and partial patterns only. African Americans' descent from the survivors of the middle passage, followed by subsequent waves of black migration, remains a defining feature of black American identity. From this vantage point, ties between African Americans and West or Central Africans adhere to a different, more lineal model of relation than do ties between African Americans and black South Africans, which are historically more recent, more politically based, and more overtly affiliative, despite the discourse of kinship. If the classic model of the African diaspora hinges upon the vertical axis of descent, the South African–African American connection emphasizes the horizontal axis of affiliation.

Numerous scholars have complicated the classical model of diaspora in important ways. Tiffany Ruby Patterson and Robin D. G. Kelley have characterized it as an ongoing process, for instance, and Brent Hayes Edwards has framed diaspora as a practice.[96] In the spirit of this complicating scholarship, the notion of constructive engagements shows that classic diasporic relationships, on the one hand, and affiliation between black South Africans and African Americans, on the other, share more common ground than generally appreciated—namely, they share the labor involved in building cross-cultural relation. Approaches to the African diaspora that privilege ancestry or cultural heritage as the link between two or more populations explore what (and who) survived the fact of dispersal, including the cultural, political, epistemic, and somatic violence of the West's transatlantic slave trade. But what should not be obscured is the generative work in the aftermath of (initial) dispersal that has actualized cultural heritage or made it salient. A wide variety of subsequent and ongoing endeavors have helped construct diasporic bonds by imagining, creating, and mobilizing black transnational relation. For example, African American efforts to preserve African diasporic cultural traditions and practices, from agricultural techniques to storytelling, involve the assertive work of making them meaningful in explicit and implicit ways. Generations of imaginative, cultural, political, and intellectual workers labored to make this past meaningful, and this, of course, extends to the intellectual labor of studying what was or was not lost in migration as well as to conceptualizing diaspora itself.[97]

Constructive engagement, then, lays bare the ongoing affiliative dimensions of diasporic relationships; it brings into view the production and continued activation of these bonds. Accounting for how the grounds of engagement are produced offers a capacious understanding of relation, even where evident lineal connections do exist, and it is an approach that can be extended to thinking about other (black) transnational relationships. In the context of black transnationalism, constructive engagements make new—and old—forms of black collectivity possible. Indeed, in the absence of efforts to articulate the terms of relation, assign them meaning, and actualize them, black collectivity is unimaginable.

Black transnationalism has been—and continues to be—a set of processes and practices painstakingly crafted across space and time, and it is propelled by deliberate action, desire, will, and overlapping interests in a liberated future. It takes place in a material world and is motivated by very material circumstances: the pernicious physical and social geographies that racial states produce. In this study, I have situated the imaginative work of black South African and African American writing within this wider frame of material relations. In addition to representing racial geographies, the texts have been part of a world in motion. The transnational circulation of writers and texts have animated, and been animated by, the ways people have reimagined cross-cultural relation. Guided by visions of a more justly arranged world, the black South African and African American writers above dedicated themselves to this necessary task of reimagining.

Langston Hughes adeptly captures the indispensability of that imaginative work in "Question and Answer," his dialogue poem raised in Chapter 1. As he looks upon the pitched battles across South Africa and the United States, the despondent interlocutor questions the significance of political struggle ("Why not go under?"). When the revolutionary reminds him that "[t]*here's a world to gain*," he cannot envision it. His nihilistic reply—"suppose I don't want it / Why take it?"—reveals his disengagement from a racist world that has no viable place for him. The revolutionary's (and poem's) ultimate answer—"[t]o *remake it*"—holds out the prospect of a new world, one that the nihilist will want to reclaim because it is a world of his own imagining. Even from this starting point, revolutionary change is no simple task. The struggle to realize the world worth taking is long, arduous, and never really finished. But among the first steps, as the writers featured here have demonstrated, is the hard, vital labor of imaginative engagement.

Notes

Chapter 1. Introduction

1. The Langston Hughes Collection at the Beinecke Library holds the bulk of Langston Hughes's papers. See Langston Hughes Collection (hereafter cited as LHC). See also Graham and Walters, *Langston Hughes*.

2. Because lives cohere around imposed and elected terms, quotation marks around racial identity markers (white, coloured, black) will not be added. But all terminology for racial identities should be understood as historically constructed, contingent, and subject to debate. As I detail later, the book employs a broad definition of blackness that includes those the apartheid regime identified as coloured. Rather than homogenizing or downplaying cultural or historical differences within South Africa and the United States, I examine the ways that blackness became a political term that numerous individuals chose to deploy. Indeed, Rive, Peter Abrahams, and Bessie Head—often designated as coloured writers—identified themselves as black at different points across the years.

3. Rive to Hughes, July 30, 1954, LHC 5; also quoted in Graham and Walters, *Langston Hughes*, 40.

4. Ibid.

5. Hughes to Rive, October 6, 1954, LHC 8; also quoted in Graham and Walters, *Langston Hughes*, 46.

6. Hughes to Rive, July 24, 1954, LHC 3; also quoted in Graham and Walters, *Langston Hughes*, 39.

7. Rive to Hughes, n/d, LHC 54.

8. See Edwards, *The Practice of Diaspora*; Gaines, *African Americans in Ghana*; Helgesson, *Transnationalism in Southern African Literature*; Makalani, *In the Cause of Freedom*; Nwankwo, *Black Cosmopolitanism*; Stephens, *Black Empire*; Sundiata, *Brothers and Strangers*.

9. Lefebvre, *The Production of Space*, 90; Neil Smith, "Contours of a Spatialized Politics," 64.

10. Soja, *Postmodern Geographies*, 81.

11. Hale, *Making Whiteness*, 6.

12. See Crenshaw, "Mapping the Margins"; Wiegman, *American Anatomies*; Felipe Smith, *American Body Politics*; Daymond, *South African Feminisms*; Elder, *Hostels, Sexuality, and the Apartheid Legacy*; Ardener, "The Partition of Space"; Massey, *Space, Place, and Gender*; and McKittrick, *Demonic Grounds*.

13. McKittrick, *Demonic Grounds*, xiv.

14. Du Bois, *The Souls of Black Folk*, 1.

15. Chrisman, "Beyond Black Atlantic," 261.

16. The term "spatialized sensibility" is Chrisman's. Ibid.

17. This idea may also inform van Wyk Smith's *Grounds of Contest*, a short survey of South African literature framed as a "record of the mythology developed by its people to justify or resist" the social struggle over land and its resources (3).

18. See "Mr. Nakasa Goes to Harlem," collected in Nakasa, *The World of Nat Nakasa*, 115–25.

19. Said, *Orientalism*, 71. Drawing on the work of Foucault, Said's treatment of Orientalist discourse underscores the ways that discourse produces its own object of knowledge. Imaginative geography, for Said, is the arbitrary distinction between familiar and unfamiliar spaces accompanied by the assignment of values and meaning to such spaces (54).

20. Carby, "Multicultural Wars," 14; Nelson Mandela, *Long Walk to Freedom*, 508; Angela Davis, *Women, Culture, Politics*, 104; Nixon, *Homelands, Harlem and Hollywood*, 13.

21. Hughes to Rive, July 24, 1954, LHC 3; also quoted in Graham and Walters, *Langston Hughes*, 39.

22. Hughes, *Collected Poems*, 549–50.

23. One of Hughes's very early poems, "Johannesburg Mines" (1925), explicitly takes up the situation of South African miners, but he would not employ his comparative poetics until after his epistolary exchanges with South African authors. Hughes, *Collected Poems*, 43.

24. I am drawing on Boehmer's use of "textual" to signify how the implementation of Euro-American imperialism *and* the resistance to it was textually carried out. For an extended discussion of textuality and imperialism, see chapter 1 in Boehmer, *Colonial and Postcolonial Literature*.

25. Literate and nonliterate community members have historically devised numerous practices to share printed knowledge and narrative—especially when operating in the same language. In the early twentieth century, for instance, African Americans

unable to read often religiously followed issues of *The Crisis* by having literate family or community members read to them (I thank Wahneema Lubiano for sharing this insight she gained from Sterling Brown). See also McHenry's discussion of reading as a "collective exercise" among members of nineteenth-century African American literary societies. McHenry, "Rereading Literary Legacy," 481. In the African context, Ngũgĩ wa Thiong'o has noted how his *Caitaani Mũtharabainĩ* was read aloud in group gatherings (even during lunch breaks) in Kenya, demonstrating the "appropriation of the novel into the oral tradition." Ngũgĩ, *Decolonising the Mind*, 83.

26. Said, "Yeats and Decolonization," 77.

27. Jameson, "Cognitive Mapping," 347–57.

28. See Harley, "Deconstructing the Map."

29. As with maps, literary texts posit particular relationships between objects (broadly understood)—spatial, social, political, psychological, and cosmological arrangements—and, in turn, shape the way we understand the world. But neither cartographic nor textual literacy necessarily yields a single, unified, and stable interpretation; texts are notoriously slippery. However, as literary texts can exert powerful imaginative force, whoever assumes the role of the cartographer has the ability to frame the terms of relation and to affirm or alter the preexisting imaginative geographies of his or her readership. See Turchi, *Maps of the Imagination*.

30. See Robinson, *Black Marxism*; Wolfe, "Land, Labor, and Difference."

31. Omi and Winant, *Racial Formation in the United States*, 77–91. In *The Racial State*, Goldberg defines some states as racial in nature because of "the structural position which they occupy in producing and reproducing, constituting and effecting racially shaped spaces and places, groups and events, life worlds and possibilities, accesses and restrictions, conceptions and mode of representation. They are *racial*, in short, by virtue of their population definition, determination, and structuration. They are *racist* to the extent that such definition, determination, and structuration operate to exclude or privilege in or on racial terms, and in so far as they circulate in and reproduce a world whose meanings or effects are racist. This is a world we might provisionally identify as a racist world." Goldberg, *The Racial State*, 104 (author's emphasis).

32. See Derrida's comparison of American and South African apartheid in "But beyond . . .," 369. Relatedly, in the 1960s a discourse on the internal colonization of black America—the notion that black Americans were subject to the same or similar conditions to those experienced by colonial subjects—emerged. In a 1962 essay entitled "Revolutionary Nationalism and the Afro-American," Cruse develops a notion of "domestic colonization" in *Rebellion or Revolution?* 75. This was followed by the analysis of internal colonization in the first chapter of Ture and Hamilton's *Black Power* entitled "White Power." Soon thereafter, Allen advanced his position on "domestic colonialism" in *Black Awakening in Capitalist America*. One year later, Tabb characterized the black ghetto as a type of colony within American national boundaries in his *The Political Economy of the Black Ghetto*. Spivak also briefly raises African Americans' subjection as an internal colonization in "Teaching for the Times," 478–79. For an early critique of this concept, see Harris, "The Black Ghetto as Internal Colony."

33. Fredrickson, *White Supremacy*, xix.

34. Fredrickson clearly acknowledges the countries' differences in *White Supremacy*; in his follow-up study, *Black Liberation*, he admits to further complexities that trouble, but also open up new avenues in, comparative history, particularly how to compare populations by race and status (versus by ideological formation) in South Africa and the United States. See his Introduction to *Black Liberation*.

35. Attwell, *J. M. Coetzee*, 35.

36. Hall, "Race, Articulation, and Societies," 57.

37. Glissant, *Poetics of Relation*, 14.

38. According to Massie, American whalers and traders off the southern tip of Africa were so numerous and frequent, one of the piers in Cape Town was referred to as the "American wharf." Massie, *Loosing the Bonds*, xiv. Moreover, from the very onset of the mineral (gold and diamond) revolution in southern Africa, the presence of American mining specialists played a key role in expediting the extraction of mineral wealth (xiii, xxi–xxii), without which the South African colonies would have quickly folded.

39. The Cape Colony ultimately favored the Confederate states as Civil War battles ensued off the coast of Cape Town. In 1863, the Confederate steamer *Alabama*, under Captain Raphael Semmes, captured the Union ship *Sea Bride*, all in view of Cape Town's residents, and was allowed by the governor to dock—contra British regulations—which, in turn, permitted it to evade another Union ship. This series of events would be framed in a still-famous folk song, "Daar Kom die Alibama" ("There Comes the Alabama"). South African Cultural History Museum, permanent exhibit; Massie, *Loosing the Bonds*, xix–xx.

40. According to Rich, the concept of "segregation" in South Africa "was not employed in an ideological vacuum for it was informed by a considerable degree of comparative historical analysis of the method of political control over blacks in the U.S. South." Rich, "Romance and the Development of the South African Novel," 122. Campbell notes the peculiar ironies and paradoxes of the mutual support between the two racial states during the mid–twentieth century: "At the very moment that the United States began tentatively to confront the problem of racial equality at home, it was deeply implicated in the elaboration of apartheid in South Africa. Stranger still, the resources that poured into South Africa in the 1950s in the name of western values of individualism and free enterprise underwrote a dramatic increase in state owner-ship and control of the economy, a process particularly evident in the steel and energy industries." Campbell, "The Americanization of South Africa," 53.

41. Marx, *Making Race and Nation*, 10–23.

42. Contrary to popular belief at the time, the BCM was not restricted by an essen-tialist definition of race or "blackness." It sought to reconstruct blackness in more expansive, inclusive terms. As Mgbako notes, the Black Consciousness journals of the day register a concerted effort to define blackness in politically strategic ways that could unify people of color in South Africa. Mgbako, "'My Blackness Is the Beauty of This Land.'"

43. See Sibley, *Geographies of Exclusion*.

44. Barnard, "Of Riots and Rainbows," 402, 405; Campbell, "Towards a Transnational Comparative History," 27.

45. Smith McKoy, *When Whites Riot*, 11–30.

46. Barnard, "Of Riots and Rainbows," 404–11. Whereas Smith McKoy highlights defining cultural patterns in white supremacist societies despite their specific differences, Barnard argues those differences make all the difference.

47. Ibid., 412.

48. Ibid., 414.

49. Meyer, "Review," 152.

50. Shih, "Comparison as Relation," 95.

51. Mignolo, "On Comparison," 112.

52. Lionnet, *Postcolonial Representations*, 106.

53. See Campbell, *Songs of Zion*; Chrisman, "Beyond Black Atlantic and Postcolonial Studies"; Couzens, *The New African*; Jaji, "Sound Effects"; Magubane, "The Influence of African-American Cultural Practices on South Africa"; Masilela, "New Negroism and New Africanism"; Nixon, *Homelands, Harlem and Hollywood*; Titlestad, *Making the Changes*; Van der Vlies, "Transnational Print Cultures."

54. See, for example, Chrisman, "Black Atlantic Nationalism," in *Postcolonial Contraventions*; Couzens, *The New African*; Masilela, "New Negroism and New Africanism."

55. See Mgbako, "'My Blackness'"; Nixon, *Homelands, Harlem and Hollywood*; Titlestad, *Making the Changes*.

56. Masilela, "New Negroism and New Africanism," 47; Nixon, *Homelands, Harlem and Hollywood*, 14–20; Titlestad, *Making the Changes*.

57. Couzens, *The New African*, 84; Masilela, "New Negroism and New Africanism," 53, 56; Vinson, *The Americans Are Coming!*

58. Mphahlele's quote is represented and reworked in Titlestad's *Making the Changes*, 60.

59. Sanders, *Complicities*, 179. See similar attributions in Mngxitama, Alexander, and Gibson, *Biko Lives!* The principal exception to these black U.S. influences is Biko's indebtedness to Martinquans Aimé Césaire and Frantz Fanon, but we should also note the Trinidadian roots of Stokely Carmichael, which points to the transnational dimensions of the term "African American."

60. Mgbako, "'My Blackness.'"

61. Rive, "Storming Pretoria's Castles," 32.

62. Masilela, "New Negroism and New Africanism," 58; Rowell, "'With Bloodstains to Testify,'" 28.

63. Es'kia Mphahlele, *Afrika My Music*, 18–19.

64. Rive, "Ethics of an Anti–Jim Crow," 12.

65. Nkosi, "The Mountain," 102; Bessie Head to Alice Walker, January 26, 1975, Alice Walker Papers, Box 85 Folder 10.

66. Blaut, *The Colonizer's Model of the World*, 1–49.

67. Nixon, Mgbako, Titlestad, and Magubane particularly make this case. So does Chrisman, who underscores how, in the early twentieth century black South African intellectuals, while borrowing from African American thought, also disagreed with their interlocutors—forming, instead of mere mimicry, a "critical, interrogative black Atlantic political culture." Chrisman, *Postcolonial Contraventions*, 92.

68. Chrisman, *Postcolonial Contraventions*, 102; Meyer, "Review," 153.

69. Crawford broaches a rare discussion of South African influence on black American art. Raising Kgositsile's literary presence in the United States, she argues that "Kgositsile's crucial involvement in the Black Arts Movement complicates the packaging of the core identity of the 1960s and '70s Black Arts Movement as African-American. Rethinking his deep immersion in the Black Arts Movement, the larger significance of his presence in [the anthology] *Black Fire*, and his Black Arts and post–Black Arts publications by Third World Press reveals that the story of the black diasporic relations during the Black Arts Movement is only beginning to unfold." Crawford, "Productive Rites of 'Passing,'" 119.

70. In *South African Literature Beyond the Cold War*, Popescu offers an alternative within the North-South axis by exploring South Africa's cultural relationship with Eastern Europe and Russia. Helgesson's *Transnationalism in Southern African Literature* finds an alternative to the North-South power differentials altogether by examining the literary dimensions of inequalities that cut across the countries and languages of southern Africa.

71. Shih, "Comparison as Relation," 96.

72. Campbell, *Songs of Zion*, viii.

73. See Barnard, *Apartheid and Beyond*; Bremner, *Writing the City into Being*; Bunn, "'Some Alien Native Land'"; Coetzee, *White Writing*; Judin and Vladislavić, *blank: Architecture, Apartheid and After*; Mbembe, "Aesthetics of Superfluity"; Nuttall, *Entanglement*; Nuttall and Mbembe, *Johannesburg*; Simone, "People as Infrastructure"; Vivan, "Geography, Literature, and the African Territory."

74. Bethlehem, "The Drift to the Map."

75. See Avilez, "Housing the Black Body"; Baker, "On Knowing Our Place"; Thadious Davis, *Southscapes*; Dixon, *Ride Out the Wilderness*; Griffin, *"Who set you flowin'?"*; McKittrick, *Demonic Grounds*; Myers, "Worlds beyond *Brown*."

76. Titlestad, "Traveling Jazz."

77. See Ntantla, *A Life's Mosaic*; Ndlovu, *Sheila's Day*; Nkosi, *Home and Exile*; Brutus, *Poetry and Protest*; Magona, *Forced to Grow*; Kunene, *Emperor Shaka the Great*; Ndebele, *Rediscovery of the Ordinary*; Mphahlele, *Afrika My Music*; Mzamane, *The Children of the Diaspora*; Harper, *Healing Song for the Inner Ear*; Wilderson, *Incognegro*.

78. Morrison, *Conversations with Toni Morrison*, 47.

Chapter 2. Race, Place, and the Geography of Exile

1. Rowley, *Richard Wright*, 355–56. Stovall also notes the symbolism of the ship's name in *Paris Noir*, 192.

2. Rowley, *Richard Wright*, 357.

3. Abrahams, *Black Experience in the 20th Century*, 20–21.

4. These consist of *Here, Friend* (1940) and *A Black Man Speaks of Freedom!* (1941). Wade, *Peter Abrahams*, 3.

5. Abrahams was considered coloured by his surrounding community in Johannesburg, but as an adult, he identified as black in a rejection of South Africa's racial categories.

6. Thadious Davis, *Southscapes*, 144.

7. The one possible exception is Langston Hughes, although he may have been more popularly known for his poetry.

8. For all the parallels and overlaps between the two writers, surprisingly little scholarship has covered this literary relationship. In the preface to the 1993 second edition of his Wright biography, Michel Fabre notes with regret that he had not more fully explored the relationship between Wright and Abrahams, while suggestively adding that their relationship "provided Wright with an inside feeling of what cultural colonization in Africa had been; it also revealed to him some of the ways conducive to de-colonization, challenging his belief that Africa had to resort to weapons of the West to liberate herself." Fabre, *The Unfinished Quest of Richard Wright*, xiii. In an essay entitled "Wright, Negritude, and African Writing" in his *The World of Richard Wright*, Fabre slightly elaborates on the similarities and differences in their worldviews. More recently, Masilela briefly notes this relationship in "Peter Abrahams in the Modern African World," as does Polsgrove in her history of mid–twentieth-century black intellectuals in England, *Ending British Rule in Africa*.

9. Fabre, "Wright, Negritude, and African Writing," in *The World of Richard Wright*, 195; South African History Online: Towards a People's History, "Peter Henry Abrahams."

10. Fabre, *Unfinished Quest*, 308.

11. The available letters in question are collected in the Richard Wright Papers (hereafter cited as RWP) at the Beinecke Library, and they constitute a partial record of their exchange; only Abrahams's letters to Wright are archived. Although its partial nature places significant limitations on scholarly analysis, the available portion of their correspondence offers glimpses into the terms of their relationship and literary productivity. Although restrictions prevent me from directly quoting from the letters, scholars are able to locate the letters for their own research. They can also find a general record of Wright's and Abrahams's literary engagement in Kiuchi and Hakutani's documentary volume, *Richard Wright*.

12. Rowley, *Richard Wright*, 357.

13. Fabre, *Richard Wright*, 4.

14. Rowley, *Richard Wright*, 357.

15. Wright, *Conversations with Richard Wright*, 124.

16. Fabre, *Richard Wright*, 3.

17. Tuan, *Space and Place*, 12.

18. My analysis focuses upon the 1945 edition of *Black Boy* initially read by Wright's contemporaries, Abrahams included, which concludes with young Richard's flight from the South. The original midcentury publication of the autobiography includes only the first portion of the two-part chronicle that Wright produced in manuscript form (with occasional alteration)—presented as Part One, "Southern Night," in the restored 1991 edition. Part Two, "The Horror and the Glory," was published posthumously as *American Hunger* in 1977, before the 1991 edition consolidated both parts.

19. Faithfully reflecting reality is rarely the case: the careful self-fashioning in African American autobiography, from the slave narrative on, is well documented. Wade has commented upon *Tell Freedom*'s novelistic, even experimental features, which he claims are at times more successful than those in his long fiction. Wade, *Peter Abrahams*, 108–9, 113.

20. Chinosole, *The African Diaspora and Autobiographics*, 37.

21. Masilela, "New Negroism and New Africanism," 58.

22. Mphahlele, "The Tyranny of Place," 76.

23. Rive, "Storming Pretoria's Castles," 32.

24. Rowell, "'With Bloodstains to Testify,'" 28.

25. Van der Vlies, "Transnational Print Cultures," 51 (author's emphasis).

26. For an elaboration of the relationship between race-making and the formation of a new American consumer culture, see Hale, *Making Whiteness*, 6.

27. Ibid., 7.

28. Tyner, *The Geography of Malcolm X*, 4.

29. Delaney, *Race, Place, and the Law*, 96.

30. Soja, *Postmodern Geographies*, 81. See also Tyner, *The Geography of Malcolm X*, 65.

31. See Smith McKoy, *When Whites Riot*; Mark Smith, *How Race Is Made*; Hale, *Making Whiteness*.

32. See Griffin, *"Who set you flowin'?"*; Stepto, *From Behind the Veil*; Dixon, *Ride Out the Wilderness*; Baker, "On Knowing Our Place"; Davis, *Southscapes*.

33. Stepto, *From Behind the Veil*, 81, 80.

34. Miller, *Topographies*, 6.

35. Davis, *Southscapes*, 158.

36. This phrase is borrowed from Adams, Hoelscher, and Till in their introduction to *Textures of Place*. For more on geographic dimensions of Wright's work, Griffin notes the persistence of the South in Wright's literary imagination, locating its power primarily in the racial violence that has marked and symbolically infused the land. The southern landscape's idyllic beauty in Wright's classic short story, "Big Boy Leaves Home," she argues, is undercut by the fact that it doubles as a terrain of racial terror. Griffin further argues that Wright's most lyrical passages in his *12 Million Black Voices* stress the harmony of black Americans with the land they work, but brutality supplants it—"lynching literally becomes part of the description of landscape"—and compels blacks to seek sanctuary beyond the South, a search that fuels the Great Migration. Griffin, *"Who set you flowin'?"* 31, 33.

37. Davis, *Southscapes*, 151.

38. After her paralytic stroke, Wright's mother's suffering—and immobility—haunts Wright to become a "symbol in [his] mind, gathering to itself all the poverty, the ignorance, the helplessness." Wright, *Black Boy*, 87.

39. Ibid., 91 (my emphasis).

40. Ibid., 34.

41. Ibid., 35, 36.

42. Ibid., 111.

43. Ibid., 222.

44. Ibid., 148.

45. Ibid., 181. See Baker's formulation of "PLACE" in "On Knowing Our Place." For analysis of the moribund dimensions of Wright's writing, see JanMohammed, *The Death-Bound-Subject*.

46. Stepto, *From Behind the Veil*, 65.

47. Wright, *Black Boy*, 7.

48. Tuan, *Space and Place*, 52.

49. See the passage in which Wright's frozen response to a white man's sexual assault on a black woman leads to the man also threatening him. Wright, *Black Boy*, 173.

50. Stepto, *From Behind the Veil*, 83.

51. Wright, *Black Boy*, 8.

52. Tuan, *Space and Place*, 162.

53. Wright, *Black Boy*, 41.

54. Ibid., 72.

55. Ibid., 172 (my emphasis).

56. Ibid., 187. Another exemplar is Wright's own father. Tracing out an Oedipal struggle in *Black Boy*, Stepto asserts that Wright's persona "does not so much slay his father as bury him alive." Like Mrs. Moss and Bess, he is fundamentally associated with the rural southern landscape that claims him: Wright characterizes him as "a creature of the earth" and "black peasant" bound to a "bleak plantation." Stepto, *From Behind the Veil*, 84–85.

57. Wright, *Black Boy*, 137.

58. Fabre has argued that too restrictive an understanding of naturalism, in Wright's case, misses the fullness of his complex style: "American naturalism, both as a philosophy and as a literary technique in the line of Dreiser and James Farrell, provided [Wright] only with a starting point; then either . . . a larger definition of naturalism must be given—if it is to encompass the many facets of Wright's writing—or it must be recognized that he often overstepped its boundaries." Fabre, "Beyond Naturalism?" 56.

59. Wright, *American Hunger*, 22.

60. Wright, *Black Boy*, 116, 219.

61. Ibid., 227.

62. We might also note the formative environments of Chicago and New York, the locales where Wright wrote after his flight from the South, especially when we consider Wright's affinity for the Chicago School of Sociology.

63. Thacker, *Moving through Modernity*, 23.

64. For a discussion of geographical scale, see Neil Smith, "Contours of a Spatial-ized Politics," 54–81.

65. Tuan, *Space and Place*, 6–7.

66. Wright, *Black Boy*, 72 (my emphasis).

67. The consequences of that absorption may be found in the "shut[ting] off" of mind and emotion that, in Wright's view, southern black psyches resort to in self-defensive response to their environment. Ibid., 172. Even maneuvering around segre-gationist regulation has its spatial dimensions. Take, for example, Wright's successful manipulation of Memphis's whites-only public library rules to check out books that he may not legally read. Wright can physically enter the space of the library—he may and does check out books for his white boss, Mr. Olin—but the color-bar denies him borrowing privileges. The library and its resources were not built for him, and he may access them only for the service and edification of white patronage. This passage is not especially wrought with spatial reference, but we see clearly that, with forged note in hand, Wright surreptitiously accesses the exclusive physical space and services for his own purposes.

68. Griffin argues that, in his *12 Million Black Voices*, black migrant pockets of south-ern simplicity, superstition, and ultimately religion are held up as the antithesis of northern modernity and progressivism. The gendered terms of belief and worldview are particularly pronounced: "While the women of the storefront churches remain premodern, those men who possess a critical consciousness are able to emerge into the modern world." Griffin, *"Who set you flowin'?"* 82.

69. Wright, *Black Boy*, 105. This regional map of American modernity, however, is considerably troubled once he encounters the northern cityscape, as he records in *American Hunger*. Chicago "mock[s] all [his] fantasies" and reveals itself to be no land of milk and honey, but instead unfolds dystopically as an unforgiving, industrially gray "unreal city." Wright, *American Hunger*, 1. Wright expounds upon the detrimental powers of place, noting how, across regions, black Americans enter "No Man's Land" (5) and black life becomes "a sprawling land of unconscious suffering" (7).

70. Wright, *Black Boy*, 147.

71. Thadious Davis notes that Wright's move to the urban North, first Chicago and later New York, gave the aspiring author access to key institutions and opportunities. As the WPA "created a political and social space that allowed a racially restricted group of individuals an opportunity to step out into a public life, a public sphere, free to declare themselves without apology as writers" (148), Wright could devote himself to the life of the writer and be paid for his literary output: "[t]he northern city, while not the imagined utopia in the migratory process, nonetheless results in the forma-tion of a new subjectivity, still mobile and in process but inviolately black. Migration enables a perspective for redefining of self in the context of new spatial geographies, not merely of built and natural environments but primarily of the institutional and organizational structures." Davis, *Southscapes*, 151.

72. See Baker, "On Knowing Our Place"; Jasmine, "'I'd like tuh see.'"

73. Fabre, *Unfinished Quest*, 310; Rowley, *Richard Wright*, 348–53.

74. Fabre, *Unfinished Quest*, 297, 363–64.

75. Wright, "I Choose Exile," RWP Box 6 File 110, 1. I quote from a hand-corrected draft of the essay collected in the Richard Wright Papers at the Beinecke Library.

76. Ibid., 3.

77. Ibid.

78. Ibid., 4.

79. Ibid., 5.

80. Ibid.

81. Wright, *Black Boy*, 228.

82. For an extensive comparative analysis of the varying American colonial practices regarding Native Americans and enslaved blacks, see Patrick Wolfe, "Land, Labor, and Difference."

83. Malcolm X, "With Mrs. Fannie Lou Hamer," 108.

84. Tyner, *Geography of Malcolm X*, 103–25.

85. In *Black Boy*, Wright makes passing reference to varying forms of resistance. With regards to political organizing along racial lines, "I could never win that way; there were too many whites and there were but few blacks"; and "[o]utright rebellion could never win. If I fought openly I would die" (221). Wright's approach appears to cede all social power to what Henri Lefebvre calls "representations of space." Lefebvre makes a distinction between "representations of space" (dictated by the planners, state agents, and designers of space from "above") and "representational spaces" (spaces inhabited by those "from below" and (re)fashioned through practices and engagements with it). Lefebvre, *The Production of Space*, 36–40. See, too, Thacker, *Moving through Modernity*, 20.

86. McDonald, *The Literature Police*, 358. While celebrated in certain circles, *Tell Freedom* was also met by considerable critique by some writers. Upon *Tell Freedom*'s publication, Richard Rive would report to Langston Hughes that numerous intellectuals in South Africa "accuse [Abrahams] of escapism and not providing tangible solutions to any problems"; and his earlier 1953 nonfiction work, *Return to Goli* (Abrahams's report on his brief return to South Africa), was panned in a local political newspaper as "slimy oozings from the pen of that Imperialistic flea." Graham and Walter, *Langston Hughes and the South African* Drum *Generation*, 43; Rive to Hughes, July 30, 1954, LHC 7. Later, Baraka would seize on Abrahams's (and James Baldwin's) privileging of "the individual" in his essay "Brief Reflections on Two Hot Shots." Baraka, *Home*, 116–20.

87. For example, the *Birmingham Post* (England) favorably associated Abrahams's *Mine Boy* with Wright's *Black Boy*. Kiuchi and Hakutani, *Richard Wright*, 218.

88. In addition to Stepto, Dixon makes this claim about Wright's work clear in *Ride Out the Wilderness*. Chinosole likewise argues that Wright's and Abrahams's autobiographies operate within this classic slave narrative tradition. Chinosole, *The African Diaspora and Autobiographics*, 46.

89. Chinosole, *The African Diaspora and Autobiographics*, 39–40.

90. Abrahams, *Tell Freedom*, 44–45; author's ellipses.

91. Chinosole, *The African Diaspora and Autobiographics*, 47.

92. Ibid., 224.

93. Ibid., 233.

94. Ibid., 238.

95. Ibid., 287; author's ellipsis.

96. Wade, *Peter Abrahams*, 127, 132.

97. Ibid., 149.

98. Ibid., 161.

99. See Couzens, *The New African*, 82–124. Chrisman argues that transnational white liberal efforts to suppress black radicalism by creating cultural institutions "paid off" in Abrahams's case: "Abraham's encounter with American literary blackness influenced his decision to pursue a professional vocation as a writer. He openly rejected both Marxism and party political affiliation in the process." Chrisman, "Beyond Black Atlantic," 267.

100. Abrahams, *Tell Freedom*, 192–94 (my emphasis); first and fourth ellipses are author's.

101. Ibid., 197.

102. Ibid., 204–5.

103. Johannesburg rested upon evident racial delineation of residential space, but both municipal and national economy required interracial proximity to service wealthy white enclaves across the cityscape. Whatever rationales segregationists offered, the plush, "modern" white residential areas depended wholly on the putatively "nonmodern" black and coloured sections deprived of the fruits of the "modern" economy they powered. As in the United States, the checkered municipal landscapes across South Africa signaled not the uneven application of modernity but, rather, the very terms of modernity itself.

The fact that Abrahams's reading of his racial geography coincides with "the aspiring" class of the Mayfair neighborhood protesting the arrival of new neighbors from the Vrededorp "slum" that so many of them had escaped brings into view a geography of highly restricted social mobility. This scene reads, then, as a recognition of this fate: spats among the aspiring who may squabble among themselves but still won't enjoy the life of the literally "enlightened."

104. Wright's experience with the practices and philosophies of communist cultural institutions in America was expressed in his contribution to Crossman's *God That Failed*, and in *American Hunger*.

105. Du Bois, *The Souls of Black Folk*, 13. The original version of this essay appeared in *Foreign Affairs* (also 1925) as "Worlds of Color." As Edwards argues, the revision of the piece for *The New Negro* "pushes towards a 'planetary' perspective on labor and imperialism rather than accepting the hierarchy of a center-periphery model." Edwards, "Late Romance," 129.

106. Abrahams, *Tell Freedom*, 199.

107. Ibid.

108. Ibid., 200 (my emphasis).

109. Intellectuals at the center of this transformative influx worked to dissolve the imperial center-periphery model that Said's formulation rests upon, although Said rightly points to the ways that many such intellectuals borrowed and clung to certain European influences, a certain form of universalism, chief among them. For more, see "The Voyage in and the Emergence of Opposition" in Said, *Culture and Imperialism*, 239–61.

110. Edwards, *Practice of Diaspora*, 5.

111. Robinson, *Black Marxism*, 260–65; Makalani, *In the Cause of Freedom*, 195–224.

112. Masilela, "Peter Abrahams in the Modern African World," 35–39.

113. Fabre, *Unfinished Quest*, 308; Robinson, *Black Marxism*, 262–63.

114. Davis, *Southscapes*, 164.

115. Ibid.

116. Stovall, *Paris Noir*, 190.

117. On dynamic places, see Smith and Katz, "Grounding Metaphor," 79.

118. Masilela, "Peter Abrahams," 35.

119. Kiuchi and Hakutani, *Richard Wright*, 235–36, 242.

120. Ibid., 244.

121. Abrahams, *Black Experience*, 84. See also 94. The biography is alternatively entitled *The Coyaba Chronicles*.

122. Masilela, "Peter Abrahams," 35.

123. Ibid.

124. Abrahams, *Black Experience*, 132–33; Abrahams, "The Blacks."

125. Kiuchi and Hakutani, *Richard Wright*, 222.

126. Ibid., 226.

127. Ibid., 236.

128. Ibid., 237; Peter Abrahams to Richard Wright, February 16, 1948, RWP Box 93 Folder 1161, 45.

129. Abrahams to Wright, February 16, 1948, RWP Box 93 Folder 1161, 44.

130. This may have taken place during Wright's brief visit to London but almost certainly in Paris after Abrahams's relocation in June 1948. Kiuchi and Hakutani, *Richard Wright*, 242; Abrahams to Wright, March 23, 1948, RWP Box 93 Folder 1161, 48.

131. Abrahams notes in his second autobiography that he went there to write his autobiography. Abrahams, *Black Experience*, 97–98. The evidence suggests a rewriting.

132. Kiuchi and Hakutani, *Richard Wright*, 242.

133. Abrahams to Wright, July 22, 1947, RWP Box 93 Folder 1161, 28.

134. Abrahams's approach bears out Chrisman's assertion that his "transnational blackness operates as an existential rather than a historical category." Chrisman, "Beyond Black Atlantic and Postcolonial Studies," 254.

135. Veit Erlmann, "'A Feeling of Prejudice'"; Zine Magubane, "The Influence of African-American Cultural Practices on South Africa," 297–319.

136. See "Acts of Betrayal" and "Their Own Histories" in Polsgrove, *Ending British Rule in Africa*, 118–74. Polsgrove argues that not only did Wright inform on George Padmore to American authorities abroad, but Padmore would also sever ties with Abrahams. Padmore wrote to Wright that he considered Abrahams "a man who had sold his political soul for money and fame" (133).

137. Masilela, "Peter Abrahams," 35.

138. On Abrahams's drift from a liberal-critical Marxism to a largely orthodox liberalism, see Wade, "Peter Abrahams," 9.

139. Abrahams, "The Blacks," 42–55.

140. Abrahams, *Black Experience*, 132.

141. Ibid., 145.

142. Ibid., 132–33.

143. Hall, "Race, Articulation, and Societies Structured in Dominance," 38–68. See Edwards's redeployment of Hall's concept of articulation in *The Practice of Diaspora*, 11–12.

144. Chinosole, *The African Diaspora and Autobiographics*, 43, 44. Masilela notes that some of this fusion was partially accomplished by Countee Cullen's use of Romantic poetics in his work. Masilela, "Peter Abrahams," 34.

145. Fabre, *Richard Wright*, 3.

Chapter 3. Remapping the (Black) Nation

1. As Cherryl Walker has argued, this breakdown represents a broad temporal and spatial overview, which does not always reflect the full extent of dispossession that transpired before and after apartheid was formally introduced. Walker, *Landmarked*, 36–50. See also Christopher, *The Atlas of Changing South Africa*, 30–33.

2. Plaatje, *Native Life in South Africa*, 6.

3. Radcliffe, "Liberation at the End of a Pen"; Mangharam, "'The Universal Is the Entire Collection of Particulars.'"

4. Crawford, "Productive Rites of 'Passing,'" 119.

5. Rowell, "'With Bloodstains to Testify,'" 35.

6. Jaji, "Sound Effects," 292.

7. Ibid.

8. Said, "Yeats and Decolonization," 77.

9. Said, *Orientalism*, 58.

10. Ibid., 54.

11. Jameson, "Cognitive Mapping," 347–57.

12. Jaji, "Sound Effects," 291.

13. Redmond, *Drumvoices*, 306.

14. Brown, *A Native of Nowhere*, 114.

15. Nakasa, *The World of Nat Nakasa*, 113–14.

16. Ibid., 115. Nakasa is presumably referring to Baldwin's "The Harlem Ghetto" and "Notes of a Native Son," collected in *Notes of a Native Son*.

17. Nakasa, *The World of Nat Nakasa*, 115.

18. Ibid., 116.

19. Ibid., 117.

20. Ibid., 116.

21. Fellow *Drum* staffer Lewis Nkosi preceded Nakasa into exile in the United States, and his rendering of Harlem and New York City, more broadly, differs from Nakasa's conflicted view. In "Encounter with New York (Part I)," he approximates Nakasa's material representation: New York "was hard and cold in the same way, I suppose, Johannesburg is, except that Johannesburg's cold is tempered by an irresistible African gaiety. . . . It is exasperatingly chaotic, tough, brutal. It also can be the loneliest place in the world." Parting ways with Nakasa, however, he admits having developed "a sneaking affection for New York." Nkosi, *Home and Exile*, 55–56.

22. Raditlhalo, "Writing in Exile," 420. See also Mphahlele, *Afrika My Music*.

23. Attwell, *Rewriting Modernity*, 111–36.

24. Ibid., 128–29.

25. Mphahlele, "Tyranny of Place," 81.

26. Mphahlele, *Down Second Avenue*; *Afrika My Music*.

27. Raditlhalo, "Writing in Exile," 420; Rowell, "'With Bloodstains to Testify,'" 29.

28. Kgositsile, "Wild Conquest," 13.

29. Brown, *A Native of Nowhere*, 155, 39–40.

30. Rowell, "'With Bloodstains to Testify,'" 28.

31. Ibid.

32. Ibid., 29–30.

33. Ibid., 29.

34. Kgositsile, *My Name Is Afrika*, 47.

35. Jaji, "Sound Effects," 288.

36. Mphahlele, "The Tyranny of Place," 83.

37. For more on the regional nature of BAM, see Smethurst, *The Black Arts Movement*.

38. Personal interview with Keorapetse Kgositsile, June 29, 2011, Johannesburg, South Africa.

39. Smethurst, *The Black Arts Movement*, 336.

40. Personal interview with Mongane Wally Serote, June 20, 2011, Johannesburg, South Africa.

41. Ibid.

42. Ibid. Serote and Kgositsile have subsequently had a history of literary cross-referencing. Serote's first novel *To Every Birth Its Blood*, takes its title from a line in Kgositsile's poem "My Name Is Afrika," and Serote's second novel, *Gods of Our Time*, alludes to a line in the same poem that reads "We are the gods of our day." See Kgositsile, *My Name Is Afrika*, 79. The title of Kgositsile's own volume *This Way I Salute You* reproduces the first line of Serote's classic poem, "City Johannesburg." Serote, *Yakhal'inkomo*, 12–13.

43. Chapman, *Southern African Literatures*, 55. Traditional indigenous language oral poetry among the Zulu is called *izibongo,* but, among Kgositsile's Tswana lineage, it is referred to as *mabôkô*; Scheub, *Poem in the Story*, 359 (note 54).

44. Chapman, *Southern African Literatures*, 55.

45. I am suggesting that Kgositsile engages in a similar revision of the oral poem (what Chapman calls the praise song) that Chapman finds in Alfred Temba Qabula's "Praise Poem to FOSATU"; both set the explicit focus of the poems on their contemporaneous moment to support an ongoing political effort. Chapman, *Southern African Literatures*, 57–58.

46. Kgositsile, *My Name Is Afrika*, 77.

47. Ibid., 76.

48. Ibid.

49. Ibid.

50. Ibid., 77.

51. Smethurst, *Black Arts Movement*, 171.

52. Horne, *The Fire This Time*, 3, 54–63; Abu-Lughod, *Race, Space, and Riots*, 218.

53. Henderson, Introduction to *Understanding the New Black Poetry*, 44 (author's emphasis).

54. Nightingale chronicles Johannesburg's early experiments in forced removals and the creation of permanent white racial zones four decades prior to the formal period of apartheid. By 1906, the city council forcibly removed all the black inhabitants from the more centrally located old Kaffir Location to Klipspruit Farm fifteen kilometers southwest of the city. Surrounded by a cordon *non*-sanitaire, the first of Johannesburg's Southwest Townships (years later dubbed Soweto) was "surrounded by fields that would soon receive a billion gallons of fresh sewage each year." Nightingale, *Segregation*, 257.

55. Abu-Lughod, *Race, Space, and Riots*, 200; Massey and Denton, *American Apartheid*, 49–51.

56. Horne, *The Fire This Time*, 3.

57. Kgositsile, "In America and Africa," 17.

58. Robinson elaborates upon the epistemic violence of the term in his classic study, *Black Marxism*. Robinson understands the renaming to be part and parcel of slave owners' "destruction of the African past": "The 'Negro,' that is the color black, was both a negation of Africa and a unity of opposition to white. The construct of Negro, unlike terms 'African,' 'Moor,' or 'Ethiope' suggested no situatedness in time, that is history, or space, that is ethno- or politico-geography. The Negro had no civilization, no cultures, no religions, no history, no place, and finally no humanity that might command consideration" (81).

59. Kgositsile, "In America and Africa," 21.

60. By August 1970, Biko began writing the column "I Write What I Like" under the pseudonym Frank Talk. See Biko, *I Write What I Like*.

61. In *Black Liberation*, his comparative historical study follow-up to *White Supremacy*, Fredrickson notes a shift in assumptions. Whereas in the first book, focusing on "structural and demographic differences" between the two racialized societies led him to a detailed comparison of African Americans and South African coloureds, Fredrickson bases his second study on ideological and political symmetries between

black Americans and black South Africans: "The ideologies of black advancement or liberation that emerged from these discourses were much closer to each other than the external circumstances had led me to expect." Fredrickson, *Black Liberation*, 5.

62. Kgositsile, *My Name Is Afrika*, 70.

63. Baraka, *The Leroi Jones/Amiri Baraka Reader*, 219.

64. Kgositsile, "'With Bloodstains to Testify,'" 34.

65. Kgositsile, *If I Could Sing*, 62.

66. Lindfors, *Comparative Approaches to African Literature*, 102.

67. Césaire, *Notebook of a Return to the Native Land*, 22.

68. Ibid., 43.

69. hooks, "Choosing the Margin as a Space of Radical Openness," in *Yearning*, 145–53.

70. Kgositsile arranges not just words on the page but also poems themselves. In his volume of selected poems, *If I Could Sing*, he suggestively orders poems, visually placing some across the binding from each other, such that "Mandela's Sermon" (19) follows "Brother Malcolm's Echo" (18) with some significance.

71. My emphasis.

72. Kgositsile, *My Name Is Afrika*, 46.

73. Goldberg, *The Racial State*, 109.

74. Chrisman, "Beyond Black Atlantic," 255, 265.

75. Kgositsile, *My Name Is Afrika*, 80–85.

76. Ibid., 80.

77. Ibid., 82.

78. Ibid., 81.

79. Ibid. (author's emphasis)

80. Ibid.

81. As Crawford notes in a similar analysis, "the space 'between' is the shared space: the space of connection, not of separation. The diasporic connections are figured as that which is created in the gap." Crawford, "Productive Rites of 'Passing,'" 115.

82. Shaw, *Memories of the Slave Trade*, 56.

83. Kgositsile, *My Name Is Afrika*, 80.

84. Rowell, "'With Bloodstains to Testify,'" 36; Kgositsile, "Keorapetse Kgositsile Interviewed by Achmat Dangor," 82.

85. De Kock, "South Africa in the Global Imaginary," 268.

86. Ibid., 287.

87. Ibid., 276.

88. Brian Jackson was instrumental in writing the music for this album; however, I restrict my remarks to the lyrics and spoken interventions in the song and thus focus on Scott-Heron's contributions.

89. Both musicians attended Lincoln after Kgositsile's one-year attendance there, and Scott-Heron's enrollment there also was brief. See Scott-Heron's posthumously published *The Last Holiday*.

90. Nielsen, "Choruses for Gil Scott-Heron 1 & 2." For full lyrics to "Johannesburg" and other song-poems, see Scott-Heron's 1990 poetry volume *So Far, So Good*.

91. Jordan, *On Call*, 1–3.

92. For more on Scott-Heron's activism during his time at Lincoln University, see *The Last Holiday*, 133–48.

93. In *Something Torn and New*, Ngũgĩ wa Thiong'o frames the processes of geographic renaming through colonial mapping as the implantation of European memory on non-European soil; for example, New York, New Brunswick, King Williamstown, Grahamstown, etc. (7–10).

94. The term is Sibley's in his *Geographies of Exclusion*.

95. See also Kgositsile's more recent poetry that maintains its geographic focus and language: "No Boundaries," "No Serenity Here," and "Letter from Havana" in *Beyond Words*.

96. Kgositsile, "Crossing Borders without Leaving," 7.

97. Ibid., 10.

98. Ibid. (my emphasis).

99. Ibid. (author's emphasis).

100. Lefebvre, *The Production of Space*, 86 (author's emphasis).

101. de Kock, "South Africa in the Global Imaginary," 270, 276 (author's emphasis).

102. Kruger, "Black Atlantics, White Indians, and Jews," 113 (author's emphasis).

103. Kgositsile, "Interview with Victor Dlamini."

104. Ibid.; personal interview with Keorapetse Kgositsile, June 29, 2011, Johannesburg, South Africa.

105. Crawford, "Productive Rites of 'Passing,'" 119.

Chapter 4. Cultivating Correspondences; or, Other Gestures of Belonging

1. Nixon, *Homelands, Harlem and Hollywood*, 112. Can Themba, who fled to Swaziland and remained there until his death in 1968, is an exception to this rule.

2. Jamaican-born Cliff arrived in the United States in her youth and studied in England, as well, but she has spent most of her time in the United States. Her presence in the United States pushes against narrow constructions of what is "American" and reminds us that "African American" is a designation that has always included more than multigenerational, U.S.-born black peoples. I employ "African American writer" in the broad sense for Cliff not to erase her origins but to position her within a social and literary tradition she has engaged over the years.

3. The phrase is from Jordan's volume of collected poems, *Directed by Desire*.

4. Lionnet, "Geographies of Pain," in *Postcolonial Representations*, 108.

5. I read Lionnet's "Geographies of Pain" as a forerunner of the more transactional analyses that she advances in her jointly edited (with Shih) volume, *Minor Transnationalism*.

6. For a correction to the narrative that Head was the offspring of a black stable hand and a wealthy white woman, whose family committed her to an insane asylum in response to her illicit affair, see Birch, "The Birch Family," 10.

7. For these and other biographical details, see Eilersen, *Bessie Head*.

8. Head was marginal to the black South African refugee community in the area, whose forms of African nationalism Head resisted after her stint with the Pan-Africanist Congress while in South Africa. Eilersen, *Bessie Head*, 104.

9. Cullinan, *Imaginative Trespasser*, 81.

10. Nixon, *Homelands, Harlem and Hollywood*, 102–3.

11. Eilersen makes the point that "Serowe was not nearly as isolated from the outside world as [Head] had [initially] supposed." Eilersen, *Bessie Head*, 83. Feeling herself a perpetual outsider, Head often kept to herself, especially during and following her two mental breakdowns. Referring to her residence as a "quiet backwater," she led a relatively secluded—at times, lonely—writer's existence, which she shared with her son, Howard. Yet Head sometimes participated in and around the local Swaneng cooperative project, spearheaded by dissident South African Patrick van Rensburg.

12. Eilersen, *Bessie Head*, 77.

13. Eilersen distinguishes between three classes of exiles in Botswana: trained freedom fighters, political and nonpolitical refugees, and village refugees from Angola and the Caprivi Strip. Eilersen, *Bessie Head*, 103.

14. Nixon, *Homelands, Harlem and Hollywood*, 113.

15. Menon, "A Local Cosmopolitan," 131–58.

16. Ibid., 135.

17. Ibid., 140 (author's emphasis).

18. Without a passport, Head journeyed to the United States on special travel documents, and after she received citizenship in Botswana, she ventured on brief trips to Germany, Denmark, Nigeria, the Netherlands, and Australia. See Eilersen, *Bessie Head*, 242–346.

19. Lewis, *Living on a Horizon*, 73.

20. Head, "Writing Out of Southern Africa," in *A Woman Alone*, 95. Note that Head's "national" is a much more local/regional construction than any identitarian alignment with a nation-state.

21. These texts, among many others, are collected as part of the Bessie Head Papers.

22. Head, "Notes from a Quiet Backwater," in *A Woman Alone*, 77.

23. Glissant, *Poetics of Relation*, 34.

24. O'Brien, *Against Normalization*, 217. Numerous critics have advanced this claim of Head's literary self-fashioning through her epistolary writing. On Head's "self-production," see Lewis, *Living on a Horizon*, 48–63. Gagiano argues for reading Head's letters as autobiography in "Writing a Life," 8–33. Lewis likewise makes this point in *Living on a Horizon*, 64. In "Making a 'Home' Elsewhere," Daymond suggests that we read Head's letters as texts that redefine (and destabilize) the meaning of "home."

25. Khumalo, "Ekukhanyeni Letter-Writers," 115.

26. Barber also underscores the ways that letter writers were "assembling and consolidating selves" through writing, evincing a self-awareness of their subjectivity

in the eyes of the modern colonial state. See Barber, Introduction in *Africa's Hidden Histories*, 9.

27. Head, for example was demanding of her interlocutors' reciprocal letter writing. Beyond this, some scholars have argued for important distinctions among Head's letters. Following François Jost's terms, O'Brien distinguishes between Head's *lettres-confidence* and *lettres-drame*; O'Brien, *Against Normalization*, 219. Lewis, meanwhile, notes two modes that Head's letters alternated between: "amicable, grateful, and obliging," on the one hand, and "'paranoid,' a position of extreme defensiveness," on the other; Lewis, *Living on a Horizon*, 48–49.

28. Khumalo, "Ekukhanyeni Letter-Writers," 115.

29. The letter also does not always escape or contravene the logic or mechanisms of the state—i.e., state interception and censorship. Head regularly worried that her letters and packages would get read and/or confiscated as a budding political activist in South Africa and as a marginal but surveilled refugee in Botswana.

30. O'Brien, *Against Normalization*, 227.

31. Dubey, *Black Women Novelists and the Nationalist Aesthetic*, 11, 12.

32. Head's problems with nationalism surface explicitly in *When Rain Clouds Gather* and *A Question of Power*. The latter novel, in particular, gives voice to concerns that black power politics could decimate the poor, create new forms of exclusivity, and mobilize brutalizing gender politics.

33. Giovanni to Head, February 17, 1974, KMM 75 BHP 15. (The Bessie Head Papers are cited as KMM BHP.) She registers in this letter her objections to Eldridge Cleaver's *Soul on Ice*.

34. Morrison has remarked upon black women writers' efforts to write beyond the mandates of a white male presence and hegemonic gaze—a tradition that includes Toni Cade Bambara, Alice Walker, Michelle Cliff, and Morrison herself. For two recent commentaries by Morrison, see "Sheer Good Fortune" (October 16, 2012) and "Reading the Writing" (March 7, 2013). Feminist critics have persuasively argued that Head's work reflects the gendered terms of Njabulo Ndebele's concept of the ordinary in South African literature. See Daymond, "Inventing Gendered Traditions," 223–40.

35. Consider, for example, the authors' editorial work in different capacities and different periods: Morrison's editorship at Random House, Walker's cofounding (with then-partner Robert Allen) of Wild Trees Press, Cliff's coediting (with her partner, Adrienne Rich) of the journal *Sinister Wisdom*, and Giovanni's editing of a volume of black women's writing, *Night Comes Softly*.

36. Moore, "The Bessie Head–Langston Hughes Correspondence, 1960–1961."

37. Eilersen, *Bessie Head*, 85. Head featured Kerina in her essay "The Woman from America" (1966 in *New Statesman*). With Kerina in mind two years later, Head penned a disquisition on revolutions sweeping across the African continent, where she posited God as a black American woman, entitled "God and the Underdog: Thoughts on the Rise of Africa" (1968 in *New African*). Both are collected in Head, *A Woman Alone*.

38. Walker, *In Search of Our Mothers' Gardens*, xi–xii.

39. Eilersen, *Bessie Head*, 278–79.

40. Head's work has been the subject of some astute queer readings; see Desai, "Out in Africa"; Munro, *South Africa and the Dream of Love to Come*, 144–69. The driving questions of my study about race, space, and representation do not permit me to fully address the matter of Head on sexuality, but it is a critical enterprise well worth engaging. It is important to resist salacious speculation on Head's sexuality, but there remains a general scholarly reluctance to wrestle with the knotty roots of her sexual depictions. Head did denounce the "drift towards lesbianism and indiscriminate love-making" and expressed her repulsion for gay men to some individuals—actions disconcertingly at odds with her radical liberatory vision. See Coreen Brown, *The Creative Vision of Bessie Head*, 194; Holzinger, "Conversations and Consternations with B Head," 51–54. But it is worth weighing this against some potentially complicating factors, including Head's befriending of some openly queer authors and—as we will see later in the chapter—Head's professed identification with characters like Clare Savage (from Michelle Cliff's *Abeng*), whose tomboyish ways are accompanied by queer desires.

41. In an unpublished letter dated August 10, 1974, Giovanni mentions that Head is Margaret Walker's "favorite writer, barring none, on or from the African continent. I gave her your latest book" (KMM 75 BHP 22), which would have been *A Question of Power*.

42. Morrison makes these claims in two separate interviews. In a 1986 interview with Christina Davis, Morrison identifies Head and Gloria Naylor as two black women writers whose works do not hang on confrontations with white male characters: "[T]he confrontation between black women and white men is not very important, it doesn't center the text. There are more important [confrontations] for them and their look, their gaze of the text is unblinking and wide and very steady. It's not narrow, it's very probing and it does not flinch." Morrison, *Conversations with Toni Morrison*, 230. In a 1994 interview with Claudia Dreifus, Morrison names several African and Caribbean writers—Chinua Achebe, Camara Laye, Léopold Sédar Senghor, Aimé Césaire, and Bessie Head—to note how "[t]hey did not explain their black world. Or clarify it. Or justify it. White writers had always taken white centrality for granted. They inhabited their world in a central position and everything nonwhite was 'other.' These African writers took their blackness as central and the whites were the 'other.'" Morrison, *Toni Morrison: Conversations*, 102.

43. Eilersen, *Bessie Head*, 341.

44. Walker, *Her Blue Body Everything We Know*, 215. (The volume contains Walker's first four volumes of poetry along with previously uncollected poems.) In "From an Interview," Walker listed several African writers "I *hope* to be influenced by" noting specific texts, including Okot p'Bitek's "Song of Lawino," Elechi Ahmadi's *The Concubine*, Camara Laye's *The Radiance of the King*, and Head's *Maru*: "These writers," she observes, "do not seem to be afraid of fantasy, of myth and mystery. Their work deepens one's comprehension of life by going beyond the bounds of realism." Walker, *In Search*, 259.

45. Walker, *Her Blue Body Everything We Know*, 267.

46. Ibrahim, "The Problematic Relationship," 202.

47. AWP, Box 171 Folder 18.

48. In an unpublished letter from September 25, 1981, Cliff informed Head that, at a reading in Detroit, she read to the audience "The Collector of Treasures," alongside her work: "[T]he "response to your story was overwhelming—women wanted to know where you were, how they could get the book, etc." KMM 313 BHP 1.

49. Young, *Haunting Capital*, 13.

50. O'Brien, *Against Normalization*, 220–22.

51. As Lewis notes, while Head "certainly shared many African-American women writers' concerns with gendered locations in the context of white racism," she also resisted categories and analytical frameworks that she believed flattened complex human experience. Lewis, *Living on a Horizon*, 71–72. She thus explicitly eschewed the formulations of feminists and black nationalists while, at times, nevertheless developing literary scenarios and analyses that aligned with their respective broader platforms.

52. Head to Morrison, January 5, 1976, KMM 42 BHP 2.

53. Morrison to Head, January 21, 1976, KMM 42 BHP 3.

54. O'Brien interprets the exchange as Head's unfortunate misinterpretation of the "formality and dignity" in Morrison's response to Head's inquiry. O'Brien, *Against Normalization*, 230–34; Eilersen, *Bessie Head*, 212.

55. Eilersen, *Bessie Head*, 184.

56. Giovanni, blurb on back cover of American edition of *Maru*.

57. Head to Giovanni, n/d 1973, KMM 75 BHP 21.

58. Ibid. (author's emphasis), and first two ellipses are author's.

59. Ibid.

60. Giovanni to Head, December 4, 1973, KMM 75 BHP 12.

61. Head to Giovanni, February 19, 1975, KMM 75 BHP 27.

62. See Cullinan, *Imaginative Trespasser*; Vigne, *A Gesture of Belonging*.

63. Lewis, *Living on a Horizon*, 58.

64. Walker to Head, September 16, 1974, KMM 76 BHP 1.

65. Nixon, *Homelands, Harlem and Hollywood*, 117.

66. Walker to Head, February 28, 1976, KMM 76 BHP 19.

67. Walker to Head, n/d, KMM 76 BHP 11; Head to Walker, October 28, 1976, AWP, Box 6 Folder 4; Head to Walker, December 22, 1974, KMM 76 BHP 6 / AWP, Box 5 Folder 4. The letters from Bessie Head may also be found in the Alice Walker Papers (cited as AWP), housed at Emory University's Manuscripts, Archives, and Rare Book Library; where the letters overlap, I cite both archives.

68. Walker to Head, December 6, 1974, KMM 76 BHP 5.

69. Head to Walker, January 26, 1975, AWP, Box 85 Folder 10.

70. After quitting the Pan-Africanist Congress and leaving South Africa, Head repudiated black or African nationalism, couching her early activism as youthful indiscretion and a sign of South Africa's desperate circumstances. She understood her writing to explore the freeing of the human mind from oppressive thought. Less

noted by scholars are the ways that Head's positions still ascribe to some black nationalist precepts.

71. Walker, *The Third Life of Grange Copeland*, 229.

72. Ibid., Afterword, 318.

73. Ibid., 113.

74. Dixon, *Ride Out the Wilderness*, 97–98.

75. As Dubey notes, Grange achieves the status of landowner only via his exploitation and self-sacrifice of Josie. Dubey, *Black Women Novelists*, 110.

76. Thadious Davis, *Southscapes*, 350.

77. Eilersen, *Bessie Head*, 98, 143–44, 156, 165.

78. Ibid., 165.

79. Quickly recognizing the literary possibilities from her work at the Radisele farm, Head wrote Randolph Vigne in a letter, "I could get all I needed on this farm in concentrated form. It's an experimental venture of old, ancient methods of farming and the very new. A good book, published, may be an open sesame to more creative, constructive work." See Vigne, *A Gesture of Belonging*, 21.

80. Head, *When Rain Clouds Gather*, 17.

81. Lewis, *Living on a Horizon*, 145.

82. Head, *A Question of Power*, 162, 158.

83. Although guided by more noble intentions than his western cohort, Gilbert in *When Rain Clouds Gather* does make questionable Eurocentric assumptions, but he also eventually corrects his approach to the villagers, respects the safeguards of tribal land tenure, and solicits local input from village elders and the crop-tending women. In *A Question of Power*, the deeply communitarian Eugene stands in sharp contrast to the condescending, racist Camilla, who makes the experimental farm appear to Elizabeth "the most miserable place on earth" (76).

84. Graham, *Land and Nationalism in Fictions from Southern Africa*, 60, 90; Fielding, "Agriculture and Healing," 20.

85. In Paustian's analysis of Head's gardens, universalism does not precede cooperative farming but rather proceeds from the collective engagement. See Paustian, "Narratives of African Improvement," 179–80.

86. Eilersen, *Bessie Head*, 165; Fielding, "Agriculture and Healing," 18; Sample, "Space," 42.

87. Beard, "Bessie Head's *A Question of Power*," 272.

88. Head, *A Question of Power*, 206.

89. Walker to Head, June 23, 1976, KMM 76 BHP 24.

90. See Walker's early poetry in *Once*, republished in Walker, *Her Blue Body Everything We Know*, 1–150. In her Steve Biko Memorial lecture in 2010, she did make some historical references to African revolutionary struggle but demonstrated little of the historical knowledge about South Africa that she would have gained from Head. See Walker, 11th Annual Steve Biko Memorial Lecture, September 9, 2010, University of Cape Town, Cape Town, South Africa.

91. Head to Walker, August 1, 1976, AWP, Box 6 Folder 3.

92. Walker to Head, September 9, 1976, KMM 76 BHP 27; author's ellipsis.

93. Head to Walker, June 23, 1977, AWP, Box 6 Folder 7; author's ellipses.

94. Head's biographer, Gillian Stead Eilersen, notes that the face-to-face encounter was not satisfactory for Head, owing in part to her disapproval of Walker's sexuality, but there seems to be room for differing interpretations on this point. Head knew about Walker's sexuality long before their meeting; moreover, Head's final letter to Walker, written upon her return to Botswana, politely emphasizes her "great pleasure" in their meeting. Eilersen interprets another portion of the same letter raising Head's weight as Head being cross about Walker's alleged bias against overweight people. Although this seems unpersuasive, Eilersen reports that Head complained to others about Walker in different letters. Eilersen, *Bessie Head*, 250.

95. Cliff to Head, September 25, 1981, KMM 313 BHP 1. She adds in a different letter that she has been passing around Head's work to fellow writers while at a writer's colony. Cliff to Head, May 19, 1984, KMM 313 BHP 9.

96. Adisa, "Journey into Speech," 275–76.

97. In a later letter, Cliff notes to Head that she "is in the process of joining together my identity and attempting to become whole. As Toni Cade Bambara says, 'wholeness is no trifling matter'—indeed." Cliff to Head, May 19, 1984, KMM 313 BHP 9.

98. Raiskin, "The Art of History: An Interview with Michelle Cliff," 60.

99. Head to Cliff, October 13, 1981, KMM 313 BHP 2.

100. Ibid.

101. Ibid.

102. Cliff, *Claiming an Identity*, 20–21.

103. Ibid., 52–53, 55.

104. Ibid., 53.

105. Ibid. See also Gourdine, *The Difference Place Makes*, 58–59.

106. Cliff, *Claiming an Identity*, 56–57.

107. Nair identifies in Cliff's work the colonial disruption of the natural order as well as nature's subversion of human designs (local and imperial) to control their environment. See Nair, *Pathologies of Paradise*, 44–45.

108. Head to Cliff, February 21, 1983, KMM 313 BHP 5.

109. Cliff to Head, May 5, 1983, KMM 313 BHP 6.

110. Head to Cliff, May 20, 1983, KMM 313 BHP 7.

111. Head to Cliff, May 7, 1984, KMM 313 BHP 8.

112. Cliff to Head, May 19, 1984, KMM 313 BHP 9.

113. Cliff to Head, August 10, 1985, KMM 313 BHP 11.

114. Mudimbe, *The Invention of Africa*, 1.

115. Western, *Outcast Cape Town*, 31–32; Dooling, *Slavery, Emancipation and Colonial Rule*, 16–18.

116. The political dimensions of the pastoral have been lucidly examined by Williams in *The Country and the City*. Said followed up by highlighting the colonial worldliness of the seemingly isolated English country estate in *Culture and Imperialism*.

A variety of other scholars have articulated the profoundly political nature of the landscape and the pastoral in South Africa. See Pratt, "Scratches on the Face of the Country"; Coetzee, *White Writing*; Barnard, *Apartheid and Beyond*; Wenzel, "The Pastoral Promise"; Klopper, "Politics of the Pastoral"; Robolin, "Properties of Whiteness." For the pastoral in early-twentieth-century African American poetry, see Honey's Introduction in *Shadowed Dreams*.

117. See, in particular, "To Name Is to Possess" and "In History" in Kincaid, *My Garden (Book)*.

118. For example, Shockley outlines the raced and gendered contours of Black Renaissance poet Anne Spencer's seemingly "raceless" and neutral "nature poetry" inspired by her Virginia garden. See chapter four in Shockley, *Renegade Poetics*, 121–44. Nair charts the thorny entanglements of human history and nature across gardens featured in Caribbean literature, which remains attentive to the region's imposed British botanical, political, and economic orders as well as its remaking. See chapter one in Nair, *Pathologies of Paradise*, 23–48. Stouck likewise stresses the ambivalence of gardening and horticulture in the Caribbean postcolony: both a sign of colonial conquest and a tool for grounding one's identity. See Stouck, "Gardening in the Diaspora."

119. Helphand, *Defiant Gardens*, 1. Helphand emphasizes the restorative properties of gardening in spaces of incarceration, including Nelson Mandela's garden on Robben Island. Mandela conceived of gardening as "an antidote to my intellectual labors," but it was also a means of exercising his will in a site of dispossession: "A garden was one of the few things in prison that one could control. To plant a seed, watch it grow, to tend it and then harvest it, offered a simple but enduring satisfaction. The sense of being a custodian of this small patch of earth offered a small taste of freedom." Mandela also understood gardening as a "metaphor for certain aspects of my life," including how "a leader must take responsibility for what he cultivates." Mandela, *Long Walk to Freedom*, 426.

120. Walker, *In Search of Our Mothers' Gardens*, 233, 238.

121. Ibid., 241.

122. Ibid.; first ellipsis is author's.

123. Wall, *Worrying the Line*, 212.

124. Dixon, *Ride Out the Wilderness*, 95–96.

125. In this section, I restrict my analysis to Head, Walker, and Cliff because land and gardens surface explicitly in their epistolary exchanges. But Morrison's *Sula*, which Head read, foregrounds land ownership at the outset: The black community lives in the hills called the Bottom due to a white slaveowner's deceitful renaming to keep the fertile flatland of the valley for himself. *Tar Baby* also raises the geopolitics of land possession and greenhouse horticulture on the Caribbean property of Valerian Street.

126. Gourdine, *The Difference Place Makes*, 58–59.

127. Gandhi, *Affective Communities*. Although Gandhi's use of "affective communities" and "elected affinities" explores relations across the boundaries separating

colonizer and colonized, this capacious vocabulary extends to lateral relationships between different subjugated communities.

128. See chapter four in Nixon, *Homelands, Harlem and Hollywood*, 101–30; chapter four in Perera, *No Country*, 122–63. In her study of proletarian literature, Perera astutely frames the socialized labor practices in Head's represented villages as the basis of international solidarities and imaginings of community.

129. Coundouriotis, "An 'Internationalism of the Planted Earth,'" 23.

130. Ibid., 32.

131. Ibid, 33.

132. On jumping scale, see Neil Smith, "Contours of a Spatialized Politics," and Tyner, *The Geography of Malcolm X*.

133. Glissant, *Poetics of Relation*, 67.

134. Email from Linda-Susan Beard, July 1, 2014. See also Eilersen, *Bessie Head*, 132.

135. O'Brien, *Against Normalization*, 220.

136. Perera, *No Country*, 131.

137. Head, *A Question of Power*, 206.

138. Cliff, *Claiming an Identity*, 41.

139. Thorsson, *Women's Work*, 23. Thorsson's study of community-forming labor focuses on cultural nationalism, as many of the African American women's writing she examines explicitly raise the nation as a category (3).

Chapter 5. Constructive Engagements

1. Nesbitt, *Race for Sanctions*, 1; von Eschen, *Race against Empire*, 61.

2. See Campbell, *Songs of Zion*.

3. Meriwether, *Proudly We Can Be Africans*, 239.

4. Nesbitt, *Race for Sanctions*, 74, 103.

5. Randall Robinson, quoted in Nesbitt, *Race for Sanctions*, 104.

6. Chester Crocker, quoted in Massie, *Loosing the Bonds*, 485.

7. Massie, *Loosing the Bonds*, 473–522.

8. I am also referencing the work of Lubiano on black common sense. Although I examine other ways of imagining black collectivity, much of these ways of imagining were quite influenced by or gave expression to black nationalist thought that is Lubiano's focus. See Lubiano, "Black Nationalism and Black Common Sense."

9. Brutus, *Poetry and Protest*, 128, 160–63.

10. Viljoen, *Richard Rive*, 180.

11. Rive, *Writing Black*, 114.

12. Rive to Langston Hughes, n/d, Langston Hughes Collection, 56.

13. Farred, *Midfielder's Moment*, 42.

14. Rive, *"Buckingham Palace," District Six*, 197–98.

15. Ibid., 191.

16. Farred, *Midfielder's Moment*, 44 (author's emphasis).

17. The class notes of Jim Kornish comprise part of a file on Richard Rive (henceforward referenced as RRP) at the National English Literary Museum in Grahamstown,

South Africa. They were procured by researcher Kathleen A. Hauke and donated to NELM upon her passing.

18. Jim Kornish, class notes (Harvard University), March 3, 1987, RRP 70.

19. Ibid., n/d, RRP 22.

20. Ibid., May 22, 1987, RRP 4.

21. Ibid., April 21, 1987, RRP 121, and April 23, 1987, RRP 166; Sepamla, *The Soweto I Love*, 17; Hughes, *Collected Poems*, 32–33.

22. Rive, *Writing Black*, 23. Rive's identification with his environment in contrast to Hughes's overlooks the fact that his mentor was tightly associated with Harlem far more than he was the abstract jungle of primitivism.

23. Ibid., 185.

24. Ibid., 104.

25. Both Rive's admirers and detractors noted the writer's "self-inflation," according to Viljoen, *Richard Rive*, 54.

26. See, for example, nightly news coverage of South Africa across the 1980s; Stevie Wonder's "It's Wrong (Apartheid)" from his *In Square Circle* album and Artists United against Apartheid's *Sun City* album, both from 1985; and Adrian Piper's 1986 *Vanilla Nightmare* Series, among others.

27. See, for example, Omond, *The Apartheid Handbook*, and Mermelstein, *The Anti-Apartheid Reader*.

28. For example, Wicomb's *You Can't Get Lost in Cape Town*, Tlali's *Soweto Stories*, and Ndebele's *Fools and Other Stories* appeared in the United States in the mid to late 1980s. For an incisive critique of the association of black (South African) writing, especially penned by women, with autobiography, see Wicomb, "Interview with Eva Hunter," 79–96.

29. Some of their characterizations of hunger are strikingly similar. Consider, for example, Wright's passage: "But this new hunger baffled me, scared me, made me angry and insistent." Wright, *Black Boy*, 13. Compare to Mathabane's rendering: "Gradually, I came to accept hunger as a constant companion. But this new hunger was different. It filled me with hatred, confusion, helplessness, hopelessness, anxiety, loneliness, selfishness and a cynical attitude." Mathabane, *Kaffir Boy*, 67.

30. Ibid., 67–68, 78.

31. Ibid., 79–80.

32. Ibid., 100.

33. Jordan, *On Call*, 1–3.

34. Ibid., 17.

35. Ibid., 18.

36. de Veaux, *Warrior Poet*, 350.

37. Lorde, "Apartheid U.S.A.," 27, 28. I am citing from the essay in Lorde's *A Burst of Light*, published two years later. This essay was also reproduced in *Art against Apartheid*.

38. Ibid., 34–35.

39. Ibid., 36.

40. Mbembe, "Aesthetics of Superfluity," 43.

41. Alexander, *African Diasporic Women's Narratives*, 44.

42. Lorde, *A Burst of Light*, 132–33; also quoted in Alexander, *African Diasporic Women's Narratives*, 45.

43. Alexander, *African Diasporic Women's Narratives*, 45–46.

44. For two brief unpublished histories of this collective, see Gloria I. Joseph, "A Brief History of SISA (Sisterhood in Support of Sisters in South Africa)," November 23, 1984, and Gloria I. Joseph and Audre Lorde, "'In Memory of Our Children's Blood': Sisterhood and South African Women," n/d, Audre Lorde Papers (henceforward noted as ALP), housed at the Spelman College Archives.

45. Gloria I. Joseph to Founding Mothers, "Dear Founding Mothers," December 10, 1991, ALP.

46. de Veaux, *Warrior Poet*, 280.

47. Lorde, *A Burst of Light*, 100–6.

48. Audre Lorde to Miriam Tlali, "Dear Miriam Tlali," n/d, ALP; Ellen Kuzwayo to "All My Overseas Friends," December 13, 1985, ALP.

49. Michelle Cliff to Audre Lorde, October 30, 1981, ALP. For antiapartheid materials Cliff sent Lorde, see the Audre Lorde Papers. For Head's full letter, see Bessie Head to Michelle Cliff, October 13, 1981, Bessie Head Papers, KMM 313 BHP 2.

50. Lorde, *The Collected Poems of Audre Lorde*, 337, 357–58, 383, 403–6, 408, and 430–31.

51. Baraka and Baraka, *Confirmation*, 70; Clifton, *Next*, 16, 17; Sanchez, *Shake Loose My Skin*, 75–76; Jordan, "A Song for Soweto," 93; Cortez, *Coagulations*, 101; Derricotte, *Captivity*, 55; Elizabeth Alexander, *The Venus Hottentot*, 50.

52. Clifton, *Next*, 17, 19; Osbey, *All Saints*, 11–14; Sanchez, *Shake Loose My Skin*, 51–53; Dent, *Blue Lights and River Songs*, 30.

53. Cortez, *Coagulations*, 44–47; Jacques, "Soweto Remembrance," 69; Reagon, "Chile Your Waters," 164.

54. Clarke, *Living as a Lesbian*, 75. See also "living as a lesbian" (55) and "an exile I have loved" (81). Citation of the poem is from the original Firebrand Books edition, but reprinted with permission from author and publishers of reissue: © 2014, Sinister Wisdom/A Midsummer Night's Press.

55. Weaver, *Water Song*, 62–63. Weaver has since outlined the context of the poem: "I wrote that poem during my journeyman period as a factory worker in Baltimore. A cop who was also in my unit of the Army Reserves . . . explained to me once that his night stick was his 'nigger knocker,' and he tried to surprise me once by jumping out at me in a 7Eleven where I used to stop on the way to work, armed with my poetry. I saw a photo of miners in S. Africa lined up for work and was inspired to write the poem." Email communication, June 28, 2014. Citation of the poem is from the original University of Virginia edition, but reprinted with permission from author and publishers of reissue: © 2000, Sarabande Books.

56. Harper, *Healing Song for the Inner Ear*, 68, 83–84, 85–87.

57. Kent, *A Life of Gwendolyn Brooks*, 241.

58. Brooks, "Introduction," 11, 13.

59. Brooks, *Blacks*, 490–91. Brooks also briefly mentions Kgositsile in *Winnie*, 4.

60. Brooks, *Blacks*, 500, 507–9, and *Winnie*.

61. Thompson, *A History of South Africa*, 228–40; Sales, "Making South Africa Ungovernable."

62. Brooks, *Blacks*, 507.

63. Ibid.

64. Ibid., 508–9.

65. Ibid., 509.

66. Melhem, *Heroism in the New Black Poetry*, 22.

67. Ibid., 23.

68. My emphasis.

69. Brooks, "kitchenette building," in *Blacks*, 20.

70. Carby, "Multicultural Wars," 14. Brooks's implied possible association between Johannesburg and Chicago is not unique. Carl Nightingale's multicity study of segregation focuses on the racially segregated histories of Johannesburg and Chicago, as well as other cities like colonial Calcutta, in *Segregation*.

71. Thanks to Maaja Stewart for bringing the issue of proximity in this poem to my attention.

72. Jordan addressed the state's cynical rhetorical acts in "Problems of Language in a Democratic State" in *On Call*, 27–36.

73. Crockett-Smith, *Civil Rites*, 52.

74. Cliff, *The Land of Look Behind*, 99. See also *Art against Apartheid*, 78.

75. Ibid.

76. Ibid., 99–100 (author's emphasis).

77. Ibid., 100.

78. Anderson, *Imagined Communities*, 22. I draw upon Anderson's evocative phrasing without relying on his term "imagined community" for reasons articulated by Felipe Smith in "The African Diaspora as Imagined Community."

79. Winichakul, quoted in Anderson, *Imagined Communities*, 173.

80. Nwankwo, "Langston Hughes and the Translation of Nicholas Guillén's Afro-Cuban Culture and Language," 60; Edwards, *The Practice of Diaspora*, 116.

81. See J. B. Harley, "Deconstructing the Map."

82. Césaire, *Notebook of a Return to the Native Land*, 43.

83. Lubiano, "Black Nationalism and Black Common Sense," 232.

84. See Rive, "Taos in Harlem," 39. The short published piece is based on a document that Rive submitted in partial completion of his master's degree at Columbia University Teacher's College. In the initial paper, Hughes responds to Rive's inquiry about soul by marking it in very culturally specific terms. See "An Interview with Langston Hughes and Arna Bontemps," Richard Rive Papers, 99.26.12, 6.

85. Neser, *Stranger at Home*, 208.

86. Ibid., 211.

87. Stephens, "Black Transnationalism and the Politics of National Identity," 605; Edwards, *The Practice of Diaspora*, 243; Chrisman, "Beyond Black Atlantic and Postcolonial Studies," 264.

88. Lorde, "Apartheid U.S.A.," in *A Burst of Light*, 36.

89. McKittrick, *Demonic Grounds*, xiv.

90. Ibid.

91. Clarke and Thomas, Introduction to *Globalization and Race*, 4.

92. Said, *The World, the Text, and the Critic*, 18–19.

93. Both Said and Wahneema Lubiano would have us keep in mind the risks of redeploying the exclusionary filial structure or reproducing the patriarchal family narrative. See Said, *The World, the Text, and the Critic*, 19–23; Lubiano, "Black Nationalism and Black Common Sense," 244–45. In the context of black transnationalism, it can certainly lead to paternalistic political stances, when democratic institutions or orientations are not safeguarded.

94. For more on the non-inevitability of cross-cultural linkages, see Patterson and Kelley, "Unfinished Migrations," 20.

95. See Hartman, *Lose Your Mother*, 76–100.

96. See Patterson and Kelley, "Unfinished Migrations"; Edwards, *The Practice of Diaspora*. I remain grateful to Marlon Bailey and Lyndon Phillip for raising labor in relation to diaspora years ago.

97. See Edwards's essay, "The Uses of Diaspora," which points to the intellectual work of this concept over time.

Bibliography

Abrahams, Peter. *The Black Experience in the 20th Century: An Autobiography and Meditation*. Bloomington: Indiana University Press, 2000.

———. "The Blacks." In *An African Treasury: Articles/Essays/Stories/Poems by Black Africans*, edited by Langston Hughes. New York: Crown Publishers, 1960. 42–55.

———. *Mine Boy*. London: Faber and Faber, 1946.

———. *The Path of Thunder*. New York: Harper, 1948.

———. *Return to Goli*. London: Faber and Faber, 1953.

———. *Tell Freedom*. London: Faber and Faber, 1954.

———. *Wild Conquest*. London: Faber and Faber, 1951.

Abu-Lughod, Janet. *Race, Space, and Riots in Chicago, New York, and Los Angeles*. Oxford: Oxford University Press, 2007.

Adams, Paul C., Stephen Hoelscher, and Karen E. Till, eds. *Textures of Place: Exploring Humanist Geographies*. Minneapolis: University of Minnesota Press, 2001.

Adisa, Opal Palmer. "Journey into Speech—A Writer between Two Worlds: An Interview with Michelle Cliff." *African American Review* 28.2 (Summer 1994): 273–81.

Alexander, Elizabeth. *The Venus Hottentot*. Charlottesville: University of Virginia Press, 1990.

Alexander, Simone A. James. *African Diasporic Women's Narratives: Politics of Resistance, Survival, and Citizenship*. Gainesville: University of Florida Press, 2014.

Allen, Robert. *Black Awakening in Capitalist America*. Garden City: Anchor, 1970.

Anderson, Benedict. *Imagined Communities: Reflections on the Origins and Spread of Nationalism*, rev. ed. London: Verso, 1991.

Ardener, Shirley. "The Partition of Space." In *Gender Space Architecture: An Interdisciplinary Introduction*, edited by Jane Rendell, Barbara Penner, and Iain Borden. Architext Series. New York: Routledge, 2000. 112–17.

Artists United against Apartheid. *Sun City*. © 1985 from EMI Manhattan Records. Album.

Attwell, David. *J. M. Coetzee: South Africa and the Politics of Writing*. Berkeley: University of California Press, 1993.

———. *Rewriting Modernity: Studies in Black South African Literary History*. Athens: Ohio University Press, 2005.

Avilez, GerShun. "Housing the Black Body: Value, Domestic Space, and Segregation Narratives." *African American Review* 42.1 (2008): 135–47.

Baker, Houston A., Jr. "On Knowing Our Place." In *Richard Wright: Critical Perspectives Past and Present*, edited by Henry Louis Gates Jr. and Kwame Anthony Appiah. New York: Amistad, 1993. 200–25.

Baldwin, James. *Notes of a Native Son*. Boston: Beacon, 1955.

Baraka, Amina, and Amiri Baraka, eds. *Confirmation: An Anthology of African American Women*. New York: Quill, 1983.

Baraka, Amiri (LeRoi Jones). *Home: Social Essays*. New York: William Morrow & Co., 1966.

———. *The Leroi Jones/Amiri Baraka Reader*, edited by William J. Harris. New York: Thunder's Mouth Press, 1999.

Barber, Karin. "Introduction: Hidden Innovators in Africa." In *Africa's Hidden Histories: Everyday Literacy and Making the Self*, edited by Karin Barber. Bloomington: Indiana University Press, 2006. 1–24.

Barnard, Rita. *Apartheid and Beyond: South African Writers and the Politics of Place*. Oxford: Oxford University Press, 2007.

———. "Of Riots and Rainbows: South Africa, the US, and the Pitfalls of Comparison." *American Literary History* 17.2 (2005): 399–416.

Beard, Linda-Susan. "Bessie Head's *A Question of Power*: The Journey through Disintegration to Wholeness." *Colby Library Quarterly* 15.4 (December 1979): 267–74.

Bethlehem, Louise. *Skin Tight: Apartheid Literary Cultural and Its Aftermath*. Pretoria: UNISA Press, 2006.

Biko, Steve. *I Write What I Like: A Selection of His Writings*, edited by Aelred Stubbs. Johannesburg: Picador Africa, 2004.

Birch, Kenneth S. "The Birch Family: An Introduction to the White Antecedents of the Late Bessie Amelia Head." *English in Africa* 22.1 (May 1995): 1–18.

Blaut, J. M. *The Colonizer's Model of the World: Geographical Diffusionism and Eurocentric History*. New York: Guilford Press, 1993.

Blythe, Ronald. *Akenfield: Portrait of an English Village*. New York: Pantheon, 1969.

Boehmer, Elleke. *Colonial and Postcolonial Literature: Migrant Metaphors*. Oxford: Oxford University Press, 1995.

Brecht, Bertolt. *Mother Courage and Her Children: A Chronicle of the Thirty Years' War*, translated by Eric Bentley. New York: Grove Press, 1963.

Bremner, Lindsay. *Writing the City into Being: Essays on Johannesburg, 1998–2008*. Johannesburg: Fourthwall Books, 2010.

Brink, André, and J. M. Coetzee, eds. *A Land Apart: A Contemporary South African Reader*. New York: Viking, 1987.

Brooks, Gwendolyn. *Blacks*. Chicago: David Company, 1987.

———. "Introduction: Where the Kind Kills Are." In *My Name Is Afrika*, by Keorapetse Kgositsile. Garden City: Doubleday, 1971. 11–13.

———. *Maud Martha*. Chicago: Third World Press, 1993.

———. *Winnie*. Chicago: Third World Press, 1988.

Brooks, Gwendolyn, Keorapetse Kgositsile, Haki Madhubuti, and Dudley Randall. *A Capsule Course in Black Poetry Writing*. Detroit: Broadside Press, 1975.

Brown, Coreen. *The Creative Vision of Bessie Head*. Madison: Farleigh Dickinson University Press, 2003.

Brown, Ryan. *A Native of Nowhere: The Life of Nat Nakasa*. Auckland Park: Jacana, 2013.

Brutus, Dennis. *Letters to Martha*. London: Heinemann, 1968.

———. *Poems from Algiers*. Austin: African and Afro-American Research Institute, 1970.

———. *Poetry and Protest: A Dennis Brutus Reader*, edited by Lee Sustar and Aisha Karim. Chicago: Haymarket Books, 2006.

———. *A Simple Lust*. London: Heinemann, 1973.

Bunn, David. "'Some Alien Native Land': Arthur Nortje, Literary History, and the Body in Exile." *World Literature Today* 70.1 (Winter 1996): 33–44.

Bunn, David, and Jane Taylor, eds. *From South Africa: New Writing, Photographs & Art*. *TriQuarterly* 69 (Spring/Summer 1987).

Campbell, James. "The Americanization of South Africa." In *A South African and American Comparative Reader: The Best of Safundi and Other Selected Articles*, edited by Andrew Offenburger, Scott Rosenberg, and Christopher Saunders. Washington, D.C.: Safundi, 2002. 23–63.

———. *Songs of Zion: The African Methodist Episcopal Church in the United States and South Africa*. Oxford: Oxford University Press, 1995.

———. "Towards a Transnational Comparative History." In *Beyond White Supremacy: Towards a New Agenda for the Comparative Histories of South Africa and the United States*. Collected Seminar Papers: 49. London: School of Advanced Studies, 1997. 22–27.

Carby, Hazel. "The Multicultural Wars." *Radical History Review* 54 (1992): 7–18.

Cell, John W. *The Highest Stage of White Supremacy: The Origins of Segregation in South Africa and the American South*. Cambridge: Cambridge University Press, 1982.

Césaire, Aimé. *Notebook of a Return to the Native Land*, translated by Clayton Eshleman and Annette Smith. Middletown: Wesleyan University Press, 2001.

Chapman, Michael. *Southern African Literatures*. Pietermaritzburg: University of Natal Press, 2003.

Chinosole. *The African Diaspora and Autobiographics: Skeins of Self and Skin*. New York: Peter Lang, 2001.

Chrisman, Laura. "Beyond Black Atlantic and Postcolonial Studies: The South African Differences of Sol Plaatje and Peter Abrahams." In *Postcolonial Studies and Beyond*, edited by Ania Loomba, Suvir Kaul, Matti Bunzl, Antoinette Burton, and Jed Esty. Durham: Duke University Press, 2005. 252–71.

———. *Postcolonial Contraventions: Cultural Readings of Race, Imperialism, and Transnationalism*. Manchester: Manchester University Press, 2003.

Christopher, A. J. *The Atlas of Changing South Africa*, 2nd ed. London: Routledge, 2001.

Clarke, Cheryl. *Living as a Lesbian*. Ithaca: Firebrand Books, 1986.

Clarke, Kamari, and Deborah Thomas. "Introduction: Globalization and the Transformations of Race." In *Globalization and Race: Transformations in the Cultural Production of Blackness*, edited by Kamari Clarke and Deborah Thomas. Durham: Duke University Press, 2006. 1–34.

Cliff, Michelle. *Abeng*. Trumansburg, N.Y.: Crossing Press, 1984.

———. *Claiming an Identity They Taught Me to Despise*. Watertown: Persephone Press, 1980.

———. *The Land of Look Behind*. Ithaca: Firebrand Books, 1985.

Clifton, Lucille. *Next: New Poems*. Brockport: BOA, 1987.

Coetzee, J. M. *White Writing: On the Culture of Letters in South Africa*. New Haven: Yale University Press, 1988.

Cortez, Jayne. *Coagulations: New and Selected Poems*. New York: Thunder's Mouth Press, 1984.

Coundouriotis, Eleni. "An 'Internationalism of the Planted Earth': The Literary Origins of Bessie Head's Idea of the Village." *Comparative Literature Studies* 48.1 (2011): 20–43.

Couzens, Tim. *The New African: A Study of the Life and Work of H. I. E. Dhlomo*. Johannesburg: Ravan Press, 1985.

Crawford, Margo Natalie. "Productive Rites of 'Passing': Keorapetse Kgositsile and the Black Arts Movement." *Black Renaissance Noire* 7.3 (2007): 112–20.

Crenshaw, Kimberlé W. "Mapping the Margins: Intersectionality, Identity Politics, and Violence against Women of Color." In *Critical Race Theory: The Key Writings That Formed the Movement*, edited by Kimberlé Crenshaw, Neil Gotanda, Gary Peller, and Kendall Thomas. New York: The New Press, 1995. 357–83.

Crocket-Smith, D. L. *Civil Rites*. San Francisco: Black Scholar Press, 1996.

Crossman, Richard, ed. *The God That Failed*. New York: Harper & Brothers, 1949.

Cruse, Harold. *Rebellion or Revolution?* New York: William Morrow & Co., 1968.

Cullinan, Patrick. *Imaginative Trespasser: Letters between Bessie Head, Patrick and Wendy Cullinan, 1963–77*. Johannesburg: Wits University Press, 2005.

Culverson, Donald R. *Contesting Apartheid: U.S. Activism, 1960–1987*. Boulder: Westview Press, 1999.

Davis, Angela Y. *Women, Culture, Politics*. New York: Random House, 1989.

Davis, Thadious. *Southscapes: Geographies of Race, Region, & Literature*. Chapel Hill: University of North Carolina Press, 2011.

Daymond, M. J. "Inventing Gendered Traditions: The Short Stories of Bessie Head and Miriam Tlali." In *South African Feminisms: Writing, Theory, and Criticism, 1990–1994*, edited by M. J. Daymond. New York: Garland Publishing, 1996. 223–40.

———. "Making a 'Home' Elsewhere: Letters of Bessie Head, 1963–1974." In *Engaging with Literature of Commitment, Volume 1: Africa and the World*, edited by Gordon Collier, Marc Delrez, Anne Fuchs, and Bénédicte Ledent. Amsterdam: Rodopi, 2012. 153–72.

———, ed. *South African Feminisms: Writing, Theory, and Criticism, 1990–1994*. New York: Garland Publishing, 1996.

de Kock, Leon. "South Africa in the Global Imaginary: An Introduction." *Poetics Today* 22.2 (Summer 2001): 263–98.

Delaney, David. *Race, Place, and the Law, 1836–1948*. Austin: University of Texas Press, 1998.

———. "The Space That Race Makes." *The Professional Geographer* 54.1 (2002): 6–14.

Dent, Tom. *Blue Lights and River Songs*. Detroit: Lotus Press, 1982.

Derricotte, Toi. *Captivity*. Pittsburgh: University of Pittsburgh Press, 1989.

Derrida, Jacques. "But Beyond . . . (Open Letter to Anne McClintock and Rob Nixon)." In *"Race," Writing, and Difference*, edited by Henry Louis Gates Jr. Chicago: University of Chicago Press, 1986. 354–69.

Desai, Gaurav. "Out in Africa." In *Sex Positives? The Cultural Politics of Dissident Sexualities*, edited by Thomas Forster, Carol Siegel, and Ellen Berry. New York: New York University Press, 1997. 120–43.

de Veaux, Alexis. *Warrior Poet: A Biography of Audre Lorde*. New York: W. W. Norton, 2004.

Dixon, Melvin. *Ride Out the Wilderness: Geography and Identity in Afro-American Literature*. Urbana: University of Illinois Press, 1987.

Dooling, Wayne. *Slavery, Emancipation and Colonial Rule in South Africa*. Scottsville: University of KwaZulu-Natal Press, 2007.

Dove, Rita. *Mother Love*. New York: W. W. Norton & Co., 1995.

Dubey, Madhu. *Black Women Novelists and the Nationalist Aesthetic*. Bloomington: Indiana University Press, 1994.

Du Bois, W. E. B. *The Souls of Black Folk*. New York: Penguin, 1996.

Edwards, Brent Hayes. "Late Romance." In *Next to the Color Line: Race, Gender, and W. E. B. Du Bois*, edited by Susan Gillman and Alys Eve Weinbaum. Minneapolis: University of Minnesota Press, 2007. 124–49.

———. *The Practice of Diaspora: Literature, Translation, and the Rise of Black Internationalism*. Cambridge: Harvard University Press, 2003.

———. "The Uses of Diaspora." *Social Text* 19.1 (2001): 45–73.

Eilersen, Gillian Stead. *Bessie Head: Thunder behind Her Ears*, 2nd ed. Johannesburg: Wits University Press, 2007.

Elder, Glen. *Hostels, Sexuality, and the Apartheid Legacy: Malevolent Geographies*. Athens: Ohio University Press, 2003.

Erlmann, Veit. "'A Feeling of Prejudice': Orpheus M. McAdoo and the Virginia Jubilee Singers in South Africa 1890–1898." *Journal of Southern African Studies* 14.3 (1988): 331–50.

Fabre, Michel. "Beyond Naturalism?" In *Richard Wright (Modern Critical Views)*, edited by Harold Bloom. New York: Chelsea House Publishers, 1987. 37–56.

——, ed. *Richard Wright: Books & Writers*. Jackson: University Press of Mississippi, 1990.

——. *The Unfinished Quest of Richard Wright*, 2nd ed., translated by Isabel Barzun. Urbana: University of Illinois Press, 1993.

——. *The World of Richard Wright*. Jackson: University Press of Mississippi, 1985.

Farred, Grant. *Midfielder's Moment: Coloured Literature and Culture in Contemporary South Africa*. Boulder: Westview Press, 2000.

Fielding, Maureen. "Agriculture and Healing: Transforming Space, Transforming Trauma in Bessie Head's *When Rain Clouds Gather*." In *Critical Essays on Bessie Head*, edited by Maxine Sample. Westport: Praeger, 2003. 11–24.

Fredrickson, George M. *Black Liberation: A Comparative History of Black Ideologies in the United States and South Africa*. Oxford: Oxford University Press, 1995.

——. *White Supremacy: A Comparative Study of American and South African History*. Oxford: Oxford University Press, 1982.

Gagiano, Annie. "Writing a Life in Epistolic Form: Bessie Head's Letters." *Journal of Literary Studies* 25.1 (March 2009): 8–33.

Gaines, Kevin K. *African Americans in Ghana: Black Expatriates and the Civil Rights Era*. Chapel Hill: University of North Carolina Press, 2006.

Gandhi, Leela. *Affective Communities: Anticolonial Thought, Fin-de-Siècle Radicalism, and the Politics of Friendship*. Durham: Duke University Press, 2006.

Gilroy, Paul. *The Black Atlantic: Modernity and Double Consciousness*. Cambridge: Harvard University Press, 1993.

Giovanni, Nikki. *Black Feeling, Black Talk, Black Judgement*. New York: Morrow and Co., 1970.

——. *Gemini: An Extended Biographical Statement on My First Twenty-Five Years of Being a Black Poet*. New York: Penguin, 1971.

——. *My House: Poems*. New York: W. Morrow & Co., 1972.

——, ed. *Night Comes Softly: An Anthology of Black Female Voices*. Newark: Medic Press, 1970.

——. *Re: Creation*. Detroit: Broadside Press, 1970.

Giovanni, Nikki, and James Baldwin. *A Dialogue*. Philadelphia: Lippincott, 1973.

Glissant, Édouard. *Poetics of Relation*, translated by Betsy Wing. Ann Arbor: University of Michigan Press, 1997.

Goldberg, David Theo. *The Racial State*. London: Blackwell, 2001.

Gourdine, Angeletta K. M. *The Difference Place Makes: Gender, Sexuality, and Diaspora Identity*. Columbus: Ohio State University Press, 2002.

Graham, James. *Land and Nationalism in Fictions from Southern Africa*. New York: Routledge, 2009.

Graham, Shane, and John Walters, eds. *Langston Hughes and the South African* Drum *Generation: The Correspondence*. New York: Palgrave Macmillan, 2010.

Gray, Stephen, ed. *Penguin Book of Southern African Stories*. New York: Penguin, 1985.

Griffin, Farah Jasmine. *"Who set you flowin'?": The African-American Migration Narrative*. Oxford: University of Oxford Press, 1995.

Hale, Grace Elizabeth. *Making Whiteness: The Culture of Segregation in the South, 1890–1940*. New York: Vintage, 1999.

Hall, Stuart. "Race, Articulation, and Societies Structured in Dominance." In *Race Critical Theories*, edited by Philomena Essed and David Theo Goldberg. Oxford: Blackwell, 2002. 38–68.

Harley, J. B. "Deconstructing the Map." *Cartographica* 26.2 (Spring 1989): 1–20.

Harper, Michael S. *Healing Song for the Inner Ear: Poems*. Urbana: University of Illinois Press, 1985.

Harris, Donald. "The Black Ghetto as Internal Colony: A Theoretical Critique and Alternative Formulation." *Black Political Economy* 2.4 (1972): 3–33.

Hartman, Saidiya. *Lose Your Mother: A Journey Along the Atlantic Slave Route*. New York: Farrar, Straus, and Giroux, 2007.

Harvey, David. *The Condition of Postmodernity: An Enquiry into the Origins of Cultural Change*. Oxford: Blackwell, 1990.

Head, Bessie. Bessie Head Papers. Khama III Memorial Museum. Serowe, Botswana.

———. *A Bewitched Crossroad: An African Saga*. St. Paul: Paragon House Publishers, 1984.

———. *The Collector of Treasures and Other Botswana Village Tales*. Harlow: Pearson/Heinemann, 1992.

———. *Maru*. New York: McCall Publishing Company, 1971.

———. *A Question of Power*. Portsmouth: Heinemann, 1974.

———. *Serowe: Village of the Rain Wind*. Portsmouth: Heinemann, 1981.

———. *When Rain Clouds Gather*. Harlow: Pearson/Heinemann, 2008.

———. *A Woman Alone: Autobiographical Writings*. Portsmouth: Heinemann, 1990.

Helgesson, Stefan. *Transnationalism in Southern African Literature: Modernists, Realists, and the Inequality of Print Culture*. New York: Routledge, 2009.

Helphand, Kenneth I. *Defiant Gardens: Making Gardens in Wartime*. San Antonio: Trinity University Press, 2006.

Henderson, Stephen. "Introduction: The Form of Things Unknown." In *Understanding the New Black Poetry: Black Speech and Black Music as Poetic References*, edited by Stephen Henderson. New York: William Morrow, 1973. 1–69.

Holzinger, Tom. "Conversations and Consternations with B Head." In *Writing Bessie Head in Botswana: An Anthology of Remembrance and Criticism*, edited by Mary Lederer and Seatholo Tumedi. Gaborone: Pentagon Publishers, 2007. 35–57.

Honey, Maureen. *Shadowed Dreams: Women's Poetry of the Harlem Renaissance*, 2nd ed. New Brunswick: Rutgers University Press, 2006.

hooks, bell. *Yearning: Race, Gender, and Cultural Politics*. Boston: South End Press, 1990.

Horn, Peter. "When It Rains, It Rains: U.S. Black Consciousness and Lyric Poetry in South Africa." In *Soweto Poetry: Literary Perspectives*, edited by Michael Chapman. Durban: University of KwaZulu-Natal Press, 2007. 162–68.

Horne, Gerald. *The Fire This Time: The Watts Uprising and the 1960s*. Charlottesville: University of Virginia Press, 1995.

Hughes, Langston, ed. *An African Treasury: Articles/Essays/Stories/Poems by Black Africans*. New York: Crown Publishers, 1960.

———. *The Collected Poems of Langston Hughes*, edited by Arnold Rampersad and David Roessel. New York: Vintage, 1994.

———. Langston Hughes Collection. JWJ MSS 26. James Weldon Johnson Collection in the Yale Collection of American Literature. Beinecke Rare Book and Manuscript Library.

———. *Panther and the Lash: Poems of Our Times*. New York: Knopf, 1967.

Ibrahim, Huma. "The Problematic Relationship of Western Canonicity and African Literature: The Not-So-Singular Case of Bessie Head." In *Emerging Perspectives on Bessie Head*, edited by Huma Ibrahim. Trenton: African World Press, 2004. 199–215.

Jacques, Geoffrey. "Soweto Remembrance." In *Art against Apartheid: Works for Freedom*. New York: IKON, 1986. 69.

Jaji, Tsitsi. "Sound Effects: Synaesthesia as Purposeful Distortion in Keorapetse Kgositsile's Poetry." *Comparative Literature Studies* 46.2 (2009): 287–310.

Jameson, Fredric. "Cognitive Mapping." In *Marxism and the Interpretation of Culture*, edited by Cary Nelson and Lawrence Grossberg. Urbana: University of Illinois Press, 1988. 347–57.

JanMohammed, Abdul. *The Death-Bound-Subject: Richard Wright's Archaeology of Death*. Durham: Duke University Press, 2005.

Jasmine, Randy. "'I'd like tuh see any man put me outer dis house': Space and Place in Richard Wright's Early Work." *Publications of the Mississippi Philological Association* (2004): 37–44.

Jordan, June. *Directed by Desire: The Collected Poems of June Jordan*. Port Townsend: Copper Canyon Press, 2007.

———. *On Call: Political Essays*. Boston: South End Press, 1985.

———. "A Song for Soweto." In *Art against Apartheid: Works for Freedom*. New York: IKON, 1986. 93.

Joseph, Gloria I. "A Brief History of SISA (Sisters in Support of South Africa)." Unpublished paper. Audre Lorde Papers. November 23, 1984.

———. "Dear Founding Mothers." Unpublished paper. Audre Lorde Papers. December 10, 1991.

Joseph, Gloria I., and Audre Lorde. "'In Memory of Our Children's Blood': Sisterhood and South African Women." Unpublished paper. Audre Lorde Papers. n/d.

Joubert, Elsa. *Poppie Nongena*. New York: W. W. Norton & Co., 1985.

Judin, Hilton, and Ivan Vladislavić, eds. *blank: Architecture, Apartheid and After*. Rotterdam: NAi, 1995.

Kent, George E. *A Life of Gwendolyn Brooks*. Lexington: University Press of Kentucky, 1990.

Kgositsile, Keorapetse. *Beyond Words: South African Poetics*. London: Flipped Eye Publishing, 2009.

———. "Crossing Borders without Leaving." *Staffrider* 4.2 (1991): 5–10.

———. *If I Could Sing: Selected Poems*. Roggebaai: Kwela, 2002.

———. "In America and Africa: Where Is the Black Revolution?" *Black World* 19.7 (May 1970): 16–21.

———. Interview with Victor Dlamini, August 12, 2008: http://victordlamini.bookslive .co.za/blog/2008/08/12/podcast-with-poet-laureate-keorapetse-kgositsile/ (accessed August 2, 2010).

———. "Keorapetse Kgositsile Interviewed by Achmat Dangor." In *Out of Exile: South African Writers Speak*, edited by Kevin Goddard and Charles Wessels. Grahamstown: National English Literary Museum, 1992. 79–91.

———. *My Name Is Afrika*, Introduction by Gwendolyn Brooks. Garden City: Doubleday, 1971.

———. Personal interview with Keorapetse Kgositsile. Johannesburg, South Africa, June 29, 2011.

———. *This Way I Salute You: Selected Poems*. Roggebaai: Kwela, 2004.

———. "Wild Conquest: An Introduction." In *Wild Conquest*, by Peter Abrahams. Garden City: Anchor Books, 1971. 7–14.

Khumalo, Vukile. "Ekukhanyeni Letter-Writers: A Historical Inquiry into Epistolary Network(s) and Political Imagination in Kwazulu-Natal, South Africa." In *Africa's Hidden Histories: Everyday Literacy and Making the Self*, edited by Karin Barber. Bloomington: Indiana University Press, 2006. 113–42.

Kincaid, Jamaica. *My Garden (Book)*. New York: Farrar, Straus and Giroux, 2001.

Kiuchi, Toru, and Yoshinobu Hakutani, eds. *Richard Wright: A Documented Chronology, 1908–1960*. Jefferson, N.C.: McFarland & Company, 2013.

Klopper, Dirk. "The Politics of the Pastoral: The Poetry of Thomas Pringle." *English in Africa* 17.1 (May 1990): 21–59.

Komunyakaa, Yusef. *Pleasure Dome: New and Collected Poems*. Middletown: Wesleyan University Press, 2001.

Kruger, Loren. "Black Atlantics, White Indians, and Jews: Locations, Locutions, and Syncretic Identities in the Fiction of Achmat Dangor and Others." *South Atlantic Quarterly* 100.1 (2001): 111–43.

Kunene, Mazisi. *Emperor Shaka the Great*, translated by Mazisi Kunene. Oxford: Heinemann, 1979.

Kuzwayo, Ellen. *Call Me Woman*. San Francisco: Spinster Ink, 1985.

La Guma, Alex. *A Walk in the Night*. Ibadan: Mbari Publications, 1962.

Lawrence, D. H. *Sons & Lovers*. New York: Viking Press, 1958.

Lefebvre, Henri. *The Production of Space*, translated by Donald Nicholson-Smith. London: Wiley-Blackwell, 1991.

Lewis, Desiree. *Living on a Horizon: Bessie Head and the Politics of Imagining*. Trenton: Africa World Press, 2007.

Lindfors, Bernth. *Comparative Approaches to African Literature*. Amsterdam: Rodopi, 1994.

Lionnet, Françoise. *Postcolonial Representations: Women, Literature, Identity*. Ithaca: Cornell University Press, 1995.

Lionnet, Françoise, and Shu-mei Shih, eds. *Minor Transnationalism*. Durham: Duke University Press, 2005.

Locke, Alain, ed. *The New Negro: Voices of the Harlem Renaissance*. New York: Simon & Schuster, 1997.

Lorde, Audre. Audre Lorde Papers. Spelman College Archives. Spelman College.

———. *A Burst of Light*. Ithaca: Firebrand Press, 1988.

———. *The Collected Poems of Audre Lorde*. New York: W. W. Norton, 1997.

Lubiano, Wahneema. "Black Nationalism and Black Common Sense." In *The House That Race Built: Black Americans, U.S. Terrain*, edited by Wahneema Lubiano. New York: Pantheon Books, 1997. 232–52.

Mackenzie, John. *Papers of John Mackenzie*, edited by A. J. Dachs. Johannesburg: Wits University Press, 1975.

Magona, Sindiwe. *Forced to Grow*, 3rd ed. Cape Town: David Philip, 2013.

Magubane, Zine. "The Influence of African-American Cultural Practices on South Africa, 1890–1990." In *Leisure in Urban Africa*, edited by Paul Tiyambe Zeleza and Cassandra Rachel Veney. Trenton: Africa World Press, 2003. 297–319.

Makalani, Minkah. *In the Cause of Freedom: Radical Black Internationalism from Harlem to London, 1917–1939*. Chapel Hill: University of North Carolina Press, 2011.

Mandela, Nelson. *Long Walk to Freedom: The Autobiography of Nelson Mandela*. New York: Little, Brown and Co., 1994.

Mandela, Winnie. *Part of My Soul Went with Him*, edited by Anne Benjamin. New York: W. W. Norton & Company, 1984.

Mangharam, Mukti Lakhi. "'The Universal Is the Entire Collection of Particulars': Grounding Identity in a Shared Horizon of Humanity." *College Literature* 40.3 (Summer 2013): 81–98.

Marx, Anthony. *Making Race and Nation: A Comparison of the United States, South Africa, and Brazil*. Cambridge: Cambridge University Press, 1998.

Masilela, Ntongela. "The 'Black Atlantic' and African Modernity in South Africa." *Research in African Literatures* 27.4 (Winter 1996): 88–96.

———. "New Negroism and New Africanism: The Influence of United States Modernity on the Construction of South African Modernity." *Black Renaissance/Renaissance Noire* 2.2 (Summer 1999): 46–59.

———. "Peter Abrahams in the Modern African World." *Current Writing* 16.2 (2004): 31–46.

Massey, Doreen. *Space, Place, and Gender*. Minneapolis: University of Minnesota Press, 1994.

Massey, Douglas, and Nancy Denton. *American Apartheid: Segregation and the Making of the Underclass*. Cambridge: Harvard University Press, 1993.

Massie, Robert K. *Loosing the Bonds: The United States and South Africa in the Apartheid Years*. New York: Doubleday, 1997.

Mathabane, Mark. *Kaffir Boy: An Autobiography*. New York: Plume/Penguin, 1987.

Mbembe, Achille. "Aesthetics of Superfluity." In *Johannesburg: The Elusive Metropolis*, edited by Sarah Nuttall and Achille Mbembe. Durham: Duke University Press, 2008. 37–67.

Mbiti, John. *African Religions and Philosophy*. London: Heinemann, 1969.

McDonald, Peter D. *The Literature Police: Apartheid Censorship and Its Cultural Consequences*. Oxford: Oxford University Press, 2009.

McHenry, Elizabeth. "Rereading Literary Legacy: New Considerations of the 19th-Century African-American Reader and Writer." *Callaloo* 22.2 (1999): 477–82.

McKittrick, Katherine. *Demonic Grounds: Black Women and the Cartographies of Struggle*. Minneapolis: University of Minnesota Press, 2006.

Melhem, D. H. *Heroism in the New Black Poetry*. Lexington: University Press of Kentucky, 1990.

Menon, Dilip M. "A Local Cosmopolitan: 'Kesari' Balakrishna Pillai and the Invention of Europe for a Modern Kerala." In *Cosmopolitan Thought Zones: South Asia and the Global Circulation of Ideas*, edited by Sugata Bose and Kris Manjapra. New York: Palgrave Macmillan, 2010. 131–58.

Meriwether, James H. *Proudly We Can Be Africans: Black Americans and Africa, 1935–61*. Chapel Hill: University of North Carolina Press, 2002.

Mermelstein, David, ed. *The Anti-Apartheid Reader: South Africa and the Struggle against White Racist Rule*. New York: Grove Press, 1987.

Meyer, Stephan. "Review of *South African and American Comparative Reader: The Best of Safundi and Other Selected Articles*." *Current Writing* 16.2 (2004): 149–54.

Mgbako, Ofole. "'My Blackness Is the Beauty of this Land': Racial Redefinition, African American Culture, and the Creation of the Black World in South Africa's Black Consciousness Movement." *Safundi* 10.3 (July 2009): 305–34.

Mignolo, Walter. "On Comparison: Who Is Comparing What and Why?" In *Comparison: Theories, Approaches, Uses*, edited by Rita Felski and Susan Stanford Friedman. Baltimore: Johns Hopkins University Press, 2013. 99–119.

Miller, J. Hillis. *Topographies*. Stanford: Stanford University Press, 1995.

Mngxitama, Andile, Amanda Alexander, Nigel Gibson, eds. *Biko Lives! Contesting the Legacies of Steve Biko*. New York: Palgrave Macmillan, 2008.

Modisane, Bloke. *Blame Me on History*. New York: Simon & Schuster/Touchstone, 1986.

Moore, David Chioni. "The Bessie Head–Langston Hughes Correspondence, 1960–61." *Research in African Literatures* 41.3 (Fall 2010): 1–20.

Morrison, Toni. *Conversations with Toni Morrison*, edited by Danille K. Taylor-Guthrie. Jackson: University Press of Mississippi, 1994.

———. "Reading the Writing: A Conversation with Toni Morrison," March 7, 2013, Cornell University: http://www.cornell.edu/video/toni-morrison-on-language-evil-and-the-white-gaze (accessed April 20, 2013).

———. "Sheer Good Fortune," October 16, 2012, Virginia Tech University: http://media1.vbs.vt.edu/content/adhoc/fall2012/Sheer_Good_Fortune (accessed April 3, 2013).

———. *Sula*. New York: Knopf, 1973.

———. *Tar Baby*. New York: Knopf, 1981.

———. *Toni Morrison: Conversations*, edited by Carolyn C. Denard. Jackson: University Press of Mississippi, 2008.

Mphahlele, Es'kia. *Afrika My Music: An Autobiography, 1957–1983*. Johannesburg: Ravan, 1984.

———. *Down Second Avenue*. Gloucester: Peter Smith, 1978.

———. *Man Must Live and Other Stories*. Cape Town: African Bookman, 1946.

———. "The Tyranny of Place." *New Letters* 40.1 (1973): 69–84.

———. *Voices in the Whirlwind and Other Essays*. New York: Hill and Wang, 1972.

Mudimbe, V. Y. *The Invention of Africa: Gnosis, Philosophy, and the Order of Knowledge*. Bloomington: Indiana University Press, 1988.

Munro, Brenna M. *South Africa and the Dream of Love to Come: Queer Sexuality and the Struggle for Freedom*. Minneapolis: University of Minnesota Press, 2012.

Myers, Shaundra. "Worlds beyond *Brown*: Black Transnational Identity and Self-Narration in the Era of Integration." PhD diss., University of Maryland–College Park, 2011.

Mzamane, Mbulelo. *The Children of the Diaspora and Other Stories of Exile*. Trenton: Africa World Press, 2000.

Nair, Supriya M. *Pathologies of Paradise: Caribbean Detours*. Charlottesville: University of Virginia Press, 2013.

Nakasa, Nat. *The World of Nat Nakasa: Selected Writings of the Late Nat Nakasa*, edited by Essop Patel. Johannesburg: Ravan Press, 1975.

Ndebele, Njabulo. *Fools and Other Stories*. New York: Readers International, 1986.

———. *Rediscovery of the Ordinary: Essays on South African Literature and Culture*. Scottsville: University of KwaZulu-Natal Press, 2006.

Ndlovu, Duma. *Sheila's Day*. In *Black South African Women: An Anthology*, edited by Kathy Perkins. New York: Routledge, 1998. 145–58.

———, ed. *Woza Afrika! An Anthology of South African Plays*. New York: George Braziller, 1986.

Nesbitt, Francis Njubi. *Race for Sanctions: African Americans against Apartheid, 1946–1994*. Bloomington: Indiana University Press, 2004.

Neser, Ashlee. *Stranger at Home: The Praise Poet in Apartheid South Africa*. Johannesburg: Wits University Press, 2011.

Ngũgĩ wa Thiong'o. *Decolonising the Mind: The Politics of Language in African Literature*. London: James Currey, 1986.

———. *Something Torn and New: An African Renaissance*. New York: Basic Civitas Books, 2009.

Nielsen, Aldon L. "Choruses for Gil Scott-Heron 1 & 2." Unpublished paper presented at Louisville Conference on Literature and Culture since 1900, February 2012.

Nightingale, Carl. *Segregation: A Global History of Divided Cities*. Chicago: University of Chicago Press, 2012.

Nixon, Rob. *Homelands, Harlem and Hollywood: South African Culture and the World Beyond*. New York: Routledge, 1994.

Nkosi, Lewis. *Home and Exile and Other Selections*. London: Longman, 1983.

———. "The Mountain: In Search of Jimmy Baldwin." *Transition* 8.3 (79): 102–23.

Ntantla, Phyllis. *A Life's Mosaic: The Autobiography of Phyllis Ntantla*. Berkeley: University of California Press, 1993.

Nuttall, Sarah. *Entanglement: Literary and Cultural Reflections on Post-Apartheid*. Johannesburg: Wits University Press, 2009.

Nuttall, Sarah, and Achille Mbembe, eds. *Johannesburg: The Elusive Metropolis*. Durham: Duke University Press, 2008.

Nwankwo, Ifeoma. *Black Cosmopolitanism: Racial Consciousness and Transnational Identity in the Nineteenth-Century Americas*. Philadelphia: University of Pennsylvania Press, 2005.

———. "Langston Hughes and the Translation of Nicholas Guillén's Afro-Cuban Culture and Language." *The Langston Hughes Review* 16.2 (1999–2000): 55–72.

O'Brien, Anthony. *Against Normalization: Writing Radical Democracy in South Africa*. Durham: Duke University Press, 2001.

Ogungbesan, Kolawole. *The Writing of Peter Abrahams*. New York: Africana Publishing Co., 1979.

Omi, Michael, and Howard Winant. *Racial Formation in the United States: From the 1960s to the 1990s*. New York: Routledge, 1994.

Omond, Roger. *The Apartheid Handbook: A Guide to South Africa's Everyday Racial Policies*. New York: Penguin, 1985.

Oosthuizen, Ann, ed. *Sometimes When It Rains: Writings by South African Women*. New York: Pandora, 1987.

Osbey, Brenda Marie. *All Saints: New and Selected Poems*. Baton Rouge: Louisiana State University Press, 1997.

Padmore, George. *Pan-Africanism or Communism? The Coming Struggle for Africa*. London: Dennis Dobson, 1956.

Pasternak, Boris. *Doctor Zhivago*. New York: Pantheon, 1958.

Paton, Alan. *Cry, the Beloved Country*. New York: Scribner's Son, 1987.

Patterson, Tiffany Ruby, and Robin D. G. Kelley. "Unfinished Migrations: Reflections on the African Diaspora and the Making of the Modern World." *African Studies Review* 43.1 (April 2000): 11–45.

Paustian, Megan. "Narratives of African Improvement: Missions, Humanitarianism, and the Novel." PhD diss., Rutgers University, 2013.

Perera, Sonali. *No Country: Working-Class Writing in the Age of Globalization*. New York: Columbia University Press, 2014.

Piper, Adrian. *Vanilla Nightmare* Series, 1986. Charcoal and oil crayon on *New York Times* text and ads. Private collection.

Plaatje, Sol T. *Mhudi*. London: Heinemann, 1978.

———. *Native Life in South Africa*, edited by Brian Willan. Harlow: Longman, 1987.

Plummer, Brenda Gayle. *Rising Wind: Black Americans and U.S. Foreign Affairs, 1935–1960*. Chapel Hill: University of North Carolina Press, 1996.

Plumpp, Sterling, ed. *Somehow We Survive: An Anthology of South African Writing*. New York: Thunder's Mouth Press, 1982.

Polsgrove, Carol. *Ending British Rule in Africa: Writers in a Common Cause*. Manchester: Manchester University Press, 2009.

Pope, Mary Elizabeth. "'I am NOT just like one of the family . . .': The Black Domestic Servant and White Family Dynamics in 20th Century American and South African Literature." *Safundi: The Journal of South African and American Comparative Studies* 2.4 (November 2001): 1–19.

Popescu, Monica. *South African Literature Beyond the Cold War*. New York: Palgrave Macmillan, 2010.

Pratt, Mary Louise. "Scratches on the Face of the Country; or, What Mr. Barrow Saw in the Land of the Bushmen." *Critical Inquiry* 12.1 (Autumn 1985): 119–43.

Radcliffe, Anthony J. "Liberation at the End of a Pen: "Writing Pan-African Politics of Cultural Struggle." PhD diss., University of Massachusetts–Amherst, 2009.

Raditlhalo, Tlhalo. "Writing in Exile." In *The Cambridge History of South African Literature*, edited by David Attwell and Derek Attridge. Cambridge: Cambridge University Press, 2012. 410–28.

Raiskin, Judith. "The Art of History: An Interview with Michelle Cliff." *Kenyon Review* 15.1 (1993): 57–71.

Reagon, Bernice Johnson. "Chile Your Waters." In *Art against Apartheid: Works for Freedom*. New York: IKON, 1986. 164.

Redmond, Eugene. *Drumvoices: The Mission of Afro-American Poetry, A Critical History*. New York: Anchor, 1976.

Rich, Paul. "Romance and the Development of the South African Novel." In *Literature and Society in South Africa*, edited by Landeg White and Tim Couzens. Essex: Longman, 1984. 120–37.

Rive, Richard. *Advance, Retreat: Selected Short Stories*. Cape Town: David Philip, 1983.

———. *African Songs*. Berlin: Seven Seas, 1963.

———. *"Buckingham Palace," District Six*, educational ed. Cape Town: David Philip, 1986.

———. *Emergency*. London: Faber and Faber, 1964.

———. "The Ethics of an Anti–Jim Crow." In *Design and Intent in African Literature. Annual Selected Papers of the ALA*, edited by David F. Dorsey, Phanuel Akubueze Egejuru, and Stephen H. Arnold. Washington D.C.: Three Continents Press, 1982. 7–15.

———. Richard Rive Papers. National English Literary Museum. Grahamstown, South Africa.

———. "Storming Pretoria's Castles—To Write or Fight?" *New York Times Book Review* January 17 (1988): BR1.

———. "Taos in Harlem: Interview with Langston Hughes." *Contrast* 4.2 (1966): 33–39.

———. *Writing Black*. Cape Town: David Philip, 1981.

Robinson, Cedric J. *Black Marxism: The Making of a Black Tradition*, 2nd ed. Chapel Hill: University of North Carolina Press, 2000.

Robolin, Stéphane. "Loose Memory in Toni Morrison's *Paradise* and Zoë Wicomb's *David's Story*." *Modern Fiction Studies* 52.2 (Summer 2006): 297–320.

——. "Properties of Whiteness: (Post)Apartheid Geographies in Zoë Wicomb's *Playing in the Light*." *Safundi* 12.3–4 (July–October 2011): 349–71.

Rochman, Rachel, ed. *Somehow Tenderness Survives: Stories of Southern Africa*. New York: HarperCollins Publishers, 1988.

Rowell, Charles. "'With Bloodstains to Testify': An Interview with Keorapetse Kgositsile." *Callaloo* 2 (February 1978): 23–41.

Rowley, Hazel. *Richard Wright: The Life and Times*. New York: Henry Holt & Company, 2001.

Said, Edward. *Culture and Imperialism*. New York: Vintage, 1994.

——. *Orientalism*. New York: Vintage, 1978.

——. *The World, the Text, and the Critic*. Cambridge: Harvard University Press, 1983.

——. "Yeats and Decolonization." In *Nationalism, Colonialism, and Literature*, by Terry Eagleton, Fredric Jameson, and Edward Said. Minneapolis: University of Minnesota Press, 1990. 69–95.

Sales, William. "Making South Africa Ungovernable: ANC Strategy for the '80s." *The Black Scholar* 15.6 (November/December 1984): 2–14.

Sample, Maxine. "Space: An Experiential Perspective: Bessie Head's *When Rain Clouds Gather*." In *Critical Essays on Bessie Head*, edited by Maxine Sample. Westport: Praeger, 2003. 25–45.

Sanchez, Sonia. *Shake Loose My Skin: New and Selected Poems*. Boston: Beacon, 1999.

Sanders, Mark. *Complicities: The Intellectual and Apartheid*. Durham: Duke University Press, 2002.

Scheub, Harold. *The Poem in the Story: Music, Poetry, and Narrative*. Madison: University of Wisconsin Press, 2002.

Scott, James C. *Seeing Like a State: How Certain Schemes to Improve the Human Condition Have Failed*. New Haven: Yale University Press, 1998.

Scott-Heron, Gil. *Black Wax*. DVD, directed by Robert Mugge, 1982; Washington, D.C.: Channel Four Films/Mug-Shot, 1998.

——. *The Last Holiday: A Memoir*. New York: Grove Press, 2012.

——. *So Far, So Good*. Chicago: Third World Press, 1990.

Scott-Heron, Gil, and Brian Jackson. *From South Africa to South Carolina*. © 1975 from Arista Records. Arista AL-4044. Album.

Sepamla, Sipho. *The Soweto I Love*. London: Rex Collings, 1977.

Serote, Mongane Wally. *Gods of Our Time*. Randburg: Ravan Press, 1999.

——. Personal Interview. Johannesburg, South Africa, June 20, 2011.

——. *To Every Birth Its Blood*. Johannesburg: Ravan Press, 1981.

——. *Yakhal'inkomo*. Johannesburg: Ad Donker, 1983.

Shaw, Rosalind. *Memories of the Slave Trade: Ritual and the Historical Imagination in Sierra Leone*. Chicago: University of Chicago Press, 2002.

Sherman, Susan, and Gale Jackson, eds. *Art against Apartheid: Works for Freedom*. IKON Second Series 5–6 (Winter/Summer 1986).

Shih, Shu-mei. "Comparison as Relation." In *Comparison: Theories, Approaches, Uses*, edited by Rita Felski and Susan Stanford Friedman. Baltimore: Johns Hopkins University Press, 2013. 79–98.

Shockley, Evie. *Renegade Poetics: Black Aesthetics and Formal Innovation in African American Poetry*. Iowa City: University of Iowa Press, 2011.

Sibley, David. *Geographies of Exclusion: Society and Difference in the West*. London: Routledge, 1995.

Simone, Abdulmaliq. "People as Infrastructure." In *Johannesburg: The Elusive Metropolis*, edited by Sarah Nuttall and Achille Mbembe. Durham: Duke University Press, 2008. 68–90.

Smethurst, James E. *The Black Arts Movement: Literary Nationalism in the 1960s and 1970s*. Chapel Hill: University of North Carolina Press, 2005.

Smith, Felipe. "The African Diaspora as Imagined Community." In *Global Circuits of Blackness: Interrogating the African Diaspora*, edited by Jean Muteba Rahier, Percy C. Hintzen, and Felipe Smith. Urbana: University of Illinois Press, 2010. 3–28.

———. *American Body Politics: Race, Gender, and the Black Literary Renaissance*. Athens: University of Georgia Press, 1998.

Smith, Mark. *How Race Is Made: Slavery, Segregation, and the Senses*. Chapel Hill: University of North Carolina Press, 2006.

Smith McKoy, Sheila. *When Whites Riot: Writing Race and Violence in American and South African Cultures*. Madison: University of Wisconsin Press, 2001.

Smith, Neil. "Contours of a Spatialized Politics: Homeless Vehicles and the Production of Geographical Scale." *Social Text* 33 (1992): 54–81.

Smith, Neil, and Cindi Katz. "Grounding Metaphor: Towards a Spatialized Politics." In *Place and the Politics of Identity*, edited by Michael Keith and Steve Pile. New York: Routledge, 1993. 67–81.

Soja, Edward. *Postmodern Geographies: The Reassertion of Space in Critical Social Theory*. New York: Verso, 2011.

South African History Online: Towards a People's History. "Peter Henry Abrahams": http://www.sahistory.org.za/people/peter-henry-abrahams (accessed March 5, 2014).

Spivak, Gayatri Chakravorty. "Teaching for the Times." In *Dangerous Liaisons: Gender, Nation, and Postcolonial Perspectives*, edited by Anne McClintock, Aamir Mufti, and Ella Shohat. Minneapolis: University of Minnesota Press, 1997. 468–90.

Stephens, Michelle. *Black Empire: The Masculine Global Imaginary of Caribbean Intellectuals in the United States, 1914–1962*. Durham: Duke University Press, 2005.

———. "Black Transnationalism and the Politics of National Identity: West Indian Intellectuals in Harlem in the Age of War and Revolution." *American Quarterly* 50.3 (1998): 592–608.

Stepto, Robert. *From Behind the Veil: A Study in Afro-American Narrative*. Urbana: University of Illinois Press, 1979.

Stouck, Jordan. "Gardening in the Diaspora: Place and Identity in Olive Senior's Poetry." *Mosaic: A Journal for the Interdisciplinary Study of Literature* 38.4 (December 2005): 103–24.

Stovall, Tyler. *Paris Noir: African Americans in the City of Light*. Boston: Houghton Mifflin, 1996.

Sundiata, Ibrahim. *Brothers and Strangers: Black Zion, Black Slavery, 1914–1940*. Durham: Duke University Press, 2003.

Tabb, William K. *The Political Economy of the Black Ghetto*. New York: W. W. Norton & Co., 1970.

Tate, Claudia. *Black Women Writers at Work*. New York: Continuum, 1983.

Thacker, Andrew. *Moving through Modernity: Space and Geography in Modernism*. Manchester: Manchester University Press, 2003.

Thompson, Leonard. *A History of South Africa*, rev. ed. New Haven: Yale University Press, 1995.

Thorsson, Courtney. *Women's Work: Nationalism and Contemporary African American Women's Novels*. Charlottesville: University of Virginia Press, 2013.

Titlestad, Michael. *Making the Changes: Jazz in South African Literature and Reportage*. Pretoria: UNISA Press, 2004.

———. "Traveling Jazz: Themes and Riffs." *Safundi* 8.1 (January 2007): 73–82.

Tlali, Miriam. *Soweto Stories*. New York: Pandora, 1989.

Tuan, Yi-Fu. *Space and Place: The Experience of Perspective*. Minneapolis: University of Minnesota Press, 1977.

Turchi, Peter. *Maps of the Imagination: The Writer as Cartographer*. San Antonio: Trinity University Press, 2004.

Ture, Kwame (Stokely Carmichael) and Charles V. Hamilton. *Black Power: The Politics of Liberation*. New York: Vintage, 1968.

Tyner, James. *The Geography of Malcolm X: Black Radicalism and the Remaking of American Space*. New York: Routledge, 2006.

van der Vlies, Andrew. "Transnational Print Cultures: Books, -scapes, and the Textual Atlantic." *Safundi* 8.1 (January 2007): 45–55.

van Wyk Smith, Malvern. *Grounds of Contest: A Survey of South African English Literature*. Kenwyn: Jutalit, 1990.

Vigne, Randolph, ed. *A Gesture of Belonging: Letters from Bessie Head, 1965–1979*. Portsmouth: Heinemann, 1991.

Viljoen, Shaun. *Richard Rive: A Partial Biography*. Johannesburg: Wits University Press, 2013.

Vinson, Robert Trent. *The Americans Are Coming!: Dreams of African American Liberation in Segregationist South Africa*. Athens: Ohio University Press, 2012.

Vivan, Itala. "Geography, Literature, and the African Territory: Some Observations on the Western Map and the Representation of Territory in the South African Literary Imagination." *Research in African Literatures* 31.2 (2000): 49–70.

Vivekananda, Swami. *The Complete Works of Swami Vivekananda*, Volume VIII. Calcutta: Advaita Ashrama, 1971.

von Eschen, Penny M. *Race against Empire: Black Americans and Anticolonialism, 1937–1957*. Ithaca: Cornell University Press, 1997.

Wade, Michael. *Peter Abrahams*. Modern African Writers Series. London: Evan Brothers Ltd., 1972.

———. "Peter Abrahams." *Dictionary of Literary Biography. Volume 117: Twentieth-Century Caribbean and Black African Writers*, edited by Bernth Lindfors and Reinhard Sander. Detroit: Gale Research Inc., 1992. 3–14.

Walker, Alice. 11th Annual Steve Biko Memorial Lecture. September 9, 2010. University of Cape Town, Cape Town, South Africa: https://www.uct.ac.za/news/lectures /stevebiko/ (accessed June 23, 2014).

———. Alice Walker Papers. Manuscripts, Archives, and Rare Books Library, Emory University.

———. *Her Blue Body Everything We Know: Earthling Poems 1965–1990 Complete*. New York: Harcourt Brace Jovanovich, 1991.

———. *In Search of Our Mothers' Gardens: Womanist Prose*. New York: Harcourt Brace, 1983.

———. *The Temple of My Familiar*. New York: Harcourt Brace Jovanovich, 1989.

———. *The Third Life of Grange Copeland*. Orlando: Harcourt, 2003.

———. *You Can't Keep a Good Woman Down*. New York: Harcourt Brace Jovanovich, 1981.

Walker, Cherryl. *Landmarked: Land Claims and Land Restitution in South Africa*. Johannesburg: Jacana, 2008.

Wall, Cheryl A. *Worrying the Line: Black Women Writers, Lineage, and Literary Tradition*. Chapel Hill: University of North Carolina Press, 2005.

Weaver, Afaa Michael. *Water Song*. Charlottesville: University of Virginia Press, 1985. 62–64.

Wenzel, Jennifer. "The Pastoral Promise and the Political Imperative: The Plaasroman Tradition in an Era of Land Reform." *Modern Fiction Studies* 46.1 (Spring 2000): 90–113.

Western, John. *Outcast Cape Town*. Berkeley: University of California Press, 1996.

Wicomb, Zoë. "Interview with Eva Hunter." In *Between the Lines II: Interviews with Nadine Gordimer, Menán du Plessis, Zoë Wicomb, Lauretta Ngcobo*, edited by Eva Hunter and Craig MacKenzie. Grahamstown: National English Literary Museum, 1993. 79–96.

———. *You Can't Get Lost in Cape Town*. New York: Pantheon, 1987.

Wiegman, Robyn. *American Anatomies: Theorizing Race and Gender*. Durham: Duke University Press, 1995.

Wilderson, Frank B., III. *Incognegro: A Memoir of Exile & Apartheid*. Boston: South End Press, 2008.

Williams, Raymond. *The Country and the City*. Oxford: Oxford University Press, 1973.

Wolfe, Patrick. "Land, Labor, and Difference: Elementary Structures of Race." *American Historical Review* 106.3 (June 2001): 866–905.

Wonder, Stevie. *In Square Circle*. © 1985 from Tamla/Motown Records. Album.

Wright, Richard. *12 Million Black Voices*. New York: Basic Books, 2008.

———. *American Hunger*. New York: Harper & Row, 1977.

———. *Black Boy: A Record of Childhood and Youth*. New York: Harper & Brothers, 1945.

———. *Conversations with Richard Wright*, edited by Keneth Kinnamon and Michel Fabre. Jackson: University of Mississippi Press, 1993.

———. *Native Son*. New York: Harper & Brothers, 1940.

———. Richard Wright Papers. JWJ MMS 3. James Weldon Johnson Collection in the Yale Collection of American Literature, Beinecke Rare Book and Manuscript Library.

———. *Uncle Tom's Children*. New York: Harper & Row, 1936.

X, Malcolm. "With Mrs. Fannie Lou Hamer." In *Malcolm X Speaks: Selected Speeches and Statements*, edited by George Breitman. New York: Grove Press, 1994. 105–14.

Young, Hershini Bhana. *Haunting Capital: Memory, Text, and the Black Diasporic Body*. Hanover: Dartmouth College Press, 2006.

Index

STÉPHANE ROBOLIN is an associate professor of English at Rutgers University.

THE NEW BLACK STUDIES SERIES

The University of Illinois Press
is a founding member of the
Association of University Presses.

———————————————

University of Illinois Press
1325 South Oak Street
Champaign, IL 61820-6903
www.press.uillinois.edu